Henry Miller

Revised Edition

By Kingsley Widmer

Twayne Publishers
A Division of G. K. Hall & Co. • *Boston*

Henry Miller, Revised Edition
Kingsley Widmer

Copyright 1990 by G. K. Hall & Co.
All rights reserved.
Published by Twayne Publishers
A division of G. K. Hall & Co.
70 Lincoln Street
Boston, Massachusetts 02111

Henry Miller © 1963 Twayne Publishers
Book production by Gabrielle B. McDonald.
Book design by Barbara Anderson.
Typeset in 11 pt. Garamond
by Compositors Corporation, Cedar Rapids, Iowa.

First published 1990.
10 9 8 7 6 5 4 3 2 1

Library of Congress Cataloging-in-Publication Data

Widmer, Kingsley, 1925–
    Henry Miller / by Kingsley Widmer. — Rev. ed.
        p.   cm. — (Twayne's United States authors series ; TUSAS 44)
    Includes bibliographical references.
    ISBN 0-8057-7607-9 (alk. paper)
    1. Miller, Henry, 1891–   — Criticism and interpretation.
I. Title. II. Series.
PS3525.I5454Z92   1990
818'.5209—dc20   90–35129
                                                          CIP

Contents

About the Author

Kingsley Widmer's several hundred publications include ten books of literary-cultural criticism: *The Art of Perversity: D. H. Lawrence* (1962); *Henry Miller* (1963); *The Literary Rebel* (1965); *The Ways of Nihilism: Melville's Short Novels* (1970); *The End of Culture: Sensibility in Contemporary Society* (1975); *Paul Goodman* (1980); *Edges of Extremity: Some Problems of Literary Modernism* (1980); *Nathanael West* (1982); *Counterings: Utopian Dialectics in Contemporary Contexts* (1988); and *Desire and Negation: Dialectical Legacy of D. H. Lawrence* (1990). He has also published critical monographs on a variety of subjects, poetry, and a range of libertarian social criticism. For many years he taught remedial English at San Diego State College. Semiretired, he lives on the Southern California coast and continues writing.

Preface

The original version of this book, the first full-scale scholarly-critical study of Henry Miller's writings, was completed in 1962. Miller went on writing for another eighteen years, and so there is additional material by him to be considered. Briefly, anyway. I have been told by an apparently reliable source that Miller intensely disliked my study but nonetheless granted that it might be the enduring scholarly-critical view of him.

The studies since then, however, leave considerable ambiguity about Miller's literary role, which suggests that I not only update both primary and secondary material but go at some of the issues yet again. Some contentiousness seems appropriate to what has been a contentious subject. When I originally engaged the material, Miller was still a much-censored author—undoubtedly the most notorious "obscene" American writer of the time—yet one also ardently defended. Between cops and cultists, between those who saw him as "the foulest writer of meaningless nonsense" and a "dirty madman" and those who considered him "the greatest living author" and a "unique saint" of American literature, it was sometimes hard to tell just what was there. Neither intellectual cop nor literary cultist, I attempted to make knowledgeably discriminating responses. In my view, Miller was a sometimes intriguing and amusing but often bad writer, a posturing minor literary rhetorician with some but insufficient truth—in sum, a rebel-buffoon of our culture. Yet he was also a figure of considerable historical importance and influence and therefore worth looking into, especially in his American context.

Since my original study, there have been a scattering of others, of which I take due account, although some have been unreasonably hostile to mine—but not so much so as to avoid borrowing heavily from it. (Amusingly, a noted "reader" for a scholarly press, commenting on my comparative use of Miller in relation to another subject, naively lectured me about acquiring the information that Miller was now considered a "rebellious buffoon." Indeed.) Perhaps this updating and restating some of the issues will be of further utility.

Miller's self-obsessed, fractured, and wandering prose probably runs to a couple of million words. Discrimination, which has not sufficiently often been applied to his writings because the usual Miller devotees oppose it (or are incapable of it) and because the usual Miller denigrators lack adequate responsiveness (unavailable in their moralist and formalist bigotries), seems worth attempting, at least for reasons of economy. A critic who refuses to play the roles of abstracted literary-theory magistrate or bumptiously ignorant virgin in American culture always has a good bit of cutting to do. Not only must the edible literary goats be separated from the overfatted, exploitative sheep, but considerable shearing must be done to get at the meat. Fortunately, a subject such as this is not fit literary flesh for genteel appreciation, pretentious methodologies, or other academic aggrandizement.

Although it is my pleasure to practice criticism as *criticism,* I do not have the usual moral axes to grind on Miller's bald literary head. I am generally sympathetic to his claimed libertarian views (pacifism, anarchism, individualism), properly amused by obscenity and wildness, and agreeably angry about America and much else in a probably doomed civilization. No doubt I lack large sympathy with Miller's occultism and his cultish notions of the artist, as well as with his considerable bad writing and silly thinking. The past issue of censorship, in which I did help defend Miller in a court case and in the mass media, will only be touched on in passing. My purpose is to put a sensitive but sharp knife to Miller's conglomerate writings, to cut away the fat, and to probe some of the major themes, meanings, and qualities that give those materials significance in our literature and sensibility.

Several cautionary points. Unlike many of the writers on Miller, I did not know him personally. This study is confined to published material (although I have looked at some other documents), and I have attempted to be reasonably thorough in going through Miller's own writings, those writings about him, and a good many of the things he has read. It has sometimes been too lengthy to cite all the sources for my generalizations, especially in this format, but this is not meant to excuse matters that are opinion and interpretation. It is almost unavoidable when discussing Miller's writings to call the central figure Henry Miller and to treat the writings as autobiography, as does Henry Miller, although this is not a claim that the events are literal experience. Indeed, at a couple of points I have indicated reasons for believing that Miller's writings about Miller are not true, in several senses.

A coherent commentary on the endlessly seamed fabric of Miller's multivolume confession-essay-letter poses problems of organization. I have settled on a separate chapter for *Tropic of Cancer,* "The Apocalyptic Comedian," leavening the analysis of his first and major book with some background. The second chapter, "The American Abroad," carries the motifs of the first chapter into Miller's other writings about and around Europe. (For reasons of theme and comparison, some writings of this period have been discussed later and out of chronological order.) The third chapter, "The Brooklyn Passion," deals only with some of the more important representative motifs of the "autobiographical romances," from *Tropic of Capricorn* through *Nexus*. The fourth chapter, "The Outsider at Home," focuses on Miller's other writings about America. The concluding chapter, "The Rebel-Buffoon," discusses some of Miller's views of literature, religion, and morals, and ends with some suggested evaluations, some brief comment on Miller's role in the American literary scene, and a broad interpretation.

Other matters are touched upon lightly or not at all: more could well be said about Miller and the attempt at American domestication of dadaism and surrealism; many biographical matters have been ignored, including the "Miller circle" (Lawrence Durrell, Anaïs Nin, and others); Miller's painting is only briefly noted; and, of course, there is no space for much of the pertinent cultural and social history of our weird times.

So I also commented a generation ago, and although I may have extended my knowledge a bit, I have found no impassioned reason for changing the direction of my views. May they equally displease intellectual cops and cultists, aggrandizing academic theorists and decorous common readers.

Kingsley Widmer

Cardiff by the Sea, California

Acknowledgments

It would seem too melancholy to repeat the personal acknowledgments of the earlier edition. All those people are, by death, divorce, or other alienation, no longer in my personal ken. As usual, I have been aided, or abetted, in my intellectual projects only in the most minimal ways—mostly in the standard use of several university libraries—by any institutions and their officials, monies, and ambience. Just as well. But the disclaimer does not apply to the publisher, who asked for the new edition, or the current field editor, Warren French, who went above and beyond in patience, tolerance of contentiousness, and helpfulness.

While all the longer quotes are from the early (noncopyrighted) editions of Henry Miller's works, the following have courteously granted additional permissions:

Grove Press: *Tropic of Cancer,* © 1961 by Grove Press, Inc.; *Tropic of Capricorn,* © 1963 by Grove Press, Inc.; *Black Spring,* © 1963 by Grove Press, Inc.

New Directions: *The Wisdom of the Heart,* copyright 1941 by New Directions; *The Cosmological Eye,* copyright 1939 by New Directions; *The Colossus of Maroussi,* copyright 1941 by Henry Miller; *The Books in My Life,* all rights reserved 1952 by New Directions; *The Air-Conditioned Nightmare,* copyright 1945 by New Directions; *Remember to Remember,* copyright 1947 by New Directions; *Sunday After the War,* copyright 1944 by Henry Miller; *The Time of the Assassins,* © 1956 by New Directions; *Stand Still Like the Hummingbird,* © 1956 by Henry Miller; *Big Sur and the Oranges of Hieronymous Bosch,* © 1957 by New Directions.

Chronology

Tropic of Cancer in Paris (book denied entry into United States). Divorces second wife.

1935 Returns to Paris. Writes miscellaneous pieces and letter-essays with Michael Fraenkel (later published as *Hamlet*).

1936 Spends first part of year in New York. *Black Spring* published.

1937–1938 Lives in Paris, except for brief visits to London and southern France, on writing income. Publishes collection of periodical sketches, *Max and the White Phagocytes* (later published in America as *The Cosmological Eye*). Has large circle of literary friends, including Lawrence Durrell. Edits *The Booster*.

1939 *Tropic of Capricorn* completed and published (Paris). Tours Greece from August through December.

1940 Returns to New York in January.

1941 Writes and publishes *Colossus of Maroussi* and *Quiet Days in Clichy*. In October starts a year-long auto tour of United States.

1942–1943 Settles in Los Angeles. Paints watercolors and writes essays and *Opus Pistorum*.

1944 Lives in Big Sur, California. Marries Janina Lepska.

1945 Daughter Valentine born. Completes *Air-Conditioned Nightmare* and *Sexus*.

1946–1947 Completes *Remember to Remember* and monographs on Rimbaud and Wasserman. Entertains many devotees at Big Sur.

1948 Son Tony born. Astrologer friend Moricand visits him at Big Sur ("Devil in Paradise"). Writes *Plexus* and paints.

1949–1952 Earns substantial income from writing. *Sexus* (Paris) and *The Books in My Life* (New York) published.

1952 Divorces third wife.

1953 Spends half year touring Europe. Marries Eve McClure.

1954–1957 Spends most of his time in Big Sur, about which he writes sketches, *Big Sur and the Oranges of Hieronymous Bosch*. Mother dies.

1958–1960 Makes several trips to Europe. Writes and publishes *Nexus* (Paris). Elected to National Institute of Arts and Letters.

1961–1962 *Tropic of Cancer* first published in United States, is repeatedly prosecuted for obscenity, and becomes best-seller. Divorces fourth wife.

1963–1966 Settles in Pacific Palisades, Southern California. Wealthy, active, traveling celebrity. First play, *Just Wild about Harry,* and sermonic pieces, *Stand Still Like the Hummingbird,* published, and earlier works republished in United States.

1967 Marries fifth wife, Haroka Takuda (Japanese entertainer).

1972 Publishes *On Turning Eighty* and Playboy picture book, *My Life and Times.*

1973–1979 Divorces fifth wife. Awarded French Legion of Honor. Publishes series of chapbooks (*My Book of Friends,* etc.) and collections of letters. Has many exhibitions of watercolors, which he continues to paint. Is physically infirm.

1980 *The Word of Lawrence* published. Dies 7 June at Pacific Palisades.

Chapter One
The Apocalyptic Comedian
Tropic of Cancer

On the first page of his first published book, Miller writes: "This is not a book. This is libel, slander, defamation of character. This is not a book in the ordinary sense of the word. No, this is a prolonged insult, a gob of spit in the face of Art, a kick in the pants to God, Man, Destiny, Time, Love, Beauty . . . what you will. I am going to sing for you, a little off-key perhaps, but I will sing. I will sing while you croak."[1] And sing he does, although in very bookish ways, with such mixture of hyperbolic romantic abstractions and Brooklyn street-corner invective. The intentionally eccentric antibook of *Tropic of Cancer* (1934) is a mélange of anecdotes, rhapsodies, caricatures, philosophizings, burlesques, and ruminations around art and sex and civilization, as well as loose documentations of a year or so of the marginal life of an expatriate American in Paris during the Great Depression. Its theme might be described as the rhetorical self-boosting of an arty buffoon into literary and self-acceptance. The gestures, historically, succeeded.

From the opening epigraph of *Tropic of Cancer* (Emerson praising autobiography) through a nearly half-century literary career, Miller's obsessive subject is himself. The first book both insists on it yet partly obscures its realities. Fortyish, slight of build, bald, and nearsighted, Miller had been down and out in Paris for some months—"no money, no resources, no hopes," as he exaggeratedly puts it. For a decade, he had hungered to be recognized as a writer. For half a dozen years he had played at the role of "Artist," practicing in New York an exacerbated bohemianism while unsuccessfully attempting to produce commercial short stories and belaboring several autobiographical novels.[2] (By his own account as well as those of others, his writing was not promising.) The only son of a lower-middle-class German-American family, he had been both indulged by a weak and failing tailor father and repressed by a narrow-spirited housewife mother. Mostly self-educated after his graduation from a Brooklyn high school (he dropped out of college his first term), his reading had been wide, and marked by a taste for late-romantics, apocalyptic philosophy, and American and European naturalism and expressionism. By both personal need and literary conditioning, he viewed art in exaltedly therapeutic and salvational terms. Thus to be an "Artist" meant for Miller a rebellious freedom from a petty past and society, an entrance into a superior, magical, larger world that justified everything. Above all, it meant the definition, expression, and regeneration of a failing and fractured self.

For the most part, Miller's personal life seems to have been as pathetically unsuccessful as his artistic ambitions. The first dozen years of his adult life consisted of a dreary succession of ordinary jobs, menial and clerical; his longest and major employment—hiring messengers for Western Union for three years—had been, he later reported, frenzied and sickening. His first galling marriage ended in divorce and the abandonment of his daughter; his second marriage, to a passionately responsive but, by his accounts, schizophrenically erratic woman who supported him and encouraged his faltering efforts as a writer, also disintegrated in the late 1920s. (She is the wife "Mona" elliptically referred to in *Tropic of Cancer* as briefly visiting, sending money, etc.) By the end of the 1920s, after a visit to Europe had increased his sense of alienation from an America which he identified with his frustrations and failures—"America is the very incarnation of doom" (86)—and after his second marriage, his finances, and his literary ambitions had reached a low point, he had desperately fled to a marginal existence in the capitol of the overripe dreams of his literary youth—bohemian Paris.

The fragmentarily autobiographical *Tropic of Cancer* draws on a bit more than a year of his Parisian experiences (1930–31, basic text completed in 1932), but its rages and longings emphatically derive from the failures of the previous decade in his life, although this is not made very clear in the book. The nuclear *Tropic of Cancer* should be understood as the saga of an aging American failure who bootstraps himself into self-acceptance as an "Artist" by writing *Tropic of Cancer*. While the materials of the book are primarily destitution, loneliness, sordidness, and misery, the almost simultaneous writing about those experiences constitutes for Miller a joyous achievement. His way down becomes his way up. Thus he can affirmatively reverse many usual senses of suffering and other feeling.

Miller's failures as a man and a writer were certainly extensive and genuine, although quite common, as was his alienation from America and himself. And his early circumstances in Paris, as the book shows, were certainly miserable enough, with much of his time dominated by the anxieties of conniving for money, food, drink, a place to sleep, sex, a job, and cleanliness. However, Miller also simultaneously felt the exhilaration of the American outcast and the intense elation of a holiday among the European ruins for the innocent abroad. It was partly by choice that he was severed from America, family, conventions, responsibilities, and certitudes. He had the *lüftmensch* intoxication of the renegade from a restrictive past. There wasn't much more to lose. His chaos, aided by exotic newness, became positive. At the Parisian end of Whitman's Open Road—as Miller trumpets late in the book, "Whatever there is of value in America Whitman has expressed" (216)—life is minimal and immediate and intense and, therefore, open for barbaric yawps.

Miller also carried some special talents into the chaos: a zesty appetite; a rebellious improvidence about conventional amenities; an accomplished unscrupulousness and ability to beg, borrow, and steal; a loquacious personal charm which had always provided a circle of responsive, indulgent, male companions (anywhere in the world the "easiest thing for me to discover was a friend" [162]); and a magical belief in himself as having the destiny of an artist—and that the "race of artists" were beyond conventional morality and thus superiorly "inhuman" (229). He also had good health (in spite of painful hemorrhoids and various infections): "When I say 'health,' I mean optimism, to be truthful. Incurably optimistic! Still have one foot in the 19th century. I'm a bit retarded, like most Americans" (45). This self-mocking manner is frequently Miller at his best. Thus he was prepared to give an exuberant report of a literary American's underground life abroad.

Because Miller settled in Paris in 1930, following the much-publicized expatriation of the previous decade which had directed him there, *Cancer* can partly be seen as posthumous literary Americana of the 1920s.[3] But while some of the book's scenes and characters can be translated out of their hyperbole and "slander" into a documentary on marginal bohemian life, such works as George Orwell's *Down and Out in Paris and London* or Eliot Paul's *The Last Time I Saw Paris* probably provide more useful social documentation without the peculiarities of Miller's prose and buffoonish gestures.[4] And responses other than social-moralist reporting and expatriate celebration can be recognized in this compatriot of Emerson and Whitman. As a twentieth-century urban Thoreau, Miller takes the stance of answering—in analogous metaphoric, wry, and iconoclastic terms—the problem of where and how the poet is to live; he, too, is fully prepared to confessionally publish to the world that meanness of life, if such he finds.[5] Miller's enchantment with the forest of European culture, and his particularized fascination with the flora and fauna of seedy nighttime Parisian streets—on the final page of *Cancer,* he speaks of humans as "strange flora and fauna" who need much "space"—belong to our major tradition of the rebellious individualist. So does the loose form of his autobiography-essay-prosepoem about a year's self-discovery. The sex, the sordidness, and the grotesquerie were just the weather on the twentieth-century side of Walden Pond. The many parallels between the cu-

rious books of the two American Henrys—libertarian egotists declaiming in
elaborate prose their defiant quests for individualistic regeneration—should
not be obscured by the historical change of scene from rural puritanism to
megapolitan amoralism, nor by the switch of nature metaphors from forest
to phallus. Miller's stance is partly that of a later, though lesser, Thoreau.

Fragments for Form

Tropic of Cancer consists of fifteen loosely connected, unnumbered and un-
titled, anecdotal chapters. The irregular shape does not quite come together
in what can be called a style (he attempts several) but rather in the merging
flow of description, fantasy, and rumination, which insists on a comic surviv-
alist egotism. In the conclusion, Miller, having ripped off a few thousand
francs from a friend he has just hurried back to America, watches the Seine
flow by on a fine spring day.[6] Determined not to go back himself to the defeating frenzy represented by New York, he drinks a *demi* in "golden peace"
and feels the organic flow of the river in him. He accepts his alienation as the
marginal outsider responding to the absurd flow of life (although in actuality
he had overcome it and become part of a bohemian community, which accounts for some of the sense of affirmation). Peace in a mean and mad world.

The garrulous flow of anecdotes (curiously, some of the best told are secondhand) wryly and outrageously turns about male expatriate "artists" booz-
ing, whoring, and scrounging. Those anecdotes are but studding, often
nailed in a fluent American colloquial manner which some argue is Miller's
main contribution to literature, for plastering with avant-garde and apocalyptic rhetoric.[7] In one of the longest of these verbal stuccoings, he takes a
trope (apparently from Joyce, a source for both the low-life detailing and the
rhetorical ornateness, although Miller was soon to condemn him as representing mortuary "head-culture"[8]): "I love everything that flows." He then
catalogues "rivers, sewers, semen, blood, bile, words . . . everything that
flows, everything that has time in it and becoming, that brings us back to the
beginning where there is never end: the violence of the prophets, the obscenity that is ecstasy, . . . all that is fluid, melting, dissolvent . . . that makes the
great circuit towards death and dissolution" (220ff.). Such recurrent metaphor, which also concludes the book, becomes a kind of musical background
for the colloquial "off-key" singing, and a desperation process-philosophy
which for Miller provides the fundamental antithesis to the authoritarian and
mechanical antihuman rigidities of the twentieth-century world.

In such apocalyptic foray, Miller starts, as he often does, with the grossly
specific—here, the bare pudendum of a prostitute—and fuses the sublime

and the grotesque. His "bloody shout of joy" attempts to turn the mean physical fact into a metaphysical trope. Uniting the disparities is often a *literary* mannerism—"the bloated *pages* of ecstasy slimed with excrement" (229; my italics). Rumination on a naked "cunt" leads to the proclamation that "out of nothingness rises the sign of infinity." Thus out of a Nietzscheanism (the "gay science" his acknowledged source), value consists in a responsiveness to the incongruous flux. "Do anything, but let it produce joy." Or, in Miller's high philosophical manner, those alive to the flux of life demand a "world that produces ecstasy and not dry farts."

Now living at the bottom of society, Miller literally exploits the literary possibilities of some of what is down under, including the gynecological and the excremental. Rebellion against decorous convention, American street-male iconoclasm about the obscured crudity of life, aesthetic and moral enlargement of literary style (via Joyce, Lawrence, Céline, the surrealists, etc.), and considerable bravado about doing an unusual book—these are many of the forces at work in Miller's once notorious but now relatively mild "obscenity." When the narrator lavishly, and often wryly, describes scenes of disgust, as in his visit to an impoverished Russian émigré to mooch a meal and a place to sleep, the filth, the odors, and a detailed view of the excrement sump soon put him to flight. From the handling of such scenes (as well as from other sources), it seems clear that Miller (contrary to some popular views) was essentially fastidious. Indeed, he shows an obsessive concern—like the compulsive cleanliness of his mother that he describes elsewhere—with mess and muck, to which his shouting and flight are exaggerated responses.[9]

Excremental Poetry

More striking than the scenes of "naturalistic" reporting are what might be called Miller's *excremental visions*. Two major burlesque anecdotes, one early and one late in *Cancer*, suggest how the mucky flux becomes metaphysical. In the first anecdote, by Miller's account, he served for a short period in Paris as a servant to a Depression-stymied Hindu pearl merchant whom he had heard earlier in New York boast of his fine life. Now Miller, who was in his early writings repeatedly an exposer of hypocrisy, finds the dirty reality behind the rhetoric as he does errands, cleans the toilet, and plays sycophant in the shabby room of his penurious, crippled Hindu patron (72ff.). The caricature achieves the amusing nasty-grotesque quality by catching the mixed piety and meanness, the tea with the rose leaf and the smug farting. Such incongruities provide much of the essence of Miller's art and wisdom. But so also does his indifference to his ostensible subject—the collector of pearls and of moldy bread simply disappears from the account. The anecdote, however, leads into a larger excremental vision. Miller, guiding a young, ostensible Gandhian through Parisian nightlife, finds the "gay disciple" to be naively pompous and vain, decked out with "a beret, a cane, a Windsor tie . . . two fountain pens, a kodak . . . some fancy underwear," and childishly self-righteous opinions. To Miller's iconoclastic eye, the would-be saint shows less fraudulence in his simple lust and avarice than in his mixture of Gandhianism and "the cheap idealism of the Americans"—his moral blather of a "contaminated saint who talks in one breath of love, brotherhood, bathtubs, sanitation, efficiency, etc." In one rather sniggeringly presented scene, the Gandhian outrages the whorehouse women by defecating in the bidet. In another, he dances with a naked, fat-creased blonde. Miller then drops the character and goes off into a self-delighting reverie around the metaphors that the encounter has suggested. He scornfully considers again the disparity between gross physical reality and man's ideal aspirations— roses in the dung, cockroach priests, and bilious ideas obscuring the truth: "And so I think what a miracle it would be if this miracle which man attends eternally should turn out to be nothing more than these two enormous turds which the faithful disciple dropped in the bidet. What if at the last moment, when the banquet table is set and cymbals clash, there should appear suddenly . . . a silver platter on which even the blind could see that there is nothing more, and nothing less, than two enormous lumps of shit" (89). The reverse miracle appeals to the iconoclasm that gives Miller's early writing much of its verve—and to the egotism of one who concludes that he is the only man who "could imagine the possibility." It also provides a kind of "epileptic" clarity (Miller got that from Dostoyevski) in which he can accept all— "everything was justified, supremely justified." And Miller draws a larger personal moral from the excremental vision:

Somehow the realization that nothing was to be hoped for had a salutary effect upon me . . . all my life I had been looking forward to something happening, some extrinsic event that would alter my life, and now suddenly, inspired by the absolute hopelessness of everything, I felt relieved. . . . Walking down Montparnasse I decided to let myself drift with the tide, to make not the least resistance to fate, no matter in what form it presented itself . . . nothing had been destroyed except my illusions. . . . I would hold on to nothing. . . . By what he called the better part of his nature, man has been betrayed, that is all. At the extreme limits of his spiritual being man finds himself again as naked as a savage. When he finds God . . . he is a skeleton. One must burrow into life again in order to put on flesh. . . . I have been trying to save my precious hide, trying to preserve the pieces of meat that hid my bones. I am done with that. I have reached the limits. As far as history goes I am dead. If there is something beyond I shall have to bounce back. I have found God but he is insufficient. I am only spiritually dead. Physically I am alive. Morally I am free. The world which I have departed is a menagerie. The dawn is breaking on a new world in which the lean spirits roam with sharp claws. If I am a hyena I am a lean and hungry one: I go forth to fatten myself. (89–90)

This stance at something like what Nietzsche described as an *amor fati* may also be viewed as a Protestant-American crisis of conscience, in which morality loses and one is liberated from lower-middle-class anxiety into artistic hobodom. While it could be taken as the amoralism which in later episodes justifies the stealing from a whore, the concluding rip-off of his friend, and other liberations—and can also be seen as hyperbolic (in the very writing of it Miller was still pursuing "history" and "spirit," if not fame and fortune, as an artist-sage)—the sense of liberation is clear, and nuclear to the narrative, and to the man. Anti-miracles have killed off some illusions, history, morals, and other false claims that obscure immediate reality. In such comic nihilism, one can laughingly live—the essential gesture of the early Miller.

But this amoral affirmation provides only one side of the excremental vision; a later anecdote in *Cancer* shows that what was only imagined becomes the actual condition of life. Miller spent a couple of months in the winter as a tutor of English (for room and board) in a lycée in Dijon. He gives some details about the slimy nineteenth-century stone school, his puppetlike colleagues, and the dreary mustard capitol in winter. But Miller's writing never stays long with narrative because of self-centered feelings, most of which in Dijon are rhetorically violent. The characteristic teacher is that "cipher who forms the nucleus of a respectable and lamentable citizenry" (246)—a trimmer in the vestibule of Hell. Humanistic ideology reveals "something obscene in this love of the past which ends in breadlines and dug-outs," and so "every man with a bellyful of the classics is an enemy of the human race" (248). Teaching is "grinding grist for that paradise which is always a wet dream"—for his own pedagogy Miller discusses the sex life of elephants because he is a "plenipotentiary from the realm of free spirits" (248, 252). The cafes of the orderly depressing city (the music "as if old Euclid had . . . swallowed Prussic acid") and the whole of provincial bourgeois life epitomize northern Europe's bitter, white winter of Christianity with its icy moral geometry. Playfully hyperbolic rage, rather than careful representation, dominate Miller's responses and style.

The capping response depends on the exacting gross imagery in which the bad food, dead spirits, and miserable winter "put the whole penitentiary into a state of constipation"; then the plumbing freezes up, human dung accumulates and spreads, and "shit" pervades the "whole stinking civilized world" (256). For stock antithesis (à la E. E. Cummings's *The Enormous Room*), Miller throws out an ornately mawkish description of the symbolic night watchman whose very drinking of wine is a pouring of rubies. This elliptically viewed nobody stands for the human dimension, for marginal Mediterranean warmth and heart, smiling above the frozen order and muck.[10] The exuberant bohemian among the pedants falters—"a fear of living separate, of staying born"—and although the message throughout *Cancer* turns on the embracement of the flowing chaos of life, here the shipwrecked bohemian finds himself at "dead center, and there you slowly rot" (259). Unable to continue shouting King of the Hill from atop the quite unmiraculous pile of everyday excrement, Miller abruptly flees Dijon for Paris where he can return to playing artist as burlesque and apocalyptic con man. This striking confession in the penultimate chapter leads to the culminating refusal to return to ordinary American life.[11] The excremental absurdity of the ordinary demands that one rebelliously be the outsider abroad, self-justifyingly called "artist."

The book's title points to related rhetorical gestures. For Miller, to devise a title is almost an end in itself: "We're all dead, or dying, or about to die. We need good titles" (36). In the following reflections on Paris as seen in one of his many walks, he adumbrates his attraction to the "leprous streets," to the malignant spirit of the place, and to the vision of the city as "a huge organism diseased in every part." The recurrent images of cancer, syphilis, plague, and decay make Paris—then the most symbolic megalopolis of modern culture—an encompassing malignancy reflecting the Spenglerian decline of the West (Miller's major conceptual source). The "tropic" of the title refers, in a somewhat muddled way, to apocalyptic geography—"the meridian that separates the hemispheres of life and death" (241)—and the metatemporal weather which "will continue bad" because the "cancer of time is eating us away" (1).[12] Medicine? It is homeopathic. As one of Miller's women reportedly tells him, "You're cancer and delirium" (53). Disease and cure are almost one and the same; the therapy for sick civilization and self consists of cancerous gestures and apocalyptic fever.

Surreal Schizophrenia

It will not do, of course, to emphasize overmuch the book's unity. Fragmentation is central to Miller in several ways. He appropriately labels his responses "schizophrenic." Fracturing provides his sensibility and his world. Disparate conjunctions provide his affirmations, as, indeed, they do in many of the modernist styles from which his often derive. If the discrete fragments and associations, as in the first two, rather weak, chapters of *Cancer*, seem beyond order, then the very disorder, by imitative form, provides the quality of his "anecdotal life." If his misery threatens all meaning, then meaninglessness becomes the trumpeted meaning. If life seems messy, then messiness becomes the life principle. He plays with his fragmentation, writing in front of a cracked mirror, exalting in his confusions, intensifying the fracturings by the disjunctions of surreal rhetoric. Powerless to change his reality, he can call it different names and thus elaborate personal chaos into cosmic proportions ("I want the whole world to be out of whack"). He purges his despair by whimsical and mannered embracement. The arty gesture is all, beyond survival to which it becomes the very means.

In a role denuded of the usual pretenses at wholeness, Miller's hyperbolic acceptance includes a desperate voraciousness and a missionary braggadocio in "the recording of all that which is omitted in books" (10). Experiences no longer fit together? Good, for they then become intensified discrete moments whose very recording is heroic. The romantic and antiromantic become simultaneous states—"the splendor of those miserable days"—in which, in conjoined sentences, he is "going mad with the beauty" of the Seine scene and "getting an erection looking at the dumb statues in the park" (14). The Baudelaire-cum-Whitman atmosphere constantly reveals "misfortune, ennui, grief, suicide," which he yet finds "exhilarating." Because everything has gone smash, Miller can only yearn for the heightening of what is—"for more and more disasters, for bigger calamities, for grander failures" (11) as an affirmation of an impossible reality, which gives him his striking role.[13]

Miller's use of prostitutes throughout *Cancer* also illustrates this stance. A cheap and genial prostitute such as Germaine, whom he cannot really relate to love or passion—"a good heart" but "without reference to any fixed point within" (41)—thus comes to represent authentic being: "She was a whore all the way through—and that was her virtue!" The callously affirmative alienation is carried further in Miller's rhapsodizing over the saleable part of Germine's anatomy just because it becomes uniquely dissociated from all other meaning: "she spoke of it [her pudendum] as if it were some extraneous object which she had acquired at great cost . . . a magic, potent treasure" (39). Unable to find anything else, Miller glories in such self-alienation, which also justifies his use and abuse of the object. Although the sentimentality of the masculine legend of the golden-hearted whore (which runs through American folk mythology, as in the Western) may have directed choice of subject and description, his stance asserts perversely residual authenticity. The genuine prostitute provides a standard in a world of ingeniously contrived prostitutes, and the very absence of love suggests a distinctive self-passion.[14] In a later low-keyed episode (188ff), Miller describes picking up a woman on the street who wheedles fifty francs out of him with nothing more than a flattering sentimental appeal. Later that night, a second prostitute mixes equal pathos with too obvious lies and avarice for services rather hurriedly rendered for a hundred francs. When she leaves the room (to check on her sick mother, she says), Miller swipes the hundred francs (plus a bit more) from her purse and flees. The fifty-franc sentimentality has been cathartically reversed to a hundred-franc cynicism. It will not do to explain this away by Miller's marginal circumstances or social defiance. Miller's cancerous world reveals no moral law, just the amoral rhythms of response and the alternating flow of sentimentality and cynicism, of acquiescence and revolt.

Thus *Tropic of Cancer*'s accounts must remain discrete and the narrator's responses fragmentary. The artists *manqué* who provide most of the cartoon figures in this ragged tapestry generally lack past, future, and depth. Boris, with whom Miller lives as the narrative opens, simply provides a silhouette target for a bit of anti-Semitic mockery of labyrinthine Jewish intellectuals. Moldorf appears only long enough to be the object of a surreal fantasy of dismemberment as illustration of Miller's contempt for familial weltschmerz. Sylvester, also a writer and one of Miller's weekly meal patrons, mostly focuses a rogue's violent interior monologue against a husband who can't seem to understand "how a change of semen can make a woman [his wife] bloom" (54). Krueger, the "sick saint" occultist painter, appears briefly to illustrate Miller's sycophancy, grotesquely ending with him being thrown out, though ill. Collins, the genially gutsy American sailor-adventurer (and apparently Proustian bisexual) may intrigue the reader, but Miller presents what he does only for Miller. Marlowe, a scholarly drunk and the editor of a literary review (which, significantly, first published Miller, as we know from outside sources), appears only in a few lugubrious strokes that show Miller's insouciant bohemianism and his delight in the grotesque. Borowski simply serves as a disembodied name for a writer with insufficient mad obsession to be a true Miller artist. These, and the rest of the fragmentary caricatures, reflect rather more Miller's sensibility than the actual-life prototypes on whom he had a continuous, though often covertly hostile, dependency.[15] While the kaleidoscopic treatment provides some of the whirl of the account, it also becomes solipsism that often leaves the art—and the reader—awkwardly dangling. It seems that Miller's quest for identity really was fractured.

Similarly fragmented is the obscured center of the personal history—wife Mona. Some scattered assertions imply that she be understood as the Dark Goddess of the city of despair. Her image, associatively arrived at in one of the narrator's journeys through the infernal city, suggests to him the cities of Dante and Strindberg and the sojourn in the depths for "the tortured, the hallucinated, the maniacs of love" (163). But Miller can only present the love mania in comic fragments.

Picaresque Patchwork

A more picaresque spirit than that of fumbled femme fatale controls the longer sections of the narrative. In one of his more sustained accounts, Miller presents a grotesque alter ego buddy—Van Norden, an American journalist and would-be literary artist, with whom Miller had a parasitic relation. Along with another refugee writer, Carl, they talk, drink, and whore together—and rather homoerotically titillate each other. I take the key to these buddies in bohemian arms to be in a Miller aside: the three call each other "Joe" because "it's easier that way. It also is a pleasant reminder not to take yourself too seriously" (93). As with the archetypal Joe of American naturalistic fictions, the "good Joe" of folk idioms, and the later pervasive "GI Joe" of World War II, we have the footloose boys on the town in the mixture of rebellion and accommodation that characterizes the netherworld of American maledom.[16] Such comic fraternal order—rather than forced images of romantic passion—provides the main world of the aging all-American-boy-in-extremis, Henry Miller.

In contrast to the rather forced tone of the surreal fantasies and apocalyptic essays, Miller's handling of the picaresque shows an artful, if sometimes too lengthy, naturalistic reporting, a deadpan recording of colloquial monologues. The episodes around Van Norden probably contain the highest proportion of verbal obscenities in the book. To flag "weather," "room," "book," "job," "idea," and many another noun, with the word "fucking" points not to Miller's dirty mind but to his accurate ear, and his sense of blasphemous decorum. (As the *OED Supplement* now notes, the term is widespread as "the coarsest equivalent of damn.")

Ostensibly burdened with the usual American artistic ambitions (a novel that "tells all") and with metaphysical despair (everything is "no fucking" good), egotistical and neurasthenic Van Norden can only pursue his griping and fucking compulsions. This devotee of Goethe displays the petty Faustian sundering of knowledge and meaning. He has, in his solipsistic disillusionment, explored the female microcosm in quantity and even, quite literally,

with a flashlight: "When you look at it [the pudendum] that way, sort of detached like, you get funny notions in your head. All that mystery about sex
and then you discover that it's nothing—just a blank. Wouldn't it be funny if
you found a harmonica inside . . . or a calendar? But there's nothing there . . .
It's disgusting. It almost drove me mad" (126).

Miller, whose own verbal elaborations on the denuded world show a similar longing to find some magic in the naked pseudomystery, commented earlier on Van Norden's Don Juan pathos: "His one fear is to be left alone, and
this fear is so deep and so persistent that even when he is on top of a woman,
even when he has welded himself to her, he cannot escape the prison which he
has created for himself. 'I try all sorts of things,' he explains to me. 'I even
count sometimes, or I begin to think of a problem in philosophy, but it
doesn't work. It's like I'm two people, and one of them is watching me all the
time. I get so god-damned mad at myself that I could kill myself . . . and in a
way, that's what I do everytime I have an orgasm!'" (118). The American
abroad has breached the last Puritan frontier only to end in the fatality of desperate self-consciousness.

One of the bemused buddy anecdotes has Carl fulsomely telling Miller of
his faltering efforts at the seduction of some tourist's rich, aging wife who,
after receiving a long barrage of ornate love letters contrived with Miller's
help, seemed willing. On the crucial evening, however, Carl needed to go to
the toilet but was too embarrassed, and was also quite repelled by the signs of
age in the woman. Nothing happened. Then the double-play: Van Norden
enviously reports to Miller the version of that same evening that Carl boast-
fully told him, in which every fantasy possibility happened. Miller's tongue-
in-cheek account shows would-be artists playing would-be rogues. But, as so
often in the pathetic American male world of the street corner and tavern, not
much but exploitative fantasy talk occurs. Miller's sly colloquial prose presents such men as they are in their self-defeating-and-placating camaraderie.
The effectiveness partly comes from the aging Brooklyn boy's lack of pretensions here to heroism, love, beauty, goodness, and the other falsifications
which make books, all of which he announced he was done with on the first
page of *Cancer.*

A more portentous deployment of Miller's iconoclasm with Van Norden's
satyriasis comes in an anecdote that Miller turns into an apocalyptic essay. In
a cafe Van Norden finishes lecturing Miller on his disgust with sex; then he
sees a whore—a hungry, gentle, and sad creature, whom he grimly gets to
agree to double-servicing for a bargain price. Miller's fractured sensibility can
sympathize with the pathetic woman, partake of her services, and bemusedly
watch his callous buddy's semi-impotent sexual gyrations. He reflects that

when the "spark of passion is missing there is no human significance in the performance" (130). (Or, as Bergson argued in *Laughter,* the human then turns into a self-propelling comic mechanism.) But at the edge of laughter lies outrage, and Miller thinks of the sexual mechanism as comparable to modern business processes or modern war, in which the machine goes on and on simply because it has started, although it satisfies no one's real desires.

Similar devastating perception of modern system-dehumanization applies to Miller's ruminations on his nonsexual activities. In the job Van Norden helps him get as a newspaper proofreader, the mechanism insists that he scrupulously place semicolons between calamities. No human response, he indicates in a verbal equivalent of dadaist collage, is allowed. The same "negative reality" in making a living also applies to his other marginal occupations as tutor, cicerone, hack and ghost writer, and so on. Miller, with his usual angry asides for America—which define much of the significance of his role abroad—claims that in Paris, at least, the viciousness of what is called "making a living" lacks the hypocritical American claims of opportunity and liberty.

But the Millerean attitude essentially goes beyond hurt idealism to transcendent insouciance. Early in the narrative he reports on casually seducing a pathetic woman: "Somehow I feel sorry as hell for her and yet I don't give a damn" (22). The art of such fractured sensibility becomes his message to Van Norden, the world, and himself. One must accept, like a "new religion," the paradoxical need to live in "a world without hope" and yet "never despair" (136). "No sorrow, no regrets. No past, no future." "Today! *Le bel aujourd'hui!*" (46) Partly, of course, this serves as literary gesture to cauterize outraged feeling and personal defeat.[17] But it also releases vitality through comic severance: "I'm not an American anymore. I haven't any allegiance, any responsibility, any hatreds, any worries, any passion. I'm neither for nor against. I'm neutral" (138). (The attitude has numerous modernist parallels, as with Henry in Hemingway's *A Farewell to Arms*: "I was not against them. I was through.")

One price of such disconnection is discontinuity—no past and no future for characters and author. Van Norden simply drops out of the narrative (except for a briefly contemptuous fillip in the final section: the Don Juan has given up women, turning to an ornate form of onanism with a cored apple). He is narratively replaced by another alter ego and American "Joe," also called Fillmore, a common 1920s expatriate, a young graduate of an Eastern college, getting money from home and not very earnestly playing artist and bohemian while working in a dull job. Miller opportunistically cultivates this American innocent. Fillmore-Collins-Miller repeat the earlier boys-on-the-town of Van Norden-Carl-Miller, including a lengthy and awkwardly done brawling weekend in le Havre that has very little point (although its pointlessness may be taken as the point).[18] It does have a wry postscript in mockery of American sentimentality and the he-man dream of the country as "a big patriotic open space with cows and sheep and tender-hearted men ready to bugger everything in sight, man, woman, or beast. It doesn't exist, America. It's a name you give to an abstract idea" (187).

Having ostensibly dismissed the American dream, Miller will soon dismiss the American dreamer and that part of himself represented by Fillmore. The genial American moves the leeching Miller into his apartment so that he has a place to write, gives him a daily allowance, and shares his liquor, literary conversations, and whores. One long deadpan report centers on an erratic down-and-out Russian emigré—a venereally diseased, aspiring movie star called "Princess," who moves in but, with a mixture of snobbery and foulness in endless domestic battle, does not sexually come across. She eventually takes up with a "castrated" sculptor. Although such grotesque material justifies itself as comedy, several other points should be noted. The description of the outrageous ménage in Fillmore's apartment, like earlier descriptions of the manners of pimps and prostitutes, provides a satiric case that devastatingly parodies more conventional-appearing domestic arrangements.[19]

Inverted Romanticism

One should also emphasize the pervasive inverted romanticism of Miller's stance. For example, when moving into Fillmore's place, he comments: "The neighborhood appealed to me, particularly at night when the full squalor and lugubriousness of it made itself felt" (200). The foul, the sinister, and the richly repulsive become objects for aesthetic contemplation—the sordid sublime. So, too, do the Princess, Van Norden, the prostitutes, the older Parisian streets—indeed, all of the cancerous megalopolis and, more generally, the whole sick ambience of the years of miserable depression filling the gap between two horrendous wars. Miller went to Paris for romantic-artist motives but sometimes discovered something rather more real. Much of his rhetorical edge comes from his role as angry man, and *Cancer* insistently (indeed, sometimes gratuitously) turns to negative images of depression, world war, and the deaths of the old faiths (God, Love, Beauty, etc.). The ornately bookish contemplation and effulgent style may be seen as ways to desperately bridge the disparities of the arty and the actual.

But the angry iconoclasm is intermittently insistent. When he and Fillmore wander, seedy and drunkenly sentimental, into the Eglise Ste.

Clotilde during Mass on Christmas Day, Miller perceives a dismal, cold tomb filled with a weird dirge and mumbling faces like "cauliflowers" sticking out of shrouds—a dumbshow in a "crepuscular glow" directed by an "epicene caterwauling" from what must be an altar. The American outsider, staring at the "dementia" of an ancient and irrelevant vestigial ritual, which "no longer contains a shred of meaning," scorns it for equally blessing babies and battleships, high explosives and lowly misery, with the "mumbo-jumbo" of Christendom (236). And this is the product of two thousand years of civilization? "Marvelous."

The American rebel abroad in the fraud of traditional culture sympathizes a bit with the long-skirted, "ridiculous" lackey who gets "sore as hell" and drives the laughing protestants out. After recalling a similar "ludicrous incident" with an uncharitable priest in Florida in the 1920s (which he had weakly written up[20]), Miller swings into a Whitmanian catalog and apocalyptic essay: "The same story everywhere. If you want bread you've got to get in harness, get in lock-step . . . production! More nuts and bolts, more barbed wire, more dog biscuits, more lawn-mowers, more ballbearings, more high-explosives . . . more toothpaste, more newspapers, more education, more churches" (240). Miller's flowing invective does reflect our One World in which all is part of the same demented productivity. So he responds with the dada-Parisianized gesture of the boy from Brooklyn: "*Salut au monde!* Salute of twenty-one guns bombinating from the rectum. 'I wear my hat as I please' . . . said Walt. To get a hat that fits now you have to walk to the electric chair. They give you a skull cap. . . . [then mocking even his hero Whitman] *The Democratic soul! Flood-tide!* Holy mother of God, what does this crap mean? . . . *Forward!* More gonococci! More streptococci! More bombing machines! More and more of it—until the whole fucking works is blown to smithereens" (241).

As he repeatedly insists, no allegiance is due such a world: "I am proud to say that I am *inhuman*, that I belong not to men and governments, that I have nothing to do with creeds and principles" (229). While the middle class "rot in comfort" (217) in their fenced-off world, compassion for the rest of suffering humanity becomes a Céline-like joke—"at the bottom of every heart there is a drop or two of love—just enough to feed the birds" (219).[21] Thus, says Miller, making a sweeping metaphor from a topical issue of the time (during his revision of the manuscript), we have gone off "the gold standard in ideas," art, and love. And as he drinks a vermouth in a cheap café, he reflects that it has the bitter taste of "the lees of our great Western civilization, rotting now like the toe-nails of the saints" (221). His sometimes well-turned rage, with its winging mixture of colloquial bluster and fancy literariness, when viewed through more than a half century of mass murder, technocratic dementia, and vestigial and counterfeit values, still has its relevance.

Miller's rage also has its self-justifying self-indulgence.[22] When we return to the narrative, we have less a doomed civilization than a roguish mess. Fillmore, apparently suffering from alcoholism, venereal disease, and a guilty conscience about his petty bourgeois-whorish girlfriend, gets locked up in a hospital. From the sly Miller perspective, Fillmore isn't "exactly nuts"—he is just going through a "a typical Anglo-Saxon crisis. An eruption of morals" (265). Since Miller no longer suffers from that malady, he bemusedly reports as the wayward daughter of a stolid French rural family terrorizes the inno-cent Fillmore to marry her and settle down to shopkeeping. Convinced that what his buddy, with his fraternity-boy conscience, really wants is to go home, Miller gets him on his way, pocketing the money that was to be a sop of conscience to the French girl Fillmore was deserting. Miller neither hides nor rationalizes his dubious motives but, with topsy-turvy charm, makes the most of them.

At the end, with a pocket full of money for once, Miller asks himself if he wants to return to America, to the Manhattan of which Whitman sang, but which Miller had earlier visualized as a fantastic prison over a void sur-rounded by mechanized crowds "who walk along like blind geese and the searchlights spray their empty faces" (62). His answer is to accept the rich spring day beside the flowing Seine and hope that "for a little while I would be able to look around me" (287). As the episodes have shown, life is only immediate and expedient. He is roguishly and apocalyptically detached from all allegiances and most actual people (up close they "appear ugly and mali-cious"). His alienation confirms both his individuality and his role abroad in life, which he has paradoxically overcome by making them into a career as the *Cancer*ous artist.

As Miller tongued his way through the underground life, he often revealed confusions as to whether his quest was an exalted or burlesque transforma-tion. The apocalyptic essays often lack convincing relation to the roguish an-ecdotes of marginal existence. *Tropic of Cancer* supposedly provides the apotheosis of his alienation. But he has treated the act of recording his rhetor-ical gestures as both the comedy of writing an antibook (24) and as the na-ively sententious salvation that will change the world if he dares tell "truly his truth" (225). He both claims the high pretensions of art—"the task which the artist implicitly sets himself is to overthrow existing values" (228)—and reduces it to mere burlesque and rhetorical gestures. He righteously makes much of the "discrepancy . . . between ideas and living" in Western civiliza-tion (219), yet repeatedly exemplifies such dissociation and fracturing. The fissure runs far, and it is deeper than style. The burlesque humor and earnest indignation in his apocalyptic essays tend to cancel each other out. His caricatures show both satiric perception and egotistical short-circuiting. His verbal gusto of irreverence often turns into a self-indulgent play with exotic words. The bravado of claiming that "art consists in going the full length" (70) produces some distinctive prose gestures but also considerable egotistical noise.

An Arty Book

Tropic of Cancer starts out with the claim to being "not a book in the ordinary sense," but, as a naive reader reports, "it sure is awful damn literary."[23] Indeed it is, not just in the cast from Emerson and Thoreau and Whitman, but in self-conscious key quotations from Joyce, Dostoyevski, and Rabelais, among others; in heavy justifications of its apocalyptism from Nietzsche and Spengler; and in rhetorical mannerisms from naturalism, expressionism, dadaism, and surrealism. It is an arty book—Miller was attempting the bookishly intellectual as his self-justification—although emphasis on its obscene documentation long obscured that obvious bent.[24] Nevertheless, it is a book distinctive for its vivaciousness, its energy, and its iconoclasm. Granted, the mockery is limited by literary posturing and was not to hold very solid. (Retrospectively, for example, we can see that the Oriental mysticism mocked in *Cancer*—"all that flapdoodle which blows out of the East like a breadth from a plague" [172]—was soon to become stock blather for Miller.) It also displays some nastiness, not in the now mild sexual obscenity or quaintly sweeping denunciations but in the parochial prejudices such as anti-Semitism (evident on pp. 8, 61, 153, 246, etc.), which he was later to compensate for with philo-Semitism, and the gross misogyny, for which he was later to pseudo-compensate with some rhetoric of romantic adoration of exploitative women. But it also has its wayward wisdom—it is a kind of perverse "wisdom literature"—with its responsive sense of the fundamental disorder and absurdity of our world and the usual claims made upon it. A hard-won, and somewhat belabored, insouciance.

There are drastically diverse evaluations of *Tropic of Cancer,* ranging from vituperative condemnation to near-scriptural admiration. Miller (as is evident in the biographies and letters) worked assiduously to acquire early literary support for his book, and he got it from such well-known writers as Blaise Cendrars and Cyril Connally, among others. In the following period (frequently most crucial for a literary reputation) the book was thoughtfully written up by such noted critics as George Orwell, Philip Rahv, Herbert Read, Edmund Wilson, and Herbert J. Muller, among others. Edwin Muir briefly but aptly discussed early Miller and a few of his themes in an academic survey. Several friends showed remarkable devotion to uncritically furthering Miller's reputation. Lawrence Durrell early wrote that "American literature today begins and ends with the meaning of what he [Miller] has done."[24] A few years later, Karl Shapiro (one of the better known American poets at the time) called Miller "the world's greatest living author." In the mid-1970s the famous Norman Mailer lavishly anthologized Miller (as earlier had Durrell, Rexroth, and others) and pronounced that *Tropic of Cancer* was one of the "ten or twenty" most important twentieth-century American books.[25] The book had a long and substantial intellectual as well as popular reputation (it sold substantially for decades in its Parisian editions—for example, thousands of American soldiers obtaining copies, as I did, in Europe during World War II—before becoming a multimillion copy aboveground bestseller in the 1960s). In several ways, *Tropic of Cancer* has been historically important.

But how shall we view Miller's book now, more than two generations later? Since I have suggested a number of the issues and limitations, I might conclude with a qualified affirmation. *Tropic of Cancer* is the drastically ragged work of an inadequate consciousness, but it has sufficient energy, rhetorical reach (at times), and truth in its rhythms of sentimentality/cynicism, grotesquerie/beauty, and misery/ecstasy to stand with the lively antibooks of American individualism, of which it is one of the most outrageously positive examples. Although appearing harshly negative—America and Europe, customs and honor, morals and society, work and ideas, culture and religion, and friendship and love get badly trounced—Miller made a brilliant, if inevitably egotistical and fractured, discovery. All collapsing in a dehumanized world, the beginning of everything remains—the gaily responsive self. However fancily buffoonish in the doing, that was the real point of his quest and testimony.

Chapter Two
The American Abroad
Black Spring

The initiation of the American into the semi-European and the transformation of the outcast into the artist, which were the results of writing *Tropic of Cancer*, inevitably changed the direction of Miller's work. Considering himself to have an identity now as a capital-A artist, and justification as a unique personality, he no longer had the underlying subject matter or point of view of his first work. Only occasionally does Miller's later writing show the early desperate confrontation with absurdity and extremity. The wild and sly gesture directed at a grotesque, fragmented, hopeless reality does not fit so well into a self-important, continuing world in which he has an exalted role. Postures tend to replace perceptions when the outsider finds a spiritual home.

Black Spring (1936), his second published book, seems to to have been written partly before and partly after the delayed publication of *Cancer*. Miller repeatedly refers to the post-*Cancer* period as "euphoric," "ultra-happy,"[1] and the title of *Black Spring* may be translated as "the grim made positive." Less at war with the world, his energy turns to artistic images and to nostalgic memories. The self-made epigraph for the first section—"What is not in the open street is false, derived, that is to say, *literature*" (9)[2]—suggests *Cancer,* as do a number of flourishes in the ten autonomous sketches: but the street leads down memory to his early Brooklyn days ("The 14th Ward") and is far less of any actual street than in his first book. That is to say, its poetic-prose rambles are largely "literature."

Even when Miller deals in *Black Spring* with the present and Paris, as in its third piece, "A Saturday Afternoon," he plays the literary man at ease rather than the anguished stranger. The epigraph is "This is better than reading Virgil" (43). What is better? The genial physical sense of Paris—bicycling on a spring afternoon, looking at the Seine, eating in a sidewalk café, taking a tourist's delight in a French urinal, and free-associating. The piece is a pleasantly effusive literary appendix to *Tropic of Cancer*.[3] Miller briefly mocks Carl and Van Norden—major figures in the earlier book but otherwise unclear here—for their difficulty in writing. They should let go like true surreal mad-

men, follow Whitman and "accept Time absolutely" (47), and leap to the
hyperbolically eternal present moment; they should make the grotesque
comic gesture, such as eating wormy cheese and being "Miguel Feodor
Francois Wolfgang Valentine Miller" (48); they should, like the Seine, let all
things freely flow into exotic images and ruminations. The longest section of
flowing association comes when Miller uses a street urinal ("To relieve a full
bladder is one of the great human joys" [52]). Thus to live in the immediate
means being a Robinson Crusoe; moral: "everyman his own civilized desert"
(54). But the classic refugees from the cancerous plague of modern life, such
as Gauguin and Lawrence, did not take enough pleasure in their alienation.
So down with Virgil and classic literary restraint and up with Rabelais and all
the "fine, lusty genuine spirits" (57). The ruminations—Parisian spring,
moldy cheese, urinals, and self-satisfaction notwithstanding—turn into literary commentaries. This prose-poem sparkles with some burlesque gestures
and amusing slogans, but it also tends toward drifting wordiness without the
very agonal and joyous concentration on the intense moment which it
advocates.

Trapped in an obsessive and fragmented self, Miller's escape most often
takes the form of exploiting his weaknesses, of flight *into* rather than *away
from* his failings. One of the most literal accounts appears in the next sketch,
entitled "The Angel Is My Water-Mark!"[4] Unlike many of the other ruminations, this has a definable subject, the "genesis of a masterpiece"—Miller's
art. He starts out describing, more or less, how he writes. As should be evident from the results, Miller is a packrat collector of odd phrases, images, and
notions. These he uses to set off reminiscences and ruminations; then he compulsively annotates his annotations. Moved by obscure hungers, he nurtures
a flow of verbal frenzy, and pours out a swirl of words linked to a phrase or
image. This self-hypnotic process of art he calls "dictation" (70), though not
specifying whether the dictator is the surrealist's unconscious or the sage's
cosmos—or just obsessed Henry Miller hungering to be a unique artist.

Gratuitousness and pose play a considerable part. A pamphlet, he tells us,
about the art of lunatics sets him off on a painting, water colors being his alternate therapy to writing. His description of his attempt to draw a horse—it
threatens to turn into a "liverwurst" and a good many other things—is amusing, but at times the performance simply becomes cute. At least according to
his description, his art shows an odd mixture of sophistication and naïvete—
primitivistic surrealism—in which he bemusedly combines fragments of fantasy and accidents. Chance and association provide the only teleology,
culminating in the gratuitous image of an angel which catches his fancy.
Memories of earlier anti-painting (such as stamping on pictures) and of

things he has seen in museums combine with his "simulating" madness and with his destructiveness (blotting out and scrubbing off) in frenzied attempts to make art reach "infinity" (85). But Miller remains too "literary"—too concerned with his personality and his verbal and imagistic associations—to reach what the abstractionists were later to call "pure" or "absolute" painting. After having blotted out the horse and put the water color under the faucet, Miller sees more rather than less associations in the blob. There also remain apt imagistic pieces representing the dual Miller—a horse's ass and the angel in the corner—and the magical sense of that gratuitous angel as being unremovable in a grandiloquent affirmation of Miller.[5]

What he did with water colors, he also attempts with words, as in one of his least interesting pieces, "Jabberwhorl Cronstadt." This wordy burlesque of a Paris friend blots out much of the image of that apparently eccentric figure in heavy wordplay: "Jabberwhorl glausels with gleerious glitter, his awbrous orbs atwit and twitter" (157). Miller drags in his usual catalogue of exotic names and miscellaneous tidbits of information (frequently spurious), and his joking delight in scientific jargon: "the great vertiginous vertebration . . . the zoospores and the leucocytes . . . the wamroths and the holenlindens . . . everyone's a poem" (159). But the long jumbled images of Cronstadt drunk equally on alcohol and on Miller's jabbering whorl, and including a swan song about sinks and time running out, have insufficient thought or satiric direction to pipe the playfulness. Though the flow may have seemed magical a generation ago, following the tiresome later work of James Joyce and the *transition* school, the flush of words washes out experience and any revealing perspective in a mere spray of avant-gardism.[6]

In another literary experiment, "Into the Night Life . . . ," subtitled "A Coney Island of the Mind," Miller develops his version of the surrealist nightmare, or rather, a dozen nightmares lumped together. This work shows the to-be-expected frenzied journeys, horrendous transformations, snakes coming out of female organs, disintegrating bodies, mechanized desert landscapes, and threatening menageries of night life. Perhaps the material would be of some interest in providing psychogenetic patterns for a biographer of Miller: the "poor, desperate father" (holding a rusty razor) with whom the son can't communicate (177); the injured girl-child (his sister or his daughter?) whom he can't save; the recurring images of surgery and dismemberment; the agonized stumbling into childhood scenes next to cemeteries and the recurrent nostalgia for the "street of early sorrows"; the horrifying reappearances of the "witch mother" (166, 194); the images of sexuality always turning into grotesque mechanisms (including wives); and the italicization of personal guilt (his customs declaration: "*I want to declare that I am a traitor to the human race*" [168]).

But Miller's hyperbolic language and literary fantasizing of guilty dream material do not seem adequate to give this overextended prose-poem incisiveness or shape. Listening to another person's dreams, even when told with Miller's verbal lushness, is a bore. The more significant public themes, such as the trail of guilt or the "coney island of the mind" motif, symbolizing the pasteboard and neon quality of modern life (173), never develop. The spatial-temporal displacements of dream life may provide vivid material for paintings or cinema; but more than thirty pages of such prose seem merely mannerism or private therapy. Reality, I think, may be significantly explored by borrowing from the nightmare, but the nightmare itself cannot provide adequate reality.

Why these derangements of sense, syntax, and reality? Miller gives varied names and titles to his purpose, but they all resolve themselves into the wild rhetoric of the search for identity, finally achieved only by self-apotheosis. In one of those pieces that I have characterized as an apocalyptic essay, entitled "Third or Fourth Day of Spring," Miller simply states his two gestures of escape: "You have the dream for night time and the horse laugh for day time" (30). But they are not really separate for Miller, and the laugh is emphatically nightmarish and diseased. Each great period, he suggestively notes, is followed by its characterizing malaise: the Crusades—Black Death; Columbus—syphilis; nineteenth century—schizophrenia. The twentieth-century laugh thus tends toward hysteria, toward cackling at catastrophe.

However, Miller also claims a different stance of "gay, hard wisdom" (33). He would like to possess the sardonic delight of Petronius (whose Trimalchio's "piss warm and drink cold" provides the epigraph here), of Rabelais and his panhuman hyperbole, and of Whitman's embracing song. But, as a point of fact, he more often sees "only catastrophes," and his longings are messianic. He claims to be on the way, with his escape from the "black curse" of America and with his awareness of millennial circumstances ("I am dazzled by the glorious collapse of the world" [32]). More crudely, he accepts himself deified: his life is of great "importance" and "significance"; his writing provides "a history of our time—a history of all time" (31); his words become "divine stuttering." His megalomania raises up an image greater than Christ or God almighty, "*MYSELF.*" He is the "new *reality*" in the "Universe of Death." True, Miller shrewdly qualifies his schizophrenic pretensions by comic hyperbole, as in his burlesque horoscope:

I am Chancre, the crab, which moves sideways and backwards and forwards at will. I move in strange tropics and deal in high explosives, embalming fluid, jasper, myrrh, smaragd, fluted snot and porcupines' toes. Because of Uranus which crosses my longitudinal I am inordinately fond of cunt, hot chitterlings and water bottles. . . . I am volatile, quixotic, unreliable, independent, and evanescent. Also quarrelsome. With a hot pad under my ass I can play the braggart or the buffoon as good as any man. . . . This is a self-portrait which yields only the missing parts—an anchor, a dinner bell, the remains of a bird, the hind part of a cow. In short, I am an idle fellow who pisses his time away. I have absolutely nothing to show for my labors but my genius. (37)

Burlesque or not, then, he does have a destiny, his role as artist; his gestures are confined to sitting before the typewriter; and the wild images ("missing parts") may cover the longing to be more than the comedian he essentially is. He ends this apocalyptic essay by using the strategy of extremes, insisting that the choice is between song and listerine, "Fourth Eclogue or 13th Arrondissement!" (41). But, on the basis of the rest of the collection, to which this seems the displaced prologue, he has not chosen either, though convinced of his transformation and that his gestures of nihilism will at least save him from the more usual "lesser, muddier annihilations" (40). And perhaps he was right, though the art would have been better if he had stuck to eclogue or, more likely, to the streets of Paris—if he had been able to follow through pure extremity as mad saint or, much better, as buffoon. As is, it seems an occasionally provocative and amusing, but often pretentious and messy, burlesque confession.

So far, I have discussed half the pieces in *Black Spring*. Most of the remaining ones, while not separate from these gestures, turn self-definition to a flight from the present into Miller's own history prior to his self-discovery as an artist. These rhapsodical memories of his Brooklyn–New York life start with the much worked first piece, entitled "The 14th Ward." With a "patriotic" love of its streets, though not of the neighborhood's Lutheran morality, Miller joys over his boy-heroes and the lost richness of the time when "foam was on the lager and people stopped to chat" (13). No doubt the pre–World War I, German-American neighborhood did have a sense of community no longer to be found; but this is not really Miller's interest since most of his nice concrete details and rhetorical flourishes point to the sense of mystery in the good old days of beer, burlesque, and boys. The simple American male ethos, which underlies so much of Miller's work and response, holds him in the "clutching brilliance" of memory. The insistence on returning to the world of memory reveals a longing for the time when his life, bounded by a simple masculine code, seemed "whole," and therefore the ways of the 14th Ward become holistic. One of the curious forces driving all through Miller's work is a sense of Edenic loss which he can never quite pin down. Maturity he sees, accurately for himself, as a "great fragmentation" (18). The awesomeness of youthful vision with its awareness of mystery in common things, and, probably later, of literary discoveries not as ideas but as rituals, had a brightness that now belongs only to dream and longing. He ends with an apostrophe to a lost world that seems to have doomed all other worlds since they cannot match the innocent eye of poignant memory.

The longest piece in *Black Spring* is "The Tailor Shop," with Miller's own pathetic-clown epigraph: "I've got a motter: *always merry and bright!*" (89). This genre piece about the days when he worked in his father's tailor shop (his early twenties, before and during World War I) reveals nostalgia going bitter. The first part consists of a series of character sketches—with broad sentiment but shrewdly sardonic detail—of cursing Irish bartenders, earnest Jewish cutters, irascible well-to-do customers, loquacious and drunken drummers, and several pathetic imposters. As he later notes, "the men who passed through my father's shop reeked with love" (133); more exactly, they were endearing failures, and Miller's recognition of that bedrock type provides a solid American motif of the pathetic role of sensitivity in our society.

In the first part of this narrative, Miller subordinates the elaborate verbal play of his other sketches to an only slightly exaggerated account. Only in his dallying with sex—the too-easy seduction of the too-beautiful widow of one of his father's customers—does reality get lost, and we have a presentation suitable to one of the "old cronies" in the shop. But as the piece progresses, customers die off, the narrator fights with his wife, and outrage grows. While Miller—again claiming the example of Rabelais (115)—insists on boisterous gaiety, the misery twists the humor. He turns from the tailor shop— never able to maintain dramatically intense narrative—to the reunions of the "freaks who made up the family tree" (116), and he catalogues the heavy food and heavy troubles of his jolly Germanic tribe. Tante Melia, who went "completely off her nut" (121) and had to be taken to the asylum by Miller, focuses the horror; the "too good"—the "half-witted angel" types—are, he says, always destroyed. He thus laments the lost innocence of Henry Miller.

As a narrative, "The Tailor Shop" now disintegrates. Hyperawareness becomes verbal hyperbole, with fragments of events (apparently drawn from various years) obscurely linked in an enlarging and often surreal rhetoric. His claimed artistic gropings (dream writing in his head a vast ancestral book, of which only the title—*The Island of Incest*—exists) attempt to counter the decline of his actual world.[7] The disordered prose insists on an anguish whose cause remains unspecific and disproportionate to the obvious problems of reaching manhood which the situation suggests. The pyrotechnical fragments would seem to mark, in Miller's consciousness, the simultaneous decline of his father's tailor shop, the prewar world, and a whole way of life. Decay, death, madness, and suffering—Miller does not want to accept them, and so shores fragments of memory against the loss that threatens to become his one reality.

Miller's wasteland is less cultural and more personal than most of those that mark the early decades of the twentieth century, and it is treated as a cry of the heart rather than as a mythic theme. The touched-on pieces of experience—erotic (the painful liaison with a much older woman), familial (the complaining, unforgiving Protestant mother), literary (the admiration for Nietzsche)—become most effective when most simply direct. But Miller's narrative impatience seems to express a more obscure anguish and pervasive sense of guilt. Maturity and the twentieth century both came hard, though the emphasis on desperation and rage and outcast state goes beyond such causes. The long sketch concludes with an hysterical apostrophe: "Now I am lost, *lost*, do you hear? You don't hear? I'm yowling and screaming—don't you hear me?" (142). The shouting, smashing, and self-exhibition insist that someone must hear, someone must understand, that the "always merry and bright" gestures won't work. This, I suspect, is not just the anguish of the loss of American innocence—though certainly that—but the terror that there may never have been anything at all, and that life, truly seen, must always have been dreary, miserable, and ordinary. And this Miller can't accept.

Miller writes, as D. H. Lawrence once said of himself, not for art's sake but for his own sake. Midway in one of his burlesque pieces, entitled "Burlesk," Miller sloganizes: "THE GREAT ARTIST IS HE WHO CONQUERS THE ROMANTIC IN HIMSELF" (245). But his own means of conquest turns out to be violent surrender. To overcome his past and his obsessions, he makes them his one subject; to cure himself of overstatement, he exaggerates and shouts. A weird and rather forced line of associations leads from the Paris of the present to the New York of his past. The mania for titles becomes the heavy repetition of capitalized signs and shouts: "*Don't Spit on the Floor*" and "AMEN! GLORY! GLORY! HALLELUJAH!" (233). These incongruities come from a store-front gospel tabernacle in New York. Then, by natural antilogic, we move to Cleo, the queen of a burlesque show.[8] The style sometimes turns from shouts and violent yokings into just bad verse: "The night is cold and men are walking in lockstep. The night is cold but the queen is naked save for a jock-strap" (239). The nuclear experience underneath these verbal gestures—"the

grotesque and the void, with the heart-breaking loneliness" (242)—
intermittently comes through the mannerisms.

The cathartic process, rather than any narrative sequence or logical coherence, apparently provides the rationale for a group of brief anecdotes. These
include a sadistic-obscene one of a friend punishing his frigid and unfaithful
wife, which is told with amoral relish (one of the few "obscene" bits in *Black
Spring*). Of the sketchy sordid-fantastic anecdotes from his youth, Miller
says, "I am speaking of things that brought me relief in the beginning" (246).
But better therapy for his longings appears in the superromantic conceit of
writing a "beautiful book" that "will contain the absolute truth" of his life
(246) and will be of religious significance. To obscure the crude naivete of
this confession, Miller switches to parody of academic explication, supposedly of the frontispiece of his projected holy writ. The burlesque concludes
with an apocalyptic longing for "a new heaven and a new earth" (250), a plea
for the absolution of his own disorder and disappointments.

There are some lively bits here, but the gusto is really hysteria. Miller is
struggling to accept himself and his world, which he is of but not in. He can
only glue the fragments with the "opiums of dream" (202) and the gestures,
but not the full substance, of art. Thus, in "Walking Up and Down in
China," he makes the magic flourish of calling his alienation "China"—a favorite and repeated "symbol"—in the attempt to give shape to the shapeless
by the transcendentalism of the exotic word. In his reflections on America,
and on his "obsessional walks" in the streets of Paris, he attempts to subsume
both worlds into the dream of art. Fragments of the city scene—street
whores, horrors, and a series of burbling clichés about Paris (208)—and
some further recollections of childhood do bring bits of reality into these poetic musings. But, as *Black Spring* shows all through, the heightened concentration on the absurd immediacy of *Cancer* will not do. To put together his
"countless egos" (202) Miller turns away from the actual and praises "those
who have the courage to close their eyes . . . , whose permanent absence from
the condition known as reality can affect our fate" (209). Thus mystery,
memory, and art increasingly replace the actual.

Part of "Walking Up and Down in China" is a series of violent and sometimes perceptive gestures against America—a rejection of that all-too-
powerful actuality with its "half-celluloid" beings and with the forced
geniality of the *"smile that never comes off!"* (205). For Miller, America appears to be the center of isolation. Yet Paris really comes off no better, as we
see in an elaborate near-paranoid fantasy of death in Paris fused with a catalogue of American place names, in each of which he left his dead body. This
hyperbole of fear makes all actual places impossible. The tumbling rush of

possessed memory also results in several pages of incantation of American proper names, from American Can through Carter's Little Liver Pills to the Banks of the Wabash. Thus alternating pathetic confession with wry burlesque, he also brings in several episodes from his Brooklyn childhood, centering again on such surrogate figures as the crazy, suffering ones he knew. The concluding set of images comes from a pleasant bohemian evening with a friend, with contrasting images of his lost childhood friends, and ending with the insistence that the whole world is lost. An apocalyptic passage prophetically suggests atomic holocaust. All the magic words, then, only exorcise his mixed fears and longings.

The brief conclusion to *Black Spring* has the acute title of "Megalopolitan Maniac."⁹ The self-made epigraph does equally well: "Imagine having nothing in your hands but your destiny. You sit on the doorstep of your mother's womb and you kill time—or time kills you. You sit there chanting the doxology of things beyond your grasp. Outside. Forever outside" (251). Outsideness is the quality of the city with its glittering desert streets and sardine people, for whom he writes a sardonic paean to the vulcanized loneliness for God. Mixing sharp mechanical tropes with swelling romantic rhetoric, he hyperbolically insists on the intensity of living the apocalyptic last moments until all is "blotted in final annihilation" (257). God and the *Song of Love,* of course, have become a stinking fraud, but they point by their absence to a new and greater dynamo of love ten thousand years hence. Waiting on a Zarathustrean mountaintop for the new revelation, he meanwhile wishes to contemplate "a lone individual, a man without name or country, a man whom I respect because he has absolutely nothing in common with you— MYSELF" (259).

Such I-am-ism of an outraged Whitman abroad must do for divinity, short of the new world. This carefully written gesturing and polished invective could well have been the epilogue to *Tropic of Cancer,* or the foreword, rather than the conclusion, to *Black Spring.* For the book which it ends had already turned away from the actuality of the city, relatively little of which (either of Paris or New York) appears in it, to self-contemplation and verbal posturing.¹⁰ His powerful subject of megalopolitan man has been increasingly obliterated by the indulgent manias of Miller. The difference between his first and his second book is, of course, only partial; but the rebirth into artist has reduced the actuality which gave tension to the comic and apocalyptic gestures of the earlier work. While the mixture of eloquence and grandiloquence may be the essential Miller, its artiness too often reveals the lack of artistic mastery of his obsessions. Only the most discrete bits—such as titles, epigraphs, some of the "Tailor Shop" details and the epilogue—achieve the polished raw material of art, without adequate context. The overall product thus falls somewhere between document and literature, and it is a provocatively suggestive but only weakly satisfying anthology of rhetorical gestures, a sort of populist artiness.

"Max" and Other Grotesques

A dozen portraits and literary experiments of the early period (many of which appeared in his third book, *Max and the White Phagocytes* [1938]) will suggest other perspectives on Miller, at both his best and worst.[11] Miller's first publication in Paris—and thus his first significant publication—was a portrait sketch, "Mademoiselle Claude."[12] The ostensible subject is a whore, and the opening gesture displays the usual iconoclasm in which the prostitute is superior to other women. But self-portraiture of course takes over, with Miller as Claude's patron and then as her "pimp." In this inverted self-aggrandizement, sentimentality and cynicism again fuse. Miller almost playfully alternates between the two, portraying Claude as both common street whore and "angel," and the narrating author as both hard-boiled and shuddering innocent.

Miller, according to this portrait, exploits Claude, taking cheap advantage of her credulity with a letter of gross flattery that includes passages lifted from Valéry (he makes a sentimental point of her natural good taste in preferring the Valéry parts). He becomes so entranced with the paradoxical notion of having a *"faithful whore"* that his fantasy runs wild. Drawing on the male sentimentality which defies puritanic sexual virtue by insisting that whores make better mates than other women, he fantasizes going off to live in some mythically sunny clime with Claude.

This inverted dream of connubial bliss with a prostitute also draws upon a recurrent homoerotic obsession of Miller's with the positive side of sexual degradation: a whore has "the whole damned current of life flowing . . . through her. . . . Give me a whore always, all the time!" (146). Apparently the vicarious love, plus the good, practical care Claude provides her *maquereau,* induces a "mystic feeling" of "the unity of life" (147). But he rather neatly undercuts this semened beatitude by being unfaithful to his faithful whore, and he ends by giving her gonorrhea. No wonder the Paris of *Cancer* looks so diseased! Moreover, he deceitfully blames the illness on Claude's other clients, though bizarrely admitting to himself that his saintly fascination with whores was to blame. He concludes with images of Claude as an angel and of himself as less than a man, and with a guilty longing to take her away to live "in the sunshine . . . birds, flowers, life streaming by, just she and me" (151).

Through a series of gestures—iconoclastic, sentimental, amoral, cynical, guilty, mythical—turning about a poor, genteel street whore, he provides not only a pathetic-grotesque confession but a paradigmatic suggestion of man's relation to woman. That Miller must place his insight—the mixture of sentiment and degradation, of romanticism and exploitation, which so often characterize erotic love—in the extreme form of the prostitute's round rather than the suburban home, should not be allowed to obscure his perception and its rather apt, if base, art..

Some of the same perspective would seem necessary for a much longer and somewhat more digressive portrait, "Max," written a few years later (apparently in 1935).[13] Max, a Polish-American Jew and middle-aged pants presser stranded in Paris without job, money, friends, or hope, provides a study of the suffering Jew and Miller's mixed responses. The anecdotal piece shows Miller cauterizing his emotions, in part, by mocking the lumbering and lamenting Jew, whom Miller finds repugnant; his suffering is too emphasized—as if by "a sort of holy, unctuous light . . . stolen from the synagogue" (9). But the image enlarges until Max becomes the quintessence of misery—"suffering itself"—and the epitome, like the cripple in Nathanael West's *Miss Lonelyhearts,* of all the anonymous victims of unemployment, defeat, and despair. Misery, of course, wears its repulsive truth like a distorted mask, which Miller occasionally catches in some apt surreal images—"the look of absolute disgust which hung about his face like a rotten halo" (13). The portrait also catches bits of the pathetic-sardonic quality of Jewish humor. One of Max's great laments is that, when most miserable, he has officially been reclassified as an American tourist. He has also been given a suit that looks too prosperous for a beggar, and Max groans, "If only I shouldn't look so well" (15).

The self-irony of Jewish lamentations may cut both ways on a gentile tongue. For Miller, product of traditional German-American anti-Semitism, displays hyperconsciousness of Max not just as the sufferer but as the suffering Jew. Miller takes Max to a friend, a more cerebrally refined sufferer, a well-to-do neurasthenic American Jewish intellectual, so as to observe sardonically the double image of the suffering Jew. The guilty detachment of the Jewish intellectual, however, sets Miller to righteously imagining himself as the suffering Jew, and in his hostile sympathy he comments: "If I were a Jew [in the 1930s] I would tie a rope around my neck and throw myself overboard" (31). Misery is almost as degrading for the observer as for the sufferer, but Miller, as imaginary Jew, counters his own hostility by gestures of compassion and by some New Testament sermonizing on the need for tangible brotherly love.[14]

Miller intermittently treats Max well, giving him a suit (which doesn't fit Miller anyway), a bath, a meal, and a good many lectures on Miller's own seriocomic role as suffering artist. With shrewd candor, he capitalizes on his own egotism. Max is literary material for the writer, who says to himself while feeding Max, "Today I'm going to listen to you, you bugger . . . listen to every nuance. I'll extract the last drop of juice—and then, *overboard you go!*" (18). But within the mixed gamesmanship of repulsion and sympathy for the suffering Jew, Miller makes several discoveries. Why is the down-and-outer of *Tropic of Cancer* not, finally, as desperate as the suffering Jew? It is not just luck Miller decides, but born "innocence" which saves him from the black luck of Max; it is his egotistical energy, his optimistic practicality, and his untragic sense of destiny of traditional American innocence. Miller, in short, never fully suffers.

The grotesque portrait, however, does not end with Miller but with Max; and this focus helps make it one of Miller's better pieces, cutting deeper than innocent egotism. The assorted Parisian scenes, shrewd bits of dialogue, and apostrophes of love-hate come to focus on Max's deepest suffering. Charity—a bath, a suit, a meal—doesn't cure Max's plight but simply opens to view the unresolvable suffering, the devastating aloneness and bitter fears of the aging outcast in an impersonal world. Max, overwhelmed with anxiety, obsessed with possible madness and death, ends the piece with a semi-literate letter to Miller, begging for help. The hopeless case, the archetypal lugubrious Jew, finally emerges simply as suffering man, grotesquely without end or solace or dignity, which one can only accept as the absurd nature of the world.

Now much of the power of a grotesque portrait like Max comes not only from the acute effort to confront agonized reality but also from the drama of Miller's mixed feelings. When Miller lacks that agonal edge, he makes more purely literary gestures, and writes badly. Another portrait of that period, "Benno, the Wild Man from Borneo," shows Miller as an accomplished, and empty, verbal manipulator.[15] The piece—all effusive praise of some vaguely identified artist friend—quite lacks conflict, time and place. As a substitute for any sort of reality Miller provides a harum-scarum bag of fanciful allusions and rococo comparisons. The last three sentences—they could just as easily be the first three—give us as much, and as little, as we are to get of the man turned into Miller's whimsical version of the surrealist tropes, mythological longings, and stock antitheses: "He is of the old line of Pelagians, the ridgerunners who traveled over the sunken Andes to found a Mexican world.

He is as tough as an old turkey, but warm-hearted and inhumanly tender. A sort of wild man from Borneo with central heating, spring mattress, castors and a boomerang in his left hand" (18).

These self-portraits, whether as mannered rhetorician, imaginary suffering Jew, or American tourist as Parisian pimp, partly indicate Miller's search for a literary role. He usually succeeds least in this when he is being most elaborate. In "Scenario (A Film with Sound)"[16] Miller, a movie buff during his Parisian years, takes over such cinematic principles as the multiple montage, the surreality of visual splicing, and odd-angle perspectives.[17] Mistranslating these directly into prose descriptions, he gives nine loosely linked visual scenes of mechanical and heavy lesbian melodrama—and kills even the limited qualities of his literary source, Anaïs Nin's *House of Incest*.

In other literary experiments in the mid-1930s, Miller plays more comic roles. In *Money and How It Gets That Way*,[18] a pamphlet apparently written in 1936, he does a parody of an economic monograph, with fanciful learned allusions, surreal free associations on gold, wisecracks at businessmen, and ornate puns. He calls for new efforts at "economic disorder" (19), for improved "Marxian diuretic," and for one sure approach to money—"*spend it*" (62). But he tiresomely overelaborates a mild joke.[19] Money is, perhaps to Miller's credit, simply too abstract for him to deal with. He does a trifle better as economist and writer when he returns to his role as belligerent beggar in another pamphlet, *What Are You Going to Do about Alf?* (1935) Part joke, part appeal for money for his friend Alfred Perlès (probably really for Miller), part justification of the artist as beggar in this "open letter,"[20] Miller insists—quite consciously against the leftist socioeconomic thinking of his contemporary writers—that plans and systems don't meet his individual needs. He and his kind are not writing "proletarian" literature but the purely personal art of "our happy life of shame" (10), so "to hell with your superior economic order" (19) which has no relevance to those who want today to eat, drink, smoke—and especially to write. The ultimate justification appears as apocalyptic rebellion: "Things are so bad, we say, that it's useless to pretend any more. Get what you can by hook or crook. Lie, beg, steal, wheedle, cajole, threaten, calumniate, whimper, wail, dance, scream, stand on your head—*anything, but don't surrender!*" (20). But what Miller really justifies is such behavior for "artists." He carries to its extreme the romantic "logic" of the uniqueness of the "creative" man and his separation from all merely human standards—except the economic!

Miller, we see, takes his role as *homme de lettres* with amusing, fantastic, and often wearying literalness—and writes, and publishes, endless letters. Apparently always a compulsive letter writer, he may have produced tens of

thousands of long rambling missives.[21] In 1935, this *blagueur* man of letters
engaged in an elaborate quasi-joke with Michael Fraenkel: the two of them
were to write one thousand pages of letters on the metaphysical problem of
our age, "Hamletic man." By 1938 they had, and the results were eventually
published in two volumes entitled *Hamlet*.[22] Somewhat more indirectly,
Miller carried out similar letter programs with other writers. Probably the
major motive of that vast verbiage of letters, and its major weakness, comes
from Miller's addressing his letters less to human beings than to readers, posterity, and a bloated self-image.[23] Most often his subject is God, alias Henry
Miller.

Though the *Hamlet* letters have occasional curious passages of description
and rumination, and a few good Miller apothegms, they certainly will not go
down among the great letters of either literature or documentation. Actually
not letters at all but loose essays, they are, Miller admits with his usual candor, a "pompous monologue" (I, 166). The fault of eliminating a sense of dialogue is in good part Miller's, for he takes advantage of the agreement
(including, apparently, Fraenkel's promise of publication) to write loose sermons on whatever pleases him. His subjects rarely include the despised
Shakespeare, Hamlet, or the Faustian death theme which obsesses Fraenkel;
but they do include Henry Miller, D. H. Lawrence, Henry Miller, and a variety of miscellaneous preoccupations of Miller as sage, writer, and moralist.
Fraenkel, a bit more reluctantly, retaliates by writing his own essays.

The countergamesmanship reaches its exhausting apogee in Miller's final
"letter" of a hundred published pages (II, 366–465) which, if nothing else,
demonstrates Miller's ultimate aesthetic: "Writing is a compulsive, and de-
lectable thing. Writing is its own reward" (II 315; also I, 348). Consequently,
no limits apply, though at one point Miller effectively argues that all other
men (but Miller) need drastic limits (I, 99ff.), including consistency, accuracy, and decency. A rather mean side of Miller comes out in his repeated vicious attacks on Fraenkel, and also on a dead friend (II, 224). Fraenkel,
reasonably enough, accuses Miller of incomprehension, inconsistency, bad
motives, and harshest accuracy of all, posing ("you are only stringing words,
making literature" [II, 237]). Yet there is an odd method in Miller's badness;
for, as he writes of the archetypal sages, "Lack of integrity can become a virtue
when raised to the highest degree" (II, 296).

Miller's strategy of excess, in his writing in general as well as in his letters,
uses egomania to overcome personal failure and chaos. When these polarities
are most evident, Miller is most successful, I think, in making egotism into
comic-pathetic drama. His buffoon-tourist role produces better art and wisdom than his artist-sage role. "Via Dieppe-Newhaven," a long autobio-

graphical tourist piece, mostly in his plain style, provides an appropriate pathetic self-dramatization.[24] The first half-dozen pages are poor—an insufficient and irrelevant account of money and emotional tribulations with his second wife in Paris. The main substance, which comes from Miller's trip from Dieppe to Newhaven and back (apparently in late 1933), shows some acute observations of the world around, a nice sense of laconic dialogue, and a wry image of himself.

Out of a job and ambivalent about his wife and Paris, Miller wants to flee to London. He goes with only a few francs in his pocket for what he claims will be a short visit, though, since he takes a trunk of manuscripts, that is uncertain. He sardonically observes the English on the boat over, shrewdly noting their firm independence of character and, especially, their irritating social-class mannerisms ("all this yes sir and no sir. *Sir my ass,* I say under my breath" [206]). But with the superior and suspicious English customs officials, Miller reveals himself as the uncertain fool in a scene of comic dialogue in which the bureaucrats shortly turn up his lack of respectable order, job, money—and then cancel his visa. He is taken over by the polite and decent constable assigned to watch him in the "hoosegow," until he can be shipped back to France the next morning. The constable watches him even in the W.C.; this, Miller says with his usual excremental impetus, inspires him to write his account.

In noting the weirdness of Anglo-Saxon law and morality—"on the one hand they manhandle you, and on the other they nurse you like a baby" (218)—he succinctly catches the genteel authoritarianism of British civilization. Miller becomes sentimental about his constable, and even comes out with praise for "civilized" England. However, as he leaves England on the boat back to Dieppe, he feels joy in rejecting "that man-made muck which we glorify with the word civilization" (221), and which has rejected him. Having been timorous all the way through, he can now, to himself, make the hyperbolic gesture of verbally justifying even crime against that civilization. The contradictory view of civilization typifies Miller, but the double-response of praise and revolt also has its own validity, for modern "civilization" really demands a contradictory response.

Miller, as the episode with the customs officials emphasized, acts inept in a mildly rebellious way. Anxiety overwhelms him on the trip back: what if the French authorities reject him, too? Then he would have to return to the States: "Better a beggar in Paris than a millionaire in New York" (222). But the less efficient French bureaucracy admits him again, and he burbles in emotional release from his anxiety, ending with a comic-apocalyptic paean to the "sense of voyage." Just how self-conscious Miller may be in playing the fool here—grandiloquently philosophizing on a ferry trip and alternating rhetorical swagger with practical cringing—must remain uncertain. The casual but lucid presentation of a shrewd fool is amusingly effective. Such a self-portrait of the grotesque tourist lacks the anguished awareness of "Max," but it goes beyond the literary posturing Miller so eagerly turns to in his inchoate desires to be something other than his rebel-buffoon American self.

Colossus of Maroussi

The 1930s and Henry Miller's decade-long tour of Europe ended with World War II. Miller had long announced impending doom, but with characteristic quick-footedness he found several ways to escape his own violent apocalypse. On one level this was by appropriately leaving France just before the war broke out for a few months' tour of Greece (August 1939 to early January 1940). And in Greece he escaped doom at a more elaborate level by self-induced revelations before quitting Europe entirely for America.[25]

The series of illuminations, given loose form in *The Colossus of Maroussi* (written the following year in New York), shine on Greece, art, friendship, and religion, and cast shadows on American and French civilization. The light also is turned towards a new saintly Miller, shadowing the enfant terrible and the wise clown dominant in his best works. *Colossus* draws to a close with a rather effective catalogue of his images of his Greek tour, and then concludes:

The Greek earth opens before me like the Book of Revelation. I never knew that the earth contains so much; I had walked blindfolded, with faltering, hesitant steps; I was proud and arrogant, content to live the false, restricted life of the city man. The light of Greece opened my eyes, penetrated my pores, expanded my whole being. . . . I refuse categorically to become anything less the citizen of the world which I silently declared myself to be when I stood on Agamemnon's tomb. From that day forth my life was dedicated to the recovery of the divinity of man. Peace to all men, I say, and life more abundant. (241)

The natural world and ethical revelation often seem intricately, if contradictorily, linked in the American imagination. Of course, the light of the Miller gospel derives less from the Greek sunshine than from antithesis to the darkness of World War II. He declares his benign lack of allegiance in flight, geographical and spiritual, from the war world. While the alienation is not new, some of the benignity is.

The Greek experience, at least in memory, was "a veritable re-birth" (237) for Miller; but, we recall, each of his experiences is credited with redemptive power. Here the motif seems to be the "blinding, joyous illumination" of the Greek landscape which soon takes on a "transcendental quality . . . something holy" (45). In good part we must understand this as humanized transcendence, man writ large, as in the entitling figure of the book, the colossal Katsimbalis, Greek poet, monologist, cicerone, egotist, drinker, self-dramatizer, and warm friend to Miller. We are told more about the entrancing effect on Miller of this favorite Miller type than about the man himself (28–32 and 73—75). Miller, as I have previously noted, rarely writes concretely well of people except from disgust or malice.

Katsimbalis serves as cicerone for the touring Miller in part of the first and last episodes of the book, and Miller seems to project onto him his own magical responses to such places as Poros, Epidaurus, and Hydra. Miller, as we know from his earlier obsessive gynecological imagery, always looks for a return to the warm womb world. The entrance to Poros harbor comes to seem "the joy of passing through the neck of the womb" (53). The genial Greeks and their confined world give Miller a sense of scene far more manageable than the frightening vastness of the purposeless cosmos, or of impersonal America.

Miller's repeated moral insists on the "human kingdom" which lies between the natural and the divine (77), and here is to be found "the peace which passeth all understanding." His more tangible values are the simplicity and individuality of a Mediterranean Thoreau. Intensity, not moderation, is the moral key. The Greek emphasis on the human, he notes, takes its tone from the belief "that *genius* is the norm, not mediocrity" (83). The anarchic lucidity of the Greek scene, the enthusiasm and passion of the Greek temper, the dense continuity and limitation of the Greek world, contrast for Miller with the antagonism and emptiness, the machines and money, of America. And not only America, for France now seems to him unfriendly, destructively skeptical, arbitrary, and petty (32ff.). At Agamemnon's tomb Miller achieves the supporting revelation:

The earth is flamy with spirit as if it were an invisible compass we are treading and only the needles quivering luminously as it catches a flash of solar radiance. We are veering towards Agamemnon's tomb. . . . Stop before the heart glows through. Stop to pick a flower. Shards everywhere and sheep droppings. The clock has stopped. The earth sways for a fraction of a second, waiting to resume its eternal beat.

I have not yet crossed the threshold. I am outside, between the cyclopean blocks which flank the entrance to the shaft, I am still the man I might have become, assuming every benefit of civilization to be showered upon me with regal indulgence. I am gathering all of this potential civilized muck into a hard, tiny knot of understanding. I am blown to the maximum, like a great bowl of molten glass hanging from the stem of a glassblower. Make me into any fantastic shape, use all your art, exhaust your lung power—still I shall only be a thing fabricated, at the best a beautiful cultured soul. I know this, I despise it. I stand outside full-blown. . . . I am going to put my foot over the threshold—*now*. I do so, I hear nothing. I am not even there to hear myself shattering into a billion splintered smithereens. Only Agamemnon is there . . . he fills the still beehive: he spills out into the open, floods the fields, lifts the sky a little higher. The shepherd walks and talks with him by day and by night. Shepherds are crazy folk. So am I. I am done with civilization and its spawn of cultured souls. I gave myself up when I entered the tomb. From now on I am a nomad, a spiritual nobody. (92–93)

This revelation, which he returns to as the crux of his Greek experience in the final pages of the book, seems to be the same one Miller is always having of direct acceptance and responsiveness. It just varies the metaphors of *Cancer*. He has come prepared to find the Greek myths vibrantly alive—in contrast to any learned niggling by a "full-fledged chimpanzee" of a professor—and he ends "knowing" Agamemnon's crime and the answer to it, in a simple faith separate from all "cultural rigamarole" (95).

So much for the first part of *The Colossus of Maroussi*, which consists of such arguments, surrounded by fragmentary descriptions of touring Greece, miscellaneous personal details, and a sermon on his revelations (76–86)—all without much significant order or sequence. Though part 2, which centers on Miller's solitary stay in Crete, carries on many of the same motifs, somewhat more art and order appear. The first preliminary incident to the Crete trip, for example, provides one of the few topical perspectives. Along with a Greek audience, Miller applauds the American film *Juarez* with its denunciation of the "tragic plight" of Mexico under Maximilian's dictatorship, so analogous to the Greek dictatorship of the 1930s.[26] For Miller, this suggests an almost favorable view of what America represents (102). It is an appropriate, if cursory, perspective, for Miller never really loses, no matter how loudly he shouts, his sense of being "thoroughly American" (222).

The second preliminary incident, which he gives in his surrealist-burlesque style, shows his American cosmic iconoclasm and exuberance. Miller and Lawrence Durrell visit an astronomical observatory in Athens. They do not respond to the "prison of logic" of the science nor to the "feeble-minded" game of its mathematical tools but to their own ecstatic visions of the cosmos. For Miller, a view through the telescope revealed "an effulgent rose window shattered by a hand grenade," an "eternity of beauty" and "cos-

mic violation," the wisdom of Hermes Trismegistus, and the power of imagination over mere fact. He counters his own portentous romanticism with the
usual rhetorical violence—several pages of free-swinging malediction on the
symbolic significance of Saturn (104–6). The catalogue of associations includes "tripe, dead gray matter, . . . rheum, ectoplasm . . . constipation . . .
feeble novels . . . red tape . . . YMCA's . . . spiritist seances . . . T. S. Eliot . . .
Chamberlin"; also germane are the "double mastoid" of "the soul," "senseless
fatality," "the diabolical sweat of learning for its own sake," and "those evil
looking shreds which one hawks up in the morning." Much more of modern
life belongs in the polemical house of this mock-astrological chart, this "lym-
phatic globe of doubt and ennui."

After yet a third preliminary anecdote and poetical flight—this one em-
ploying rather sentimental praise of Greek gamins and peasant women for an
epode on Greek beauty—he finally gets to Crete and then to his description
of a trip to Phaetos (156–66). This includes a forceful account of that harsh
countryside which provides counterpoint for the benign revelations that follow. Miller exalts over the view from the car of a brutalized earth "wherein
God abdicated" and nature set "in a frozen vomit of hate" the destructive "absolute" that forces all meaning to be purely human (158).

The Minoan palace ruins provide the Edenic antithesis. Walking the final
stage of his pilgrimage, Miller is overcome with reverential bliss. A persuasive
Greek tourist guide greets him by announcing that God has sent Miller to the
Minoan monument (gross flattery always charms Miller). When the guide
also picks him a flower, cleans his shoes, serves lunch with a good wine, and
continues to flatter him, Miller becomes ponderously benign: "I had reached
the apogee, I wanted to give, to give prodigally and indiscriminately of all I
possessed" (161).

Miller does not really describe the scene apart from the sycophantic sensitivity of the tourist guide, but he insists on his own regal reactions. Apparently, part of his lavish feeling derives from his fancies of the beauty of
mysteriously ancient civilizations. The fancy provides the experience, and encourages the fortuitous priestliness in which he wants to "send out a benediction in every direction" (161) and to feel "united with the whole world"
(162). His twenty-year dream of seeing such a place (112, 153), and his
primitivistic romanticism combined with creaturely well-being on that particular day, produced a foregone unitary revelation of the standard sort. The
magical reverence for life provides, at the end of part 2, a moral fulcrum for
hurling angry condemnations at the Western world for doing little about the
Smyrna slaughter of 1922, and all the similar outrages that make "civiliza-

tion . . . a wordy phantom suspended like a mirage above a swelling sea of murdered carcasses" (173).

Miller, of course, had been a violent pacifist and righteous condemner of the barbarism of civilization for at least a decade, so the Cretan "illumination" has little particular relevance, and it is not effectively presented. More common-sense perceptions show more art and verve. His stay in Herakleion, presented with a sharp eye for the visual and anomalous, shows an equally wry awareness. With several local literary figures, Miller plays the American artist, mocking a pompous Greek's "cataract of flowery horse shit" (119). He scorns the local literati's worship of things American, their belief in the United States' cultural renascence and role as "the hope of the world" (141). With usual hyperbole, he insists that America is more impoverished than Greece, and that America's one virtue is that men have faith in their "own powers" and not in America (133–34).

France, now that Miller is out of it, becomes the subject of a diabolical parody of its pervasive petit bourgeois virtues of parsimony, insularity, and self-righteousness. The French proprietress of a Cretan souvenir shop, who comments scornfully on Crete's lack of civilization, provides the focus. In joyous reaction against Franco-American culture, Miller writes a burlesque directed against the petty and nasty civilization represented by such a woman. He sentimentally exalts in "the great Negro race which alone keeps America from falling apart" (138), and its supercivilized aristocracy of Duke Ellington, Count Basie, and other true descendants of Isidore Ducasse and "the great and only Rimbaud." He elaborates this surrealist conceit into a long "barbaric passacaglia" (138–45) directed at the proprietress of petty civilization. The mélange consists of jazz terms and song titles of the 1930s, figures from Greek mythology fused with his Whitmanesque delight in American names, and burlesque puns and denunciations. Miller fuses the glory that was Greece—its violently lucid mythologies—with another impassioned cultural form, American jazz mythology, to mock a pseudo-civilization represented by the souvenir shop mentality and the culture of mechanized murder.

Also practicing that major lively art of meditatively walking the streets, Miller contrasts Paris, New York, and Herakleion: "By comparison Park Avenue seems insane and no doubt is insane. The oldest building in Herakleion will outlive the newest building in America. Organisms die; the cell lives on. Life is at the roots, embedded in simplicity, asserting itself uniquely" (146–47). Miller is one of those longing Americans who is questing for *the* civilization, the mythological roots. He also idealizes Knossus where "before the dawn of that blight called Christianity" there was produced a richly superior style of life (154).

The third and final part of *The Colossus of Maroussi* draws on Miller's last weeks in Greece as he waits to leave the war-threatened country. Most of that time centers on Athens, with a few side "excursions" (Delphi, Eleusis, Sparta). The account is miscellaneous, generally good-humored, occasionally pompous. For those who assume Henry Miller to be mortal, the silliest section is his earnest description of his visit to an Armenian "soothsayer" (201–7). This astrologer commmonsensically notes that Miller is "schizophrenic"; the rest consists of flattery and fantasy that Miller ponderously reports and seems to take seriously. Miller asks if his writings will make him "immortal," and the charlatan goes one better and insists that Miller will literally "never die" and that he has "all the signs of divinity" (203). Miller insists, without giving examples, that all the astrologer's predictions were amazingly true (one of the few concrete ones—that Miller would never have money—proved patently false). The writer was "profoundly impressed" by the interview, which seemed to confirm his childish image of himself as a great artist and sage; he has become his own colossus.

Part of Miller's charm is that his egomania and silliness are so gross, so simpleminded, and so uncensored as to be poignant. His quaintness also comes out in his love of shabby hotels and just as shabby people—an easy exoticism for anything which has "an aroma of the past" (177). His reactions to Thebes (177), Delphi (195), and Sparta (221) are gratuitous subjective connections with quaint memories of his own past or with magical word associations. The responsiveness of the free-floating psyche flows both ways: back to the child's amorphous dreams of the classical world but also in revolt against his real childhood. The mythic view of Greece and the scorn for America provide continual counterpoint. Miller mocks the Americanized Greeks he encounters for their worship of American success; back in New York, he praises two Greek Americans for their intelligent failures as a lavatory attendant and a night elevator operator in a hotel (235). While Miller's rage against things American has a lack of discrimination which suggests inchoate rebellion against his own lack of success, he also reveals an inverted snobbery—the traditional American folk delight in finding the "humble" better than the successful. Given what many successful people in rootless America are, the inversion has some truth. Unfortunately, however, Miller simply asserts the merit of the lowly rather than demonstrating it, perhaps because of his own righteous conceit.

Miller went to Greece, as to Paris, to affirm himself and his myth. In Greece he finds his image of himself simply and joyously reflected in his literary friends who were "open, frank, natural, spontaneous, warm-hearted" (210). His American individualist's vision of a small, communal, vital, fully humanized world shines in the actual Greek light (236–37). An American innocent, carrying within an exuberant freshness of the legendary past, he went prepared for the revelations of a colossal land of the heart's desire; and, of course, he found them in moments of illumination in the obvious, fabled places. Since he was an enthusiastic tourist coming upon the scenes with sketchy literary "familiarity" and a priori "intense adoration" (209–10), the ordinariness had little effect. And even with the ordinary, Miller was so un-abashedly ready to find reflections of his memories and desires in slums, women, ruins, scenery, and friends that they all took on a childlike, and often childish, subjective wonderfulness.

The art of *The Colossus of Maroussi,* as has been indicated, is frequently defective—often vague, strident, sentimental, and silly.[27] Rhetorical asser-tions repeatedly override any sense of time and place, thus undercutting its own *raison* as a "travel book." The experiences in which Miller discovers his post-Parisian doctrine of a peace which passeth into bland truisms and egotis-tical projections are only slightly balanced by comic defiance—the satiric asides on false culture and authority and the burlesques on science and on American, British, and French ersatz civilizations. The rather dubious mysta-goguery on peace and unity may well be less an authentic reaction to Greece than to the world war that only peripherally comes into the book in his apoca-lyptic asides. It is a weak and poorly done book.

Several years after writing *The Colossus of Maroussi* Miller wrote an ex-ceptionally tiresome coda, as it were—"Today, Yesterday and Tomorrow."[28] In this sermon on the Greek resistance to the Nazi invasion, Miller forgets his pacifist revelations and shouts in praise of violent Greek heroism. His thesis seems to be that fifth-century B.C. Greek values—all abstractly superhuman—inhere in modern Greece. The careless supporting examples all come from nonpersonal and learned materials. Miller always goes bearing gifts—the literary man's legacy. His conclusion from his ten-year tour of Eu-rope is more characterized by culture-mongering than by distinctive personal experience; in Europe he found and affirmed the literary life.

But the more powerful gesture of the American abroad is that of lively disaffiliation—*Cancer*'s "I haven't any allegiance." This expresses, I suspect, a more essential American role when confronted with the European burden. "The American," he observes, "is a born anarchist. He has no genuine concern with the ideals of the European."[29] This was his claim rather more than his practice. He asserts a mocking individuality, a joyous nihilism when it comes to playing the traditional "civilized" games. Such gestures have been made often enough (especially with American antiheroes abroad, such as Hemingway's Frederick Henry and Donleavy's Sebastian Dangerfield) that we should recognize them in Miller's Henry Miller. Perhaps such a stance of the outsider is the "new man," the "true American"—as much as there ever will be one—whom D. H. Lawrence called for in *Studies in Classic American Literature*. Lawrence, however, insisted that all he could see was a "sort of recreant European." Miller became such.

Henry Miller's distinctive qualities were the iconoclasm, exuberance, hyperbole, alienation, and utopianism, of the true American, especially when confronted with the cultural religiosity and repressive falsity of the Good European—the gay renegade. But as he took himself with earnestness as the man of letters and sage of the traditional unitary vision, his distinctive qualities were obfuscated. As a buffoonish outsider, Miller had something to tell us; as a *faux naif* propagandist for art and religion, what he offered was rather less, indeed.

Chapter Three
The Brooklyn Passion
The Dark Lady

Miller's major obsession as a writer, after his first works, is the life that led up to his identification as an "artist," and henceforth his literature becomes the endless re-creation of the myth of his own history. Of this, we can no longer discuss specific works, only the motifs running through thousands of pages of episodic, garrulous ruminations and fanciful poeticizations of his Brooklyn past and self. The American alien in Europe flees his vivacious outcast role to find a home and an identity in willed acts of memory-fantasy. Miller had several ways of sustaining his role as artist-sage, but his perplexed and nostalgic account of how he became *the* Henry Miller dominates them all. At his best a sardonic and ecstatic maker of rebel gestures, and at his worst a diffuse and bombastic rhetorician, Miller mostly writes in egotistical, fragmented, exaggerated ways. When these characteristics are directed toward complex people, a life pattern, and mythologies of romance and salvation, the results can only be a weird mélange.

The several thousand published pages that comprise Miller's "autobiographical romance" about the artist as topsy-turvy Horatio Alger had an ostensible master plan. In a chronological summary, Miller put down as one of the key entries for 1927: "Compiled notes for complete autobiographical cycle of novels in twenty-four hours."[1] Elsewhere, he several times restated this plan, perhaps most significantly in *Nexus*. According to that source, the day Lindbergh completed his "Homeric feat," Miller planned one of his own, "My Doomsday Book" (199). Writing much of the night, he sketched out page after page of his "tragedy," he says, which would run from the time he met his second wife (apparently 1923) to that day in 1927. According to *Nexus*, he informs his wife that she will be "immortalized" in the long work which will tell the truth about their life. When an interior voice asks if it will qualify as literature, Miller answers: "Then to hell with literature! *The book of life*, that's what I would write." And when the mocking inner intelligence asks whose book it will be, Miller replies, "*The Creator's*" (262).

Miller's attempt to give his life cosmic shape, or at least to re-create with an imitation of divine plenitude, became a megalomania. A decade later, he partly presents that plan in *Tropic of Capricorn*. After he returned to America, he apparently shifted focus, style, and plan; he then retells the story in a multivolume series under the general title of *The Rosy Crucifixion: Sexus* (two volumes), *Plexus* (two volumes), *Nexus* (one volume). He vaguely announced several more volumes, but apparently abandoned them.[2] While the more than two thousand pages of autobiographical romance center on the 1923–27 period, they extend beyond it at both ends and incorporate (frequently by loose association) much material drawn from other periods of Miller's life. Where Miller's earliest books attempted to defy "literature," these half-dozen volumes attempt to turn dreary, perplexing reality into a purely literary life.

Several portentous themes very loosely connect these six volumes of fantasy and autobiography. The metaphor of "The Rosy Crucifixion," for example, suggests joy through suffering or, if we judge by the results, a burlesque messianic role.[3] A more tangible form of this odd suffering comes out in the misery and inspiration connected with the Dark Lady of passion. She is partly the femme fatale of the romantic, an inverted traditional muse of the artist, the Eve-Lilith of primordial knowledge, a witch-goddess of sexuality and power, and, according to Miller's insistence, his second wife. Under the names of Mona and Mara, she haunts much of Miller's work. In *Tropic of Cancer* she briefly appears as the sensual woman of the first chapter who wakes with lice in her beautiful tresses. Later, she becomes a Strindbergian metaphor, a destructive dream-woman in a dance of death (163) as the narrator wanders the Parisian streets. He says that for seven years he was more faithful to her than the Christian to his God—"even when I was deceiving her" (160)—and that she is the source of both his anguish and his power.

With this Dark Lady, the literal woman quickly turns into a metaphor. In *Quiet Days in Clichy,* Miller, in anecdotal reflections about his post-*Cancer* Parisian period, writes of the wife who visited him in Paris in 1933: "my life seems to have been one long search for *the* Mara who would devour all others and give them significant reality."[4] In sharp contrast we get a present tense, more prosaic-pathetic view of the irresponsible wife he can't live with in the opening pages of "Via Dieppe Newhaven."[5] But two decades later, she has become pretentiously literary. Miller discusses "Her" in relation to H. Rider Haggard's "She" (the heroine of *She,* Haggard's crude late-Victorian exotic-fantasy romance that Miller eulogizes):

I dedicated the cornerstone of my autobiography [*Tropic of Capricorn*] to "Her"! . . . "Her" also strove desperately to give me life, beauty, power, and dominion over others, even if only through the magic of words . . . if "Her" dealt me death in the Place of Life, was it not also in blind passion, out of fear and jealousy? What was the secret of her terrible beauty, Her fearful power over others, Her contempt for her slavish minions, if not the desire to expiate Her crime? *The crime?* That she had robbed me of my identity at the very moment when I was about to recover it . . . having dedicated myself to the task of immortalizing Her, I convinced myself that I was giving Her Life in return for Death. I thought I could resurrect the past, thought I could make it live again. . . . All I accomplished was to reopen the wound. . . . I see the meaning of the long Odyssey I made; I recognize *all* the Circes who held me in their thrall . . . immeasurably more: I found at last that all is one.[6]

The Dark Lady, Mona/Mara, "Her," has become the "She" of murky Circe-myth in which personal failure is not understood, explained, or presented but simply heightened into the unitary vision. Some sly personal mystification, and literary-occult "oneness," subsumes a bad marriage under the guise of eternity.

Midway in the mythicizing of his muddled love and identity comes a curious document, "Letter to Anais Nin Regarding One of Her Books," in which Miller discusses Mona as she appears as a character in one of Nin's books. Alternately quoting and commenting upon Nin's portrayal, he characterizes Mona as the "insatiable one," and he approvingly quotes the description of her as "copulating with cosmic furies and demons." He says that Nin caught the essential qualities of "the nymphomaniac in her, the aura of drugs, the sadism, the necrophilia, the infantilism, the regressions, the Stavrogin complex." Miller goes on, quite contrary to the image of himself he encourages in the sexual scenes in his books, to express his horror at her excessive sexuality. But, leaving aside the biographical peculiarities, the real literary key appears to be in another comment—my "deepest feelings about her: that I had *invented* her qualities!"[7] For whatever the facts about Miller's second wife (and whatever other women he draws upon), the Mona/Mara we meet in the quasi-autobiographical passion emerges as a mythic female monster who serves as schizophrenic muse to the boy from Brooklyn. And the real pathos may be the inadequacy of that literary invention.

Tropic of Capricorn, dedicated "To Her," and with an epigraph from Abelard, ostensibly centers on the story of his castrating passion. Actually, she remains peripheral in *Capricorn* as well as *Cancer.* The narrating author of *Capricorn* briefly mentions meeting her in a Broadway taxi-dance hall (80),[8] but he develops nothing more until two-thirds through the book when he identifies himself as the product of a "wound," and names the Dark Lady as the cause (238). To transcend his perplexity he enlarges the passion to religious dimensions: "In the tomb which is my memory I see buried now, the one I loved better than all else, better than the world, better than God" (239). But it was a demonic passion, a "black" love in which he "penetrated to the very altar and found—nothing" (240). He so insists on the demonic enigma of Mara that the whole description clots around the claustrophobic "blackness" of his own response, and the woman remains an indefinite force of narcissistic and nymphomaniacal sexual diabolism. The descriptions expand the metaphors rather than the character: "She dressed in black almost exclusively, except for patches of purple now and then. She wore no underclothes, just a simple sheet of black velvet saturated with diabolical perfume" (241). Their life? "We lived in black holes with drawn curtains, we ate from black plates, we read from black books. We looked out of the black hole of our life into the black world" (241). It was, in sum, the "long dark night of the soul" (241).

Mythically Mona belongs under the aegis of a black star, the "dead black sun," and is surrounded by an emblematic imagery of snakes, predatory birds and animals, violent monsters and machines, and appropriate demons for "the conjugal orgy in the Black Hole of Calcutta" (244). Miller asserts that the enigma belongs to her in large part, for she seemed a witch of shifting identities: "a bag of lies, of inventions, of imaginings, of obsessions and desires" (249). We are told, but not shown, that she alternately treats Miller as a dope fiend, a god, a madman, and as an extension of herself. But he also admits he can neither present nor understand her because he remembers "too much" (242), and too closely identifies himself with her shifting image. Miller, I should say, falls between the literary desire to present that Dark Lady of our traditional myths of passion, and the autobiographical need to exorcise (even to revenge perhaps) a confusing personal experience. Thus he produces mostly a prose of clogged anguish.

At the end of this episode, Miller simply breaks off, reminded of other sexual matters in other times and lands of fantasy. A hundred pages later in *Capricorn* the associations bring him back to Mara and to their first meeting in the dance hall. A few tangible details slip through the swirling prose, but the treatment tends to be summarized literary talk of Strindberg's evil women. It also becomes the myth of, as well as on, Broadway, U.S.A.:

She is America on foot, winged and sexed. She is the lubet, the abominate and the sublimate—with a dash of hydrochloric acid, nitroglycerine, laudanum and powdered onyx. Opulence she has, and magnificence. . . . For the first time in my life the whole continent hits me full force. . . . America the emery wheel of hope and disillusionment. Whatever made America made her, bone, blood, muscle, eyeball, gait, rhythm; poise; confidence; brass and hollow gut. (356)

Actually, Miller uses Mara to condense the major theme of *Capricorn*—the American horror (which I shall return to in a later chapter)—and not for the earlier theme of the Dark Lady who serves as muse and witch. At least implicit in his surreal metaphors and the leap to the outrageous analogy is his rhetorical extension of the Dark Lady into the machined American love goddess.

Miller does suggest that Mara's power derives from her very lack of identity and reality, although the overstatement of mythic rhetoric confuses that analysis. She who came "disguised as Venus" turns out to be "Lilith" (361). In perplexity at the cosmic shape he has given her—or at the shifting American reality?—he chooses to submit to this "destroyer of the soul" (362). *Tropic of Capricorn* ends here, with the incomplete act of exorcism. He hopes for rebirth by accepting the flow of destruction—even more, by burrowing into the horrendous womb of blackness.

The story of Mara/Mona and his regenerative suffering Miller both tells and doesn't tell again in the volumes of *The Rosy Crucifixion*. While Mona/ Mara provides the ostensible focus of the five volumes, only a small part of them actually centers on her. A novelist with any feminine identification might have done much with the Dark Lady, but Miller is no novelist, or even an apt storyteller, and he misogynistically lacks the skill to project into the feminine sensibility. Thus we never get his heroine's thoughts, feelings, motives, or sense of existence. Another difficulty appears in the grandiloquent role Miller unfortunately gives himself at the start of his history: "I was approaching my thirty-third year, the age of Christ crucified" (*Sexus*, 9).[9] With his messianic destiny, no wonder that he must plaintively insist all through the account of these years that she never understood him (21). His commitment alternates between rhetoric and indifference: she was the "one woman in the world whom I can't live without" (20); but he has hardly announced his deep love for Mara to his best friend when he is already backing another woman, just met, against the bathroom door. And he oddly refuses to be upset or jealous when he learns of Mara's relation with a wealthy old man (66). Later, in *Plexus,* he is more than cooperative in not inquiring into his wife's meetings with a series of elderly male admirers. Miller's and Mara's passion has hardly been consummated when we are teasingly presented with a scene in which he wishes to exchange her for another girl with a friend. Similarly, after his guilty break with his first wife for the "great adventure" (212) of a new life with Mona (she changed her name), he is planning to visit another woman (235) and is regularly making sexual visits to the wife whom he claims to find repulsive, despite Mona's jealous suicide attempt. Further-more, such scenes with his first wife, including an elaborately implausible three-way orgy with a neighbor girl (477–88), give a gross comic tone to what we are told is a romantic saga.[10] Such confusions of material and tone are pervasive and turn the "romance" into an uncertain parody.

In order to maintain the mystification about Mona, the narrator must re-main absurdly obtuse while slyly explaining how Mona got her dance hall job, obtained money from elderly men both before and after her marriage to Miller, and how she maintained her schizophrenic role playing. Whether he be willful mystifier or dupe, Miller certainly lacks artistic intelligence in his presentation of the Dark Lady. Actually, romantic passion appears to be un-congenial to Miller—as does internal understanding of other persons. More to his taste is the elaborately detailed story of how Mona had been brutally, though rather willingly, raped. Miller's natural cast of mind constantly dredges up materials antithetical to his announced theme.

For example, Miller and Mona mark their nuptials by going to a bur-lesque theater—a congenial and favorite subject for this Brooklyn boy—to celebrate "the rites of spring with rubber emotions" (605). (Miller is both te-diously fascinated and sarcastically critical with his own gross sensibility). Part of the author's implicit theme seems to be the polymorphous perversity of passion. As we know from the tradition of the romance, passion roots itself in adulterous ambiguities of feeling and violent reversals of emotion not sus-ceptible to moralistic treatment.[11] But Miller's confused and amoral gusto, as we have seen in his earlier fascinated treatment of whores and similar mate-rial, belongs to quite a different kind of perversity. His sensibility is alto-gether too crude to present the labyrinthine ways of romantic passion, and so, when he becomes concrete, he turns to gross sexual contradictions, inter-spersed with the camouflage of sentimental avowals, which simply confuse the myth of his demonic Dark Lady.

Perhaps the garbled art rests on a deeper confusion. Miller takes on the ro-mantic mantle of a prophet of love, and his passion for Mona, apparently, aims to provide an education of the heart. But the pathos of whatever per-sonal trauma he draws upon runs contrary to the artifice of his later intelli-gence. Thus, early in *Sexus* Miller inserts a pompous self-analysis, made by a mysterious woman melodramatically introduced for this sole purpose: "Be-cause the woman can never give you what you want you make yourself out to be a martyr. A woman wants love and you're incapable of giving love" (54). (This occult woman closely resembles a similar figure, Iris, in *The Renegade* [1941], a novel by Miller's friend, Alfred Perlès.) While his version of the

Dark Lady myth aims to show Miller as the victim of love, he really presents himself as the victim of his own lovelessness.

That Miller generally accepts, despite some nagging irritations, the role of quasi-panderer for his wife may thus be seen as something other than his vaunted "acceptance" of life. "Why was it that I always got a thrill when I thought of someone making love to her?" Answer: "The more lovers she garnered the greater my own personal triumph" (326). She, who "had offered herself to hundreds and perhaps thousands of others" now gives that accumulation of feeling to loveless Miller.[12] "I had become worshipful." Often religious feelings of love are the mark of inability at actual human love. With his Dark Lady Miller has the same cult of vicarious love that made whores— like Claude and Germaine—objects of veneration. "I had asked for a woman and I had been given a queen" (541). Promiscuity creates her royal power, and his as consort. The debased receptacle of "love," by a peculiar synecdoche, gives all love. Secondhand love provides one way to get, or at least to get near, the love of mankind. And the bad boy retelling his confused longings in *The Rosy Crucifixion* hopes to immortalize his inchoate lovelessness and thus garner the indulgent love of that part of mankind which reads books.

Miller's exaltation of such consubstantial love, as represented by the prostitutes and Mona, seems to draw on the male fascination with the despoiled woman, and thus glorifies the despoiling. The degraded sexuality of *Sexus* may be the inverted worship of female power as well as part of the revenge on women that pervades this son of a puritanic mother. Miller talks incessantly of love-ecstasy and so, of course, lacks it. The physical acts of love in his writings usually emphasize detachment and dehumanization—often hilariously so. Even early in his supposedly exalted passion with Mona he describes part of himself as feeling "as if it were made of old rubber bands . . . it was like pushing a piece of stiff suet down a drain pipe" (180). With bemused self-alienation, he also views that part of his anatomy as "disgustingly like a cheap gadget from the five and ten cent store, like a bright colored piece of fishing tackle minus the bait" (181).

The arresting candor of such perception, totally severed from all other values, also applies to Mona who is viewed not as a person but as "just a mass of undefinable contours wriggling and squirming like a piece of fresh bait seen upside down through a convex mirror in a rough sea." Such news from down under—we all live there part of the time—has authentic freshness and evokes the poet in Miller. Like his antiheroes Van Norden (in *Tropic of Cancer*) and MacGregor, Miller reveals himself as the self-alienated man, who is significant as a writer in his ability to report such extreme fractured sensibility.

But what has this to do with Miller's ostensible story of a romantic passion for a Dark Lady? That manifest content becomes a tedious sentimental masquerade for the pathetic portrayal of a dehumanized character named Miller.

Mona receives some small development, mostly additive, in *Plexus* and *Nexus,* where we read casual detailings of her fluctuations in identity and jobs of taxi-dancer, actress, candy seller, proprietress of a speak-easy, village waitress and predator on wealthy men and lesbians. Much of these volumes centers on other characters, and her peregrinations in bohemia and her weird friends remain flat and disconnected.[13] Miller wrote that "People have had enough of plot and character. Plot and character don't make life" (*Sexus,* 47).[14] Certainly the traditional novel's interior analysis, climactic sequence, and verbal and character patterns show arbitrariness; but one cannot so readily dismiss plot and character and analysis *if* he is doing exactly what they were developed for, as Miller intermittently attempts to do in the Dark Lady story. For example, when Miller presents what should be a crucial scene, Mona's turning to lesbianism (*Plexus,* 625ff.), it is sandwiched between a chapter of deadpan reportage on a crude genre scene in an Irish bar and the concluding chapter of *Plexus,* Miller's long essay about the effect on him of Oswald Spengler's *Decline of the West.* The chopped up, willful, egotistically indifferent presentation of Mona does not even achieve minimal character analysis or dramatic coherence.

Nexus, a somewhat better volume than *Plexus,* shows a more conscious effort to explain and interweave, with its fulsome discussion of Anastasia, Mona's lesbian friend, and with the repetition of motifs in *Sexus* and of the Strindbergian metaphors of *Cancer* and *Capricorn.* The lesbian material of *Nexus* may receive somewhat more incisive handling because of Miller's detachment from it.[15] The passing revelation of his inability to love, made in *Sexus,* is picked up again as he thinks back over more than three decades: "How simple and clear it all seems now! . . . *I had lost the power to love"* (44). Miller has a platitudinous way, in and out of his autobiographical romances, of repeatedly making that same discovery. His absence of love becomes his great mystery and even his one passion—his motive not only for telling his history but for becoming a writer.

More interesting is the revelation that rises out of his "underground life" (*Plexus,* 417). Miller lives in a dark basement with Mona and her girlfriend while he is ecstatically reading Dostoyevski and sinking "deeper and deeper into the pit. Hysteria became the norm. The snow never melted" (*Nexus,* 53). The "hero of love," as he oddly calls himself, finally gets an underground man's courage, after years of inexplicable dallying, to look into Mona's past. Briefly coming out into the ordinary day, he visits Mona's mother and brother and learns—unkindest cut of all—that Mona is merely pathetic (*Nexus,* 172–79). Mona's background shows "nothing unusual or remarkable" (177): she is the wayward and self-romanticizing daughter of a perfectly ordinary Jewish family. After this discovery he cannot, he says, relate his black passion for the pedestrian girl. Thus, "Neither of them existed any more. Nor did I perhaps" (179). The pathetic revelation, then, is that Mona as the Dark Lady of passion did not exist except as the product of Miller's own naivete and fantasy.

While Miller, with his absence of dramatic narrative, does not directly relate the collapse of his Dostoyevskian underground anguish and passionate "love" to the usurpation of the ordinary, that seems to be the heart of it. He soon finagles an ordinary job in a park department office, and Mona and her girlfriend run off to Europe. It is during this period that Miller plans the work we are discussing. It might be viewed as an obvious compensation for the anguish of being betrayed by two girls; better, it can be seen as a pathetic effort to give his love a shape that reality seems to have denied it. In either case, art provides a desperate refuge from the power of ordinary fact.

Then the ordinary takes over on all levels: Anastasia runs away from Mona with a man;[16] Mona stays on with some other men but soon drifts back to Miller. Now her real function as practical muse to a would-be writer becomes clearer, and she establishes Miller, with money she obtains from another man, in lavish circumstances while he attempts to write a novel. Miller, not concerned with Mona but with his role as "artist," says that how she obtained the money "in no way disturbed the smooth relationship we had established" (224). Their life of about a year is summarized, with Miller devoting himself to the arts of good eating, self-gratifying whimsies, ruminative walks, and other hobbies in his retirement from ordinariness. Mona's "other man" gives her sufficient money so that she can indulge Miller in another of his dreams of comfortable culture—a year's tour of Europe. Here the first volume of *Nexus* breaks off with a wry Whitmanesque catalog of good-byes, mostly addressed to the folk heroes who provide the mythic boys' America Miller can accept. But what happened to the passion for the demonic Dark Lady? She merely turned into an ordinary woman to be exploited—the somewhat erratic female who indulged, supported, and encouraged Miller in his ambitions to lead an "artistic" life. The rhetorical, romantic mythology of the Brooklyn boy who finally found the literary life to be the be-all and end-all of a perplexing reality turns out to be a buffoonish fantasy.

An apparently crucial scene with the Dark Lady is the one, placed out of chronological order, which concluded the first double-volume, *Sexus,* as if Miller were insisting that this confession must be blurted out regardless of what happened to the rest of the story. Curiously, Miller's most confessional episodes, such as this, are the least direct. During the wedding celebration at the burlesque theater, Miller slips into a parabolic fantasy about a synthetic assassin-flaneur, Osmanli, who wills his own death because he does not love.[17] The episode apparently represents the "immeasurable emptiness" (614) of the mind carrying the fantasy—Miller's. Another horror-fable follows, this one apparently relating to the ménage à trois developed more literally in *Nexus*. The narrator presents himself as confused, petulantly destructive, and unable either to stop or to flee his wife's lesbian and adulterous relationships. He repeatedly imagines himself a brutalized and whimpering dog. In the concluding episode, he is a dog on exhibit; the beloved woman takes a knuckle-bone he wants, which is encircled by a wedding ring, sucks out the marrow, and places it over the metaphorically appropriate part of the dog's anatomy. But the bone and the wedding ring fall to the ground, and the inadequate dog-Miller ends with a plaintive "Woof, woof, woof!" (634). This bitter image of self-degradation seems to be an elaboration of colloquial adages about a husband in the doghouse—given a bone by the powerful wife, his marrow and manliness are sucked out and his degradation is complete. Despite some of the usual fragmented lapses of tone and order, it is an intense, and perhaps intensely self-pitying, episode.

Separated from the narrative to which it belongs, and climactically concluding the volume, it becomes a nuclear confession. Explicitly fused to the nuptial celebration—and to the hallucinatory figure of burlesque queen Cleo with her rubber contortions and emotions, and to the paradigmatic empty husband, Osmanli, who becomes an assassin-flaneur and suicide—it is a devastating bit of marital debasement and confession. We might "explain" at several levels the causes of this hallucinatory bitterness: by the diabolically elusive Mara/Mona, by Miller's self-defeating dependence on and resentment of women (which harks back to his cold-hearted mother), or, more generally, by the destructive pattern of the ersatz American love-goddess and the hollow, boneless, modern man in his role of doggy American innocent. Miller's explanation may be that the suffering was part of his fate which led to the benign rebirth as saintly artist—the "rosy crucifixion" of the general title. Or, as he puts it in *Nexus,* in his greatest misery he discovers he was emotionally defeated and dead because he had "striven so vainly and ignominiously to protect his miserable little heart." A "guardian angel" has restored his heart after this pseudo-suffering; he can now accept and pass his benediction on to all mankind—"Take heart, O brothers and sisters. Take heart!" (213–14).

Self-forgiven and self-canonized, the narrator leaves us perplexed about the obscure candor of his confession. The murky and mechanical dallying with Mona/Mara does not allow her much significance as a fictional character or as a coherent image of reality, but as a figure out of rhetorical mythology she is demolished by the irrelevant messages of the narrator. The rest of the context of the narrator's life in Brooklyn, to be discussed next, also destroys her appropriateness and meaning. What we end up with is a dragged-out and unadmitted parody of the Dark Lady of passion. As actual confession, the work is tedious; as artifice, it is pointless. Miller acknowledges that the burden of "suffering," which he endlessly manipulates and inflates, only provides a "pseudo-tragedy," and in detail the suffering generally lacks authenticity as applied to the self-indulgent, obtuse, and frequently indifferent narrator. The work, then, must be an exposé of a fraudulent lover, an ersatz artist, and a bumbling and fragmented human being. But to what end? Within and without the work, Miller claims, after all, that we are dealing with the self-discovery of a passionate lover, a unique artist, and even a near-saint. The ambiguous candor of undercutting his own claims remains the one large and genuine confession of *The Rosy Crucifixion*. His most ambitious work of art and quest for identity reveals pathetic buffoonery. Saddest jape of all, an occasionally talented prose writer spends decades of obsession and thousands of pages to produce a monument that contains only a few bits of literature—and a weirdly murky confession of art as an escape from life.[18]

The Brooklyn Boys

To discuss the confused dark passion of Miller's autobiographical romance may suggest a concentration that the half-dozen volumes do not have. In Miller's free-associative ragout, the Dark Lady provides the bone, but that hardly defines the meal. As with most of Miller's work, loose narrative sequences alternate in a casual way with comedy and fantasy episodes; and these often culminate in ruminative or apocalyptic essays on Miller as philosopher, genius, or occultist. Among the characteristic Milleriana are the sometimes deadpan, sometimes rhetorically sentimental, vignettes of his buddies over thirty-odd years. In these, at least, Miller achieves a kind of semi-artistic social documentation of a significant, if limited, hunk of American reality.

None of the portraits in the half-dozen volumes on his Brooklyn days achieves the sardonic immediacy of Van Norden in *Tropic of Cancer*. One reason may be sentimentality. When he describes a taciturn Irish cop, O'Rourke, who appears as a detective for the "Cosmodemonic Telegraph Company" in *Tropic of Capricorn* and as a friend in *Sexus,* the author blandly informs us that he knew "absolutely nothing" about the man's private life

(*Sexus,* 368); and he does not imagine one for him, except for the mawkish assumption that O'Rourke may have suffered from a "frustrated love." A kind of functional father figure for Miller, this quietly persevering and kindly cynical detective receives Miller's highest accolade as "a unique being" (367) who "symbolized" an "inscrutable cosmic law." The inscrutability of both cosmos and cop partly comes from a lack of detailed dramatization.

With some of his characters, as with Mona, Miller insists on presenting portraits almost solely in terms of his feelings. In this solipsism, the characters achieve hardly any existence outside of their relation to the narrating Miller, and thus they become simply metaphors. However, in *The Rosy Crucifixion* there does seem to be some conscious but crude effort to fill in some of the figures. The musician he calls Arthur Raymond may serve as an example. First presented (397ff.) as an intense romantic artist of diverse talents in the 1920s when Miller and Mona lived with him, we are informed, by leaping out of the narrative, that he later became a Communist, and finally a middle-aged failure—just how and why remains quite vague. Miller, meeting him on the street for a moment many years later, finds his talk "effusive gush" and his hopes for his son "pitiful" (407). Miller flatly rejects the man for all time. He moralizes his contempt: "If he [Raymond] had stopped anywhere along the line and fought his way through, life would have been worth while" (408). This playing the Norman Vincent Peale (or Rev. Robert Schuller) of bohemia is one of the less attractive sides of the later Miller, but it has some unintentional humor.[19]

Miller does better when dealing with considerably lesser and more Miller-like types in his rambling, episodic caricatures that mix sentimentality and malice with sly, sharp-eared observation. MacGregor, in many ways a parallel to the Van Norden of *Cancer,* must have more than a hundred pages devoted to him in *Capricorn* and in the later volumes. We first see Mac, an old Miller friend now in his early thirties, telling the gross but observant story of his seduction of a pious Catholic girl (*Capricorn,* 96–97). Miller wryly comments that the pudendum "cunt" "was always the opening theme, and the closing theme" of Mac's conversation since it "was his way of saying *futility*" (98). Mac also endlessly laments his own weakness and failure, as he compulsively pursues another female (109ff.), or reports past seductions and crudities. Miller dryly presents much of this in the apt dialogue of the American male, but he also shrewdly summarizes the basic characteristics of all the American MacGregors: tough-guy manners masking weakness and outrageous sentimentality; the compulsive "dirty story" telling that indicates the "limited horizon"; "the contempt for the rich, the hobnobbing with politicians, the curiosity about worthless things, the re-

spect for learning, the fascination with the dance hall, the saloon, the burlesque" (281–82). The pool-hall philosopher, cursing and timid, genially
talkative and desperately lonely, reveals a smattering of ideas and information completely split to accord with his cynical accommodation to his petty
job and with his earnest fantasies of something different. Miller clearly perceives the type and—wittingly or unwittingly—himself; for this lower class
American male, with his unformed rebellion and frustrated sensibility, provides Miller's basic gestures—and, I suspect, the type of Miller's basic audience. The very qualities that Miller identifies as his own appetite,
curiosity, geniality, malleability, and dreams (291) make him simply a
spokesman for the MacGregor world.

In the various volumes of *The Rosy Crucifixion* MacGregor again appears
in Miller's deadpan reportage style, though in a somewhat debased ventrilo-
quistic function. In a long episode in *Sexus* (150–78), MacGregor discusses
Miller's great potential as an artist and—in an only slightly vulgarized version of what Miller writes in his essays—expounds Miller's views of art.
While the portrait of the aging, cigar-chewing Brooklyn bull-artist is obviously satiric, the Millerian similarities override the mockery. MacGregor, like
Miller, makes much of the artist's mistreatment by society, though he finally
inverts Miller's view: "Fuck you, Jack. You're not putting anything over on
me! You ain't making me starve to prove that I'm an artist. No siree" (174).
Miller, of course, made the hungry leap into Parisian semi-starvation, as if to
prove to a world of MacGregors that he was an artist.

The long friendship, the similarities, however parodied, and the good tangible sense of MacGregor which we get in Miller's suitable dialogue, give a
poignancy to the final confrontation of the Brooklyn boys in *Nexus*.
MacGregor tracks down Miller, who has been avoiding him for some time
while playing the superior artist, and he complains of his rejection by his
buddy and alter ego. Miller scorns him, and adds that they "haven't a thing in
common" (348) because MacGregor, though apparently the same as ever,
now appears "tame" to Miller and inside the usual social "straight-jacket."
They also argue, rather improbably, about a much later interest of Miller's—
Eastern religion. For inexplicable reasons, Mac gives in—even humbly begs
Miller to repeat one of his pseudo-profundities (the purpose of life is "to
drink of its undying essence" [352])—but the sycophantism doesn't work,
and Miller righteously sends his oldest friend away.

The narrating Miller, a man supposedly in his late thirties, wants to grow
up. But he carries his own MacGregor: his longing to escape his Brooklyn
identity and to find exotic horizons belongs to that same limited masculine
ethos. The MacGregor world—a large part of the autobiographical materials

belongs within it—generally appears, despite Miller's loving prolixity, as tedious, callow, nasty, and pathetic; yet that mean life is of major importance in American experience. Miller does, in *The Rosy Crucifixion,* partly weaken the independent reality of that material by rather fatuously trying to prove that he was a genius who broke out of the Brooklyn boy's world.

There is a representative comic episode in *Plexus* that illustrates the characteristic weakness of his art. He tells the story of working as an assistant to Lundgren, "a human adding machine" (365) compulsively dedicated to self-defeating projects. This traditional American eccentric—a basement inventor, backyard mystic, and suburban fanatic—is the proper butt of Miller's street-corner skepticism; the narrator's gusto of contempt applies well to his technological mentor with his "cold-blooded nonsense" who cannot enjoy the tangible verities of food, drink, dreams, and laughter. But much of Miller's comedy becomes a forced joke, as when the earnest Lundgren and the Schweikish Miller go to shingle a roof and Miller spills hammer, nails, etc., in a predictable slapstick crescendo. Then, too, Miller uses Lundgren not only to set off his own responsive humanity but also as a dull foil to develop his own explication of Nostradamus—a representative figure of wisdom to crank intellectuals like Lundgren and Miller. The humor in this egotistical silliness seems unintentional. Lundgren's mother provides an excuse for Miller to play with words and to effuse an arty two pages of rhetorical free-associating praise—rather imitation Rabelais—while forgetting to show us the actual woman (376–77). Finally, Miller gets back into focus with the Lundgrens' filthy town apartment, in which everything, including worn-out shoes, is properly indexed and filed. But there the story stops and Miller flees, covering his drawn-out but disintegrated anecdote with hyperbole, a grossly satiric note that ends, "To be filled under C, for catarrh . . . cantharides . . . constipation, cirlicues . . . cow-flop . . . cunneform . . . Czoglas" (379–80).

The whole episode might also be filed under "corn-doctor comedy." For the comic possibilities of Lundgren and his mother are lost in free association, easy slapstick, petty sadism, occult mumbo-jumbo, and Miller's lack of discipline and his indifference towards anything but Miller. The episode is all too paradigmatic for hundreds of pages of Miller's ostensible autobiography. The occasional satiric shrewdness and the endless self-indulgence characterize a garrulous joker gone on too long in telling the anecdotes of his one passion: his desire to transcend a narrow American ethos. But he has fallen back into being just one of those boys from Brooklyn.

The Imaginary Jew

In his longings to transcend the Brooklyn boy ethos and himself, Miller sought a new identity—in an exotic Europe, in the roles of artist and sage, in memory and fantasy—that would separate him from a tediously bland America, provide a communal heritage, and create a richer and more responsive self. The American ghetto Jew, alien yet with a community, bottom dog yet intellectual, suffering and ecstatic yet living in Brooklyn, provided an antitype of what Miller could become. Miller puts in the mouth of one of his oldest friends, in his autobiographical romance, the announcement "You're no *goy*. You're a black Jew" (*Sexus*, 87–88), and claims to have often passed for a Jew (*Nexus*, 226). In attempting to create a myth of himself, the fascinated gentile also makes his Dark Lady of passion Jewish, proclaiming to her, "I love you just because you *are* a Jew" (*Plexus*, 39).[20] And, almost in the same breath with which he rejects his Brooklyn-boy alter ego, MacGregor, he gives a Jew, one of his last remaining American friends, the power of dubbing him: "Miller . . . you're what I'd call a good Jew" (*Nexus*, 358).

Now Miller is also aware that his inversion of his anti-Semitic heritage into Jewish identification poses some curious ambiguities. He aptly develops several of them near the end of *Sexus* when Eisenstein, a superior "cloakie" (from Odessa, of course), mistakes Miller for a Jew, and lovingly expounds to him the magical power and resiliency of the mélange that constitutes Jewishness. When Miller informs him that he is not a Jew but intends to become one, Eisenstein gets upset, insists that Jewishness is only a religion, and properly notes that Miller may only be searching for exotic repentance—"violently in love with what he once hated" (532). Then follows a set piece of apocalyptic prose, to give the Jewish-gentile relation cosmic proportions (534–39). The former Jewish ghetto of New York, which Miller describes in his hyperbolic fashion, becomes the best part of the city.[21] The rest of New York he views as an inhuman "abstraction" gone "*insane*." The description emphasizes the rich physicality of the Jewish community—the food, the sexuality, the talk, the crowding, the suffering, the pervasive intensity—and ends with a chiliastic apostrophe to the gentiles: "Build your cities proud and high. . . . Underneath, below the deepest foundations, lives another race of men . . . dark, somber, passionate . . . the scavengers, the devourers, the avengers. They emerge when everything topples into dust" (539). Thus Miller's rather effective lyrical praise of a historical actuality, the ghetto, turns into mythical invective. The humanity of the Jewish saving remnant somewhat obscurely becomes the demonic vengeance of the underground pariah against the soulless megalopolis.

While we need not argue the obvious point that Miller's fascination with Jewishness contains, like the Jewish heritage, odd mixtures of love and hatred, the imaginary Jew role also expresses Miller's love of the grotesque and apocalyptic for their own sake. Miller identifies with the Jew—"Whenever I bump into a real Jew I feel I'm back home" (*Nexus*, 227)—not just because of the warmth, humor, and intensity of the community, nor just because of the lost gentile's desire to join the alien, but also because the Jew often plays the major role of bittersweet clown. Many of these grotesques appear in Miller's work, such as "Crazy Sheldon" who always loans money to Miller. A grimacing, kindly refugee from Cracow pogroms, he carries secret money and jewels, and a hidden revolver and terrors, which come forth in paranoid gestures (*Sexus*, 251–54; *Plexus*, 171–74, 178–86). Miller's favored mad innocents naturally include relatives (Tante Melia) and gospeling Christians (Crazy George); but all of them, and especially the Jews whom he treats with passionate interest partly born of repulsion, express the nearly irreparable cruelty of the world. Miller reverentially praises the intuitive wisdom of the forlorn, outcast, and defeated.

Of the many other Jews touched on in *The Rosy Crucifixion*, perhaps the most self-sufficient dramatization is that of Elfenbein near the end of the first volume of *Nexus* (276–86).[22] Having renounced his gentile world, Miller spends most of his time with Jews. During a Jewish family party, Elfenbein drops in. Miller, sensing a kindred clown, asks, "From Minsk or Pinsk?" "From the land of the Moabites," replies Elfenbein, and the elvish Jewish monologist, the burlesque "Yiddish King Lear," takes off on his flying sequences of "Old World Talk, his crazy grimaces, his stale jokes" (281). Dialectician of the mad city streets, "leaping from subject to subject like a chamois," he discusses Elizabethan drama, Yiddish actresses (of half a century ago), and Old Testament patriarchs, as if they were all contemporary. An apocalyptic moralist, he also discusses "the sickness of the Gentiles, which he likened unto *eine Arschkrankheit*," and the modern lost world, in one long song of mangled English. With wry passion, he presents Miller's real moral doctrine—a kind of comic Sabbatain heresy: "Drown yourself in the pleasures of the flesh, but hang on [to the vision of God] by a hair" (282). Elfenbein is also the mouthpiece for Millerian theology: "man has been chosen to continue the work of creation"; but of the collaboration with God, the "Jew has forgotten . . . and the Gentile is a spiritual cripple" (281).

A Brooklynized Old Testament denouncer and rabbinical clown, the fervent monologist and joking, raging, sentimental old Jewish actor provides one of Miller's more charming portraits. In his pastiche of genre sketch and self-conscious folk parable, Miller presents the gesturing Jew both as

"*meshuggah*" and as the portentous figure from Deuteronomy 13 (the un-
heeded prophet) who longs to dance at the funeral of the sick *goyim*. And so
does Henry Miller. For Americans as such lack, among other things, a collective origin and rich folk history; and wherever Henry Miller goes—Paris,
Greece, Louisiana, Big Sur, or the Brooklyn of memory and fantasy—he
hungers for a community and communion that appears not as the "tradition-
alism" of the genteel authoritarian in the academy but as a sensuous, comic,
intense, tangible world. Miller's ghetto, of course, arises from a synthetic
nostalgia—the return to a Jewish world to which he never belonged and that,
at the time of his writing, had become submerged in nationalistic and suburban pseudo-communities. But for Miller to have passion in Brooklyn meant
to create an identity as an imaginary Jew, so long as the Jew was vital and
marginal American.

Part of the Jewish identity, Miller explains in a long speech on the subject,
arises from the Jew's relating himself to those who are "in distress, hungry,
abused, despised" because of his knowledge of "poverty, misfortune, dis-
grace, humiliation." In short, Miller and his authentic Jews belong to the
communion of "pariahs" (357). But pariahs face two ways in this gentile
world: into warmth, zest, responsiveness—as Miller illustrates with such
Jews as Eisenstein, Yood, Essen, and Elfenbein—and into the underground,
"the deep subcellar of the human heart" (*Sexus*, 539)—as Miller illustrates
with Max, Boris, Sheldon, and especially Kronski. For with many of his Jewish characters, we return to Miller's savage grotesqueries and to the tortured
psychic shape of both the Jew and the gentile's dream of him.

Dr. Kronski, for example, first appears in *Tropic of Capricorn* as an intern
working for the Cosmodemonic Telegraph Company and as one of Miller's
buddies in the pursuit of food and underground experience. In an only partly
developed episode, Kronski, whose wife has just died, walks in the park with
Miller, alternately lamenting her death and mockingly discussing with Miller
a girl they have both been pursuing. He also informs Miller that he has the
making of "a Jew bastard . . . only you don't know it" (88). Miller, fascinated
with Kronski's destructive friendship, listens to Kronski announce that
Henry Miller will be a great man if he only learns to "*really suffer*"—a lesson
which Miller seems never quite to understand. Miller's fascination with
Kronski, as with Max, turns about the question of suffering; the "hopeless
Jew" is a strikingly miserable summation of the calamity so alien to Miller,
the "dumb and lucky goy" (95). In a long and outrageous monologue Miller
thinks about suffering, about the Jews' special mission to gentiles who lack
both suffering and joy, and about the dead wife of Kronski and the longing

for death—and "the more I thought about it, the happier I grew" (93). Miller approaches the existential boundaries, only to flit fantastically away.

We see Kronski more fully in *Sexus* where he appears as repulsive, a "leering, bantering pale-faced toad" (91), always talking compulsively, always helping Miller, even moving him into a lugubrious room in his own place, "Cockroach Hall." Miller sees Kronski as the secular Jewish fanatic who wishes to understand and reform the world rather than to accept and enjoy it. To the Brooklyn boy's street-skepticism, Kronski seems the neurotic intellectual "full of crap" and a bore with "a screw loose" (96). Yet Miller, himself a *lumpen* intellectual, remains peculiarly fascinated with the neurotic Jewish intellectual while he mocks him as a "walking cemetery of facts and figures," a sick reformer "dying of statistical indignation" (98). But the most grotesque misery of the Jewish intellectual—one not noted by Miller—is that an exuberant, sly, predatory *goy* is both his disciple and his tormentor.

Miller also sees Kronski's malaise as a destructive *Weltschmerz,* an endless hunger for love that turns into "anthropophagous tenderness" (205). Such a "perverted Galahad" would "pull the house down about a friend's ears in order to rescue him from the ruins" (203). And Kronski helps Miller, for the reward of endless insults. It is Kronski, not the actual men that Mara/Mona has, whom Miller fears as a sexual competitor in a long, detailed fantasy he has about the slobbering Kronski and the nymphomaniacal Mara (103ff.). Kronski also insists, despite the Dark Lady's denials, that she is Jewish; he thus incites Miller's passion both by the sense of rebellion from a cold, niggardly lower-middle-class Protestant (and anti-Semitic) German American background and by the exotic-demonic sense of the Dark Lady myth.

Kronski appears, as a gross, knowledgeable, Jewish voice, several times in *Plexus* as well as in *Nexus.* But his penultimate appearance, and the systematic revenge that Miller reserves for his friends, comes as an interpolation in the latter part of *Sexus.* Apparently drawing on materials from a decade later (Miller's return to New York in 1936), the narrator presents a Dr. Kronski grown fat and pathetic in a neurotic withdrawal from life. Although a practicing psychiatrist, Kronski lets Miller talk him into being psychoanalyzed—by Miller. As analyst, Miller shows great confidence; his willingness to play analyst is heightened by the desire for comic revenge on Kronski, by the need for money, and by the bland conviction that Henry Miller rightfully belongs with Sigmund Freud and Mary Baker Eddy as a "healer." He insists on charging Kronski ten dollars an hour, following the usual hilariously specious logic of the profession that the height of the price will raise up the patient. The compulsively talking Kronski suddenly falls silent, and Miller further deflates the patient with a mild parody of the usual analytic double-talk (414ff.).

As so often, Miller short-circuits the comedy by drowning the episode in one of his apocalyptic essays, an excursus on psychiatry and religion. Kronski's illness, Miller ruminates, comes from knowing too much—far more than he can feel or truly live with (418). His layers of obese fat, Miller suggests, are layers of pride, and the doctor further protects himself by the false superiority of being conscious of every weakness and misery around him. Kronski also becomes a monster "because he always saw himself as strange and monstrous" (421), and he remains miserable because he picks his friends (such as Miller?) to play Judas to him. Miller poses an acute analytic question for the patient: "*What kind of drama do you want to stage?*" (421). In sum, Kronski "wanted a failure so brilliant it would outshine success," and only to use his intelligence destructively. He succeeded in failing. It is too bad that Miller does not dramatically develop his intriguing analysis of this paradigmatic case.

Miller's main concern turns to the religious role gained from his own shaman-power over Kronski: "I realized at once that by the mere act of assuming the role of healer one becomes a healer in fact" (415). It is Miller's fundamental belief that any gesture produces a role, and any role produces the reality. The earnest exposition frequently becomes hilarious, as when Miller, of all people, announces that "*everybody becomes a healer the moment he forgets about himself*" (425). Miller, in the fragment we are given of the mock-analysis, never forgets the role Miller is playing, though he forgets Kronski easily enough. This, of course, does not deny his perceptions, as when he notes that some people, such as Kronski, exist primarily as cripples, and must go on being cripples. For, following D. H. Lawrence and related artists of malaise, Miller finds the main psychic disease to be rooted in self-consciousness; thus modern intellectuals cannot confront the reality that "is here and now, everywhere." Thus, too, the greatest analysts are not psychiatrists and artists but "awakeners," like the Buddha, who "electrify you by their behavior" (426). And the real cure means both self-confidence and "an abiding faith in the processes of life" (427). Once again, Miller draws the moral of amoral acceptance (Nietzche's *amor fati*)—one of the main gestures of his work from *Tropic of Cancer* to *Nexus*. Those who are truly well will have "confidence in the fitness and rightness of the universe. When a man is thus anchored he ceases to worry about the fitness of things, about the behavior of his fellow men, about right and wrong. . . ." Miller does rebelliously add that this religious acceptance does *not* mean "Adapt yourself!" to this "rotten state of affairs" but "*Become an adept!*" (427).

Miller's verve in restating this wisdom pays the literary price of junking all art of narrative and character, and perhaps of intimate human concern. Poor Kronski! He seems to have drowned in the tidal deeps of Miller's prose, to have become one of those "Piscean malingerers" with "fluid, solvent egos . . . in the uterine marshes of their stagnant self"—a fish of "surrealist metempsychology" (422). Such types may even be beyond the "plastic job" done by the usual psychiatric therapist, for they themselves are therapists: "Their most successful disguise is compassion. How tender they can become! How considerate! How touchingly sympathetic!" Such is the guise of the "egomaniacs" who act as "professional mourners" glorying in "misery and suffering" so that they finally reduce "the whole kaleidoscopic pattern of life to a glaucous glue" (423).

As so often with Miller, he stirs some genuine profundity in with such silliness as Mary Baker Eddy and literary religiosity in an uncertain mixture of parody and perception. On the serious side, he expounds the modern religious rebel's theme of the illness of reformist moral benevolence. Giving a rotten system a humanitarian gloss destroys essential vitality, freedom, and joy. Blake, Thoreau, Nietzsche, and Lawrence, among others, attacked just such moral sentimentalism. But Miller, simultaneously the mawkish and unitive salvationist, should bleed a bit from his own sharp awareness.

The Kronski fragments—unfortunately badly scattered through four books, unlike the story of Max—show a powerful suggestiveness, and nothing more. Miller longed to be an imaginary Jew, to transcend *goyische* America. Well-equipped, at least by fervent individualism, fundamental alienation, and uninhibited vigor, not to fall into the American Jew's defeating labyrinthine self-consciousness and assimilative softness, Miller dallies, sentimentally and satirically—and occasionally effectively—with the imaginary Jew as a parabolic outsider and intense prophet of a richer life. But Miller, apparently unable to take on the heritage of suffering and day-by-day commitment, always ends by escaping into easy roles of ersatz healer and joker. He makes some gestures at being an imaginary Jew, throws out candid fragments of his sensitive American's love and repulsion for the saving remnant, even tries to fuse it with his myth of a passionate destiny, via the Dark Lady as Jewish witch and muse; but he always dissipates his powerful theme. Miller settles for being only that quaint and amorphous self-hero, Henry Miller.

The autobiographical romances bunch some bits of poignant documentation of the Brooklyn ethos and the longing for a fuller identity with occasional brilliant or playful flashes, but it all adds up to a tedious testament of Miller's lostness. Ostensibly writing the history of how he gained the experience, the suffering, and the imaginative knowledge to break out of his narrow time and place to become a saintly artist, Miller reveals that he never did get out, never did learn, never did fully become an "artist." Much of *Sexus, Plexus,* and *Nexus* fails because Miller does not seek to comprehend the Dark Lady, the Brooklyn boys, or the Jewish pariah archetypes but only his artist role: "What a wonderful life, the literary life!" (*Nexus,* 297).[23]

Miller thinks of art as an escape from the ordinary life of "a paid employee" into a will-less world of personal whimsy where one can "revel in one's thoughts and emotions" (*Sexus,* 43). He aims, despite occasional ponderous claims, not at truth, not at meaning, not at art, but at his role (*Nexus,* 158; *Plexus,* 410; *Sexus,* 313, etc.). Literally dozens of passages illustrate that Miller has experiences for art's sake, and the major meaning of what did, or could, happen to him was that he would someday write it. He literally had a "frenzy to live the life of a writer" (*Sexus,* 55), and that, almost only that, is what all the fuss was about. Miller sometimes had a hard life, "struggling to visualize on the faces of all my coming readers this expression of unreserved love and admiration" (*Sexus,* 37).[24]

While he may have succeeded in playing the role of artist he did not so generally succeed in producing art. Miller believes that art must be inspiration, frenzy, free-association, comic flow, and the supercession of intellect, effort, criticism (*Sexus,* 307–13; *Plexus,* 612; *Nexus,* 235, 297, 389ff.). But for these volumes the inspiration was long gone and far removed. The two decades and more devoted to them were a willed, arbitrary violation of Miller's own esthetic. In the forced style of much of *The Rosy Crucifixion,* Miller's colloquialism becomes dominated by triteness (note the dozen stock clichés on the *first* page of *Plexus,* and throughout). The thought, lacking confrontations and defiance, becomes equally trite. The earlier Miller drew outrageous but sometimes suggestive analogies about America; now he often falls into cantankerous stock moralizing, as when he says that earlier generations of American "men were made of sterner stuff . . . more industrious, more persevering, more resourceful, more disciplined" (*Plexus,* 80). The prophet in the purlieus has moved downtown to preach in the clubrooms, in painful self-parody of the very things he supposedly despises.

Part of the verve of *Tropic of Cancer* and some of his burlesque sketches and apocalyptic essays depend on sheer revolt. But, in the self-satisfaction of resurrecting his past and trumpeting his garrulous role-playing as Artist in his six-volume "book of life," he loses his saving humor and defiance. Egomania without the struggle and immediacy of a crisis or the shattering confrontation with the actual, tends only to bloated posing; and the only surprise is that in spots Miller forgets his self-congratulatory romance of memory and fancy to achieve the amusing and the suggestive. On the whole, these volumes are just a mildly weird ruin of egotistical verbiage, from which can be extracted some stray bits of grotesque wisdom and some archaeological curiosities about a dubious Brooklyn passion for playing, at any price, the artist.[25]

Chapter Four

The Outsider at Home

"Reunion in Brooklyn" and *Tropic of Capricorn*

Miller's passion to escape the Brooklyn ethos by the identity of an artist-outsider—with such aliases as the cancerous rogue, the lover of the Dark Lady, and the imaginary Jew—swells into polemics and burlesques about America as Nemesis. In Miller's prolix writings of five decades, no matter what the ostensible subject, we repeatedly find his gestures of rage against his birthright. While the rediscovery of America furnishes one of the obsessive themes of our literature in the twentieth century, Miller makes his eternal return as an artistic Columbus in chains, shouting that he will be imprisoned on a vast desert island blocking the way to the China of the imagination.

The world of the good old Brooklyn days changes, leaving the rebel-voyager adrift; but America, he always hollers, remains the one certain place of shipwreck. Put another way, Miller's role-playing as Artist becomes a compulsion in which America *must* play the villain. But much of this polemical game is bad and clichéd since Miller takes it with stock literalness rather than with rich seriousness. Fortunately, a few of the American pieces show confessional and burlesque verve. *Tropic of Capricorn,* his most ambitious journey into his native wasteland, is usually taken as the key document of Miller's America; however, I find that "Reunion in Brooklyn"[1] provides a better and more nuclear confession where we poignantly see him at home. This autobiographical sketch and ruminative essay, written largely in his plain colloquial style, draws upon the author's return to his family from Greece in 1940. Because he had mixed feelings in confronting the reality of his Brooklyn, he achieves a significant sense of anguish. When he looks at his family's puritanically ordered, lower-middle-class home, it is both "the same modest, humble place it had always been" and the "polished mausoleum in which their misery and suffering had been kept brightly burning" (68). More generally, Brooklyn is both the place where he found everyone "dying of malnutrition of the soul" (76) and the locus of his own vision of paradise where he fuses memories of childhood and adult dreams around an obscurely sacramental street scene (100–2). In these curious mixtures of the maudlin and the sar-

donic we may detect the outraged sentimentality which infuses Miller's relation to everything American.

Some of Miller's best art comes forth in the bittersweet portrayal of his all-
too-ordinary American family life. With painful candor, he sketches the fastidious, nagging, penurious mother whose one moment of "tenderness"
comes when she picks a thread off his coat (86); the pious, resentful, half-
witted spinster sister; and the weak, kindly, dull, father slowly dying of cancer of the urinary tract. The family life centers around radio programs,
household appliances, and ritualized little anxieties, sentiments, and hatreds.
It all provides a devastating portrait—quite without the doctrinaire qualities
of the prevalent "naturalistic" treatment of such a milieu—with highlights
on the trivial "stupidity, criminality and hypocrisy" that form the sad epito-
mization of a death-in-life domesticity. Yet, for Miller, this is home, and a
heartrending part of himself, as well as the frustration of every fuller self: "By
the time I was ready to leave my throat was sore from repressing my emotions" (86).

In the animus of such devotion, Miller attempts touching gestures of expi-
ation. Burdened with guilt (93), he brings gifts, longs to do more to "prove"
himself, and rages against the machines and mass culture which both enmesh
and reflect his representative family. He hopefully contrasts a supposedly
richer European way of life, and alternately weeps over and flees into fantasies
from his identification with that narrow Brooklyn world. He cannot, of
course, prove himself to his family; his flight into the role of artist merely
confirms his failure in their eyes. Reliving the humiliation of his attempts to
write at home, when his mother insisted he hide from a visitor in a closet because it was shameful for a full-grown man not to be more usefully em-
ployed, he still feels "like a criminal" (67) and sobs like a guilty child.[2] What
can he do but wildly rage at the befuddled mixture of comfort and emptiness
that provides the American way of family life?

The complementary alternative is flight into the subject of his writing, the
romance of memory that attempts to remold the past into some now lost significance. The one bond middle-aged Miller can establish with his dying father is to listen, enchanted, to the old man's reminiscences of the 1880s. Life
then, before son Henry ever existed, must have been richer and fuller. Or,
harking back to a horrendous episode in his past when his second wife threat-
ened suicide, Miller escapes the actual by involuntary memory. His anxiety
triggers a vision of "the whole of my life" (89), which obliterates all actuality.
As with the involuntary memory some people have when drowning, the fearful connection with the present snaps and life becomes an uncontrollable
surge of the past. Only then, he tells us, does he find himself "alive again";

the whole significance of life becomes the surrender to the nonpresent, and it is "marvelous to have lived, to remember so much" (90). Should the memories be too painful, the mind will make its own distortions: Brooklyn, he says, becomes for him a "dream" that "was far more vivid than the actual scene" (100). And if not the dream of the past, then there is the dream of the future. In his fiftieth year Miller displays the spontaneous egotism of the very young. He sees himself moving toward a future that will reveal him to be a "great man" (98). So down with the mere Brooklyn actuality! He ends the piece by trumpeting his separation from family and America and by insisting grandiloquently on his "allegiance to mankind," to "God," and to his "private destiny" (106)—all apparently the same thing. This vision separates him from the painful reality of time and place. Hence there can be no reunion in Brooklyn.

Despite his bombast and muddle, and because he remains the sobbing child who flees into spastic memory and fantasy, Miller testifies with considerable effect to some of the most pervasive and crucial American experiences. His bedrock personal America—our most fundamental social pattern of lower-middle-class triviality, acquisitiveness, sentimentality, vacuousness, repression, and petty virtue—remains unacceptable to anyone's intelligence and sensitivity. Such family life can never achieve, can never be given, authentic passion, heroism, or style. To accept such a way is death-in-life. But to break with it is to be sundered, forever outside oneself, essentially outside of an America that apparently can only be defied, not transcended. With this implicit insight, Miller's art of artless confession sometimes achieves a poignant documentation superior to much art. To see this, we must not take Miller literally as the great artist-prophet from Brooklyn; when self-consciously the artist-prophet, he becomes painfully bombastic in style. But we can recognize his artist-prophet gestures as a pathetic part of a dramatic confession, as a part of the buffoonery of anguish of one who testifies—perhaps with an art he did not intend—to the lack of "inside" in America, the "home" of the outsiders.

The earlier *Tropic of Capricorn* (1939) may fairly be seen as a more ornate description-confession of the outsider at home in America. While *Capricorn* provides the first of Miller's half-dozen volumes of autobiographical romance—some motifs of which I have already discussed—it is also a work of more elaborate and peculiar artifice. In *Capricorn,* the outraged artist-prophet most fully escapes into involuntary memory and auto-fantasy, thus providing a pathetic-grotesque document of a self-alienation that aims to describe hyperbolically the spiritual climate of America. Or, to put it in terms of one of Miller's own metaphors, he creates in *Capricorn* a fantastic, monstrous verbal construct that parodies the communal American imagination: "Perhaps I regret not having been able to become an American. *Perhaps.* In my zeal now, which is again *American,* I am about to give birth to a monstrous edifice, a skyscraper, which will undoubtedly last long after the other skyscrapers have vanished, but which will vanish too when that which produced it disappears" (56).

Some of the fantasia, apparently, misleads readers as to the nature of the book. Because of the title, it has usually been considered a sequel to or continuation of *Tropic of Cancer,* but the title may suggest parallels with *Cancer* that do not really exist. Where *Cancer* was a series of roguish episodes, *Capricorn* carries anti-art a step further in its free flow of fantastic associations and disassociations, to express the transcendental power of the subjectivity of Henry Miller. Reality, in most senses, is rather less in *Capricorn* than in *Cancer,* while an ornate poetic prose—of the type Miller calls "dictation" or "cadenza"— takes greater prominence.[3] The purgative process in *Capricorn,* covering a more variegated time, space, and attitude, often lacks the incisive gestures of *Cancer*; and it certainly lacks much of the humor of the first book. The Parisian of *Capricorn,* turning back to memories of more than a decade earlier in distant America, dallies with his materials and his perplexities. The mixed feelings about his Dark Lady and about his own identity in the pre-artistic days, including the uncertain jumbling of repulsion, nostalgia, gusto, injury, rage, and confusion, allow less exuberant, sly defiance of a hopelessly cancerous world. In the home of memory Miller does not just confront chaos, he *is* the American chaos.

In the more or less prefatory essay opening of *Capricorn,* Miller insists upon his hatred of America as the most degrading and humiliating of all places: "I wanted to see America destroyed." The motive, he says, is "vengeance" to force "atonement for the crimes that were committed against me and against several others like me who have never been able to lift their voices and express their hatred, their rebellion" (12–13). We see in this statement one of Miller's most basic pervasive motivations; it is, as Nietzsche might note, the religiosity of resentment. Most simply, of course, he resents his heritage: "My people were entirely *Nordic,* which is to say *idiots*" (11). They had, that is, most of the miserable virtues of the dominant American culture. They were of northern European, Protestant, petit bourgeois stock. They had the appropriate ideology of cleanliness, righteousness, prudence, literalness, and hard work—Americans of Americans—and were unable, therefore, to live richly, openly, fully in the present. Miller accuses them, and himself as well, of being cowards, self-aggrandizing hypocrites, and spiritless somnambulists unable to embrace life.

Yet, in most of the remaining three-hundred-odd pages, Miller avoids talking much about any such mere reality as his family, except for one fine scene about his father; and when he does it is to insist on his disconnection—he "was born in the wrong household" (326). What he does discuss intermittently in the first section of manic flowing, ruminative narrative is his work as messenger-employment manager for the "Cosmodemonic Telegraph Co." Though essentially intriguing material, Miller's years with "Cosmodemonic" are not well told. Besides the usual defective characterization—such a crucial figure as the black woman Valeska lacks detail and is even killed off without our knowing why and how—Miller's account suffers more generally from disproportions between rhetoric and reality.[4] The job as messenger-employment manager turned out to be a "hideous farce" of the stupid bureaucratic hiring and firing of a marginal population of pathetic and grotesque people. Miller treats the experience as unique, when much of the point should have been that a multitude of other American jobs were equally absurd. Any sensitive and intelligent person who has held a variety of urban jobs could report similar details of frenzy, inhumanity, grossness, and farce. With the exception of some hyperbole, such as the sexual scenes, Miller reports the ordinary; but he so loads his scattered details by comparing American enterprise to a sewer, an endless war, and a contagious ward, that the fragmentary narrative will hardly carry the burden. His responses become arbitrary shouts of manic compassion and depressed resentment. He makes too much of the fact that the horrors happened to *him;* he does not probe the more profound truths of just *how* and *why* they happened.

Crudely sketching in a few of the more extreme cases of violent messengers, Miller provides no sense of motive, no rounded figures, no rich immediacy. These inverted Horatio Alger caricatures—"the dream of a sick America"—culminate in the self-portrait of one who succeeded in bullying his way into a job because one official was maliciously out to get another, then proved himself as a company spy, and ended by becoming a properly frenzied, griping, submissive, and self-punishing underling with sick dreams of glory: "If I had had real power . . . I could have used the Cosmodemonic Telegraph Company . . . as a base to bring all America to God" (27). In some of his other burlesque gestures Miller perceives that his madness is part of the system: a communication "service" speeding up things not worth communicating; "personnel policies" which are simply wild fluctuations of depersonalization and bigotry. In short, he portrays an archetypal American enterprise as not only stupid, fraudulent, and cruel but horrifyingly meaningless as well.

Miller also discovered in the Cosmodemonic mechanism that D. H. Lawrence was right in seeing the "lawless, violent, explosive, demonical" (41) under the bland efficiency and optimism of America. Miller's best case in point is Henry Miller, whose euphoric frenzy—"violent and phlegmatic at the same time" (76)—becomes the key response. Miller serves as a weather vane for the American climate in which the "whole continent is sound asleep and in that sleep a grand nightmare is taking place" (42). But perhaps Miller's most apt responses, and style, may be found in his laconic common-sense asides, such as "nobody knows what it is to sit on his ass and be content." In either case, Miller's reactions, usually flip-flopping from violent rages to fantastic sentimentality, do not present the real nature of the Cosmodemonic mechanism. There is a large, ostensible pattern: "Everything I endured was in the nature of a preparation for that moment when . . . I walked out of the office . . . to liberate [myself] from a living death" (64). This Brooklyn Sherwood Anderson theme doesn't quite fit the facts as given in his autobiographical romances; for Miller only slowly withdrew from his job, from his embittered domestic arrangements, and from the desperation of ordinary life. The transformation from employment manager to expatriate bard depended more upon the years of underground bohemian life than upon mad American enterprise.

In Miller's touchingly confused account of his quest for a private salvation from the purgatory of ordinary America, there always arises a didactic and Thoreauvian moral fervency: "I want to prevent as many men as possible from pretending that they have to do this or that because they must earn a living. *It is not true.* One can starve to death—it is much better" (37). The nihilistic twist at the end, of course, is what separates the nineteenth century, self-sufficient provincial individualist from the twentieth-century, anxious megalopolitan rebel.

Miller's amoralism and rhetoric of roguery occasionally serve him well. His bemusement and gusto at moments amidst the dreariness of the Cosmodemonic mechanism, or his comic overadjustment when he is willing to buy everything on the installment plan, or his kaleidoscopic wanderings through dance halls, burlesque theaters, vaginas and many other odd corners, provide his best gestures of defiance. But much of what he supposedly presents is *not* present, such as his summary of Myrtle Avenue, Brooklyn, which only emerges as a long series of negatives—"this street no saint ever walked . . . nor any poet" (311). Miller too often simply asserts the American drought; he fails to let us see the landscape. Broadway, however, does call forth the dadaist poet:

From Times Square to Fiftieth Street all that St. Thomas Aquinas forgot to include in his magnum opus is here included, which is to say . . . hamburger sandwiches, col-

lar buttons, poodle dogs, slot machines . . . orange sticks, free toilets, sanitary nap-
kins, mint jujubes, billiard balls, chopped onions . . . patchouli, warm pitchblende,
iced electricity, sugared sweat and powdered urine drives one on to a fever of delicious
expectancy. Christ will never more come down to earth nor will there be any law-
giver . . . and yet one expects something, something terrifyingly marvelous and absurd. (98–99)

There are half a dozen pages of this, and much of it is good—not just because
of the shrewdly rich surreal Whitmanianism, but because he also catches the
mixture of feverishness and negation that constitutes the crucial city experience. The "frenzied nothingness" makes Miller sing; but the melancholia that
follows the mechanized orgasm of the city vision also provides him with the
awareness that nothing—nothing short of apocalyptic violence—can make a
Christian, or any other, order out of the modern megalopolis.

Miller's strength as an urban poet, though weakened by his near epic pretensions, is not simply primitivism. Near the end of the book he recalls, with
the pathos that overwhelms much of *Capricorn,* his being frightened and
alone in the North Carolina countryside during one of his few flights from
the loved and hated city. In this episode Miller realizes "what a terribly civilized person I am—the need I have for people, conversation, books, theatre,
music, cafés, drinks, and so forth" (308). Such ruminations, which run
through all of his works, and his concern for elaborate meals, varieties of
wines, books, painting, as well as his endless geniality and garrulousness, re-
inforce the self-aggrandizing myth of being an artist. Caught between "complicated needs" and "this infernal automatic process" that demands too
much, he must find a devious path in which outraged rebellion itself can become a profession within the comforts of society—thus making him a man of
letters.

In contrast, his simplest rebellion and his direct flowing colloquial laments
often give his best stance:

I'm here to live, not to calculate. And that's just what the bastards don't want you to
do—to live! They want you to spend your whole life adding up figures. That makes
sense to them. That's reasonable. That's intelligent. If I were running the boat things
wouldn't be so orderly perhaps, but it would be gayer, by Jesus! You wouldn't have
to shit in your pants over trifles. Maybe there wouldn't be macadamized roads and
loudspeakers and gadgets of a million-billion varieties. . . . there certainly wouldn't
be any cabinet ministers or legislatures because there wouldn't be any god-damned
laws to obey or disobey, and maybe it would take months and years to trek from place
to place, but you wouldn't need a visa or a passport or a *carte d'identité* because you
wouldn't be registered anywhere and you wouldn't bear a number and . . . you

wouldn't own anything except what you could carry around with you and why would you want to own anything when everything would be free? (281–82)

Natural skepticism about the social fraud arises, through native American exuberance, to natural anarchism. But both the modern rebel and his modern world inevitably achieve a more complicated alienation. For both are disorganized, and so a more fundamental violation becomes necessary. Thus Miller connects the "lucid" and the "daffy" and becomes, he claims, "the unique Dadaist in America" (286). The ultimate negation of society and of any possible larger order becomes an ultimate affirmation of himself, and Miller can then say "yes, yes, yes" by acts of annihilation.

Confronted with the urban chaos and meaningless frenzy of life, Miller, by a kind of "implosion" of the psyche, finds himself back in the land of childhood. For a major example, he recalls that he and his cousin, in a boy's fight in a park near Hell Gate, accidentally killed an eight- or nine-year-old opponent with a rock. They then returned to Miller's Aunt Caroline, whose sour rye bread provides "tacit but complete absolution" (128). Like Proust's cake—Miller's source here—the dark bread, used as the memory key, opens corridors of enchantment into "a primitive world ruled by magic" (129) with the numinous power of incomprehension and nonresponsibility.

Miller pours out a long run of fragmented anecdotes about his Brooklyn childhood. One whole series centers on magical companions—a Jewish boy, a French lad, an exotic Cuban—who carried some penumbra of enrichment not yet throttled by the Brooklyn daily world. These figures represent the escape from the ordinary that provides Miller's great curse but also his identity. The Brooklyn heroes also stand for the whole childish ethos, the "enlarged world" of "anarchic man" (145). Childhood was "crazy and chaotic but not [as] crazy and chaotic as the world" of adults. The last of the series of youthful heroes, arriving and departing when Miller was twenty-one, was Roy Hamilton, a self-educated westerner in search of his father, who Miller claims revealed to him the highest virtue—"a minimum of discord between those truths which were revealed to him and the exemplification of those truths in action" (147). Apparently he was part of the impetus for Miller going West himself, an episode weakly described and insignificant in effect. Yet—proper irony—Miller was to claim repeatedly for the rest of his life that this trip West was the "turning point" in his life because of his hearing Emma Goldman lecture, meeting her, and buying Nietzsche from her consort, Ben Reitman, in San Diego (Miller was working as a casual laborer in Chula Vista). That made him into a dissenting intellectual writer. Yet it almost certainly did not happen that way.[5] Anarchist-feminist Emma Goldman, the

most notorious intellectual radical of the time, who defiantly came to San
Diego as part of a prolonged "free-speech" campaign in one of America's po-
litically ugliest cities, was not allowed to give the announced lectures (as I
discovered by chance in going through an old file of San Diego newspapers)
but was instead forced by the police to leave town while Reitman was kid-
napped by righteous San Diego businessmen-vigilantes and taken to the desert, where he was beaten and tarred. (In a return trip Goldman was not
allowed into town, although she did lecture in San Diego a couple of years
later, when Miller was long gone.) Why did Miller fabricate such a story, and
repeat it for the rest of his life? Perhaps he did it to give himself the aura of
radical credentials and tradition—adult instead of childish anarchism, and
perhaps to repress less admirable actions of his publicly timorous character.
When one looks into such a story (or talks to the more perceptive who knew
Miller) one may reasonably bring considerable skepticism to many of Miller's
claims.

But *Capricorn* mostly centers on burlesque accounts. Back in Brooklyn, he
elaborates such a description of his father, who swore off drinking too fast
and fell into, and then out of, the inebriation of Protestant religiosity, and
then finally into gross somnambulism. His snoring gets a hyped, two-page
description. But in a typically portentous reversal, Miller uses it for anxious
lament of the loss of authority in the child's world: *"Father, sleep, I beg you, for
we who are awake are boiling in horror"* (1967). Since all maturity becomes alienation to Miller, the very sequence of memories, leading inevitably into unacceptable adulthood, destroys the child vision of life. Other mantic flights
become imperative; other methods for producing a manic "euphoria" must
be found if the chaos of adult America is to be overcome.

So he uses music, sex, and a dadaistic derangement of sensibility to
provide new ecstasies. *Capricorn,* outside of one early chapter division and a
number of irregular breaks in the free-associating run of prose, has only two
formal divisions. Drawn on musical analogies, these are an "Interlude" of
fantasy composition and the concluding apocalyptic essay about the Dark
Lady entitled "Coda." Music—Miller's piano playing as a youth—becomes
sexual burlesque. His first sexual conquest of his piano teacher at fifteen
leads to the use of musical situations for the next seven (or more) gross seductions, which seem presented with traditional young American male
exaggeration.

Sexual epiphany more explicitly provides an organizing trope in the irregular development—perhaps on some vaguely musical analogy—of the
motto for *Capricorn*: "On the Ovarian Trolley." On one level, this simply refers to the compulsive train of sexuality, the pursuit of dozens of pudenda

that dominates his "The Land of Fuck." But the trope intends much more: the ovarian trolley, beginning with Miller's bemused comments about his reluctance to leave his mother's womb, in the opening pages, to his final violent assertion of nailing on the wall the black womb of his Dark Lady, would seem to be Miller's wildly splayed version of Otto Rank's *The Birth Trauma*.[6] While Miller intermittently exploits some of the metaphoric possibilities— being misborn, regressive states, a changeling child, burrowing back into the womb of memory and fantasy, the metaphysical womb journey into rebirth, and so on—Miller's mind and art depend upon fortuitous, even gratuitous, exfoliation of metaphors rather than on elaborate Dantean or Joycean metaphoric architectonics.

The "ovarian trolley" image has several forced developments in terms of auto-fantasy, ending in an apocalyptic vision. The starting point comes from that kind of gross literal fact Miller delights in: his Cosmodemonic clerk, Hymie, is married to a woman with diseased ovaries. While on a trolley ride, Hymie asks Miller to explain ovaries to him. In Miller's state of associative mania and intentional derangement, this request starts him off: "from the idea of diseased ovaries there germinated in one lightning-like flash a sort of tropical growth made up of the most heterogeneous sorts of odds and ends" (49–50). A few pages later he revealingly explains that "I had never done what I wanted and out of not doing what I wanted to do there grew up inside me this creation which was nothing but an obsessional plant, a sort of coral growth, which was appropriating everything" (53). *Tropic of Capricorn* and, indeed, the whole autobiographical fantasia are the verbal equivalents of that obsessional growth.

Miller wants to purge his failures as a human being—not to understand or to transform into a meaningful structure but explosively to unload in bursts of heightened language. At times he grows pretentious in the process: *Capricorn* is "the equivalent of that Purgatory which Dante has described" (208) (he also compares *Cancer* to Dante's *Inferno* and his Big Sur writings to a description of *Paradiso*). Actually, a kind of schizophrenic verbal gesturing remains central. I have previously noted the defining self-alienation that Miller cultivates with his discreet actions (theft, sex), discreet things (vaginas, words), and discreet feelings (sentimentality, malice), which are given heightened isolation from a full human context. In *Capricorn*, discussing his fascination with the image of ovaries, he writes, "Only the object haunted me, the separate, detached, insignificant *thing*" (54). His cannibalism of the sensibility he neatly perceives as "a perverse love of the thing-in-itself." And it rests, of course, on romantic inversion; where William Blake found truth only in "minute particulars," such as the symbolic grain of sand, Miller finds his in "minute particles" that always take form as a "blemish" or a "grain of ugliness which to me constituted the sole beauty of the object." From such fragments he compiles his obsessive growths that give shape, such as it is, to his world of dismembered imagination, mixing times and fantasies, rages and longings. This self-alienation can be given continuity and identity only by the insistent rhetoric which tries to create a distinctive voice for that naturally surreal being, Henry Miller.

Thus, though Miller will attempt, rather unsatisfactorily, to claim the American way of life—Cosmodemonic labors, Brooklyn philistinism, the loss of innocence—as the purgatory which explains him, just as he claimed the down-and-out inferno in Paris as the explanation of *Tropic of Cancer*'s gestures, the ostensible causes explain very little. His lively nihilism, his "ferocious gaiety" that he occasionally achieves by "balancing at the edge of the abyss" (62), may sometimes provide appropriate comic comment on the more general alienation, frenzy, and loss of center of the twentieth-century world, but it inheres most fully in the subjectivity of the author. The longing in the *Tropics* for cataclysm, for destruction and annihilation, is also the longing for the metamorphosis into new being and purpose—the desperate lunge out of partial chaos, as in modern wars and social manias, into the ultimate chaos.

The "ovarian trolley" trope is replayed in the "Interlude" section that Miller also calls "The Land of Fuck." In meditating on the impersonal compulsion of life represented by sex, "my soul would leave its body and roam from place to place on a little trolley such as is used in department stores for making change. I made ideological changes and excursions; I was a vagabond in the country of the brain" (202). And what he finds, *Cancer* style, is that every exit is marked "ANNIHILATION." He again exploits the destructive process, a "Gentile Dybbuk." In this section impersonal and dehumanized sex with an idiotic babysitter turns into a monstrous growth of fantasy to reach toward some sort of meaning. In yet another variation on the "ovarian trolley" trope, he makes the actual pudendum into a superpudendum "not of this land at all" but of the "bright country" of the imagination (196). More specifically, he imagines the womb at hand to be an ornately furnished Pullman car. By such fantasy processes the fragmented and nearly meaningless experiences can be turned into something portentous—"eschatological, ecumenical"—and the gross, pathetic, and compulsive become excitingly rich.

However, the Miller of *Capricorn* is not quite the Miller of *Cancer*. During his years in Paris, he became increasingly influenced by the visionary in a more impersonal sense—astrology, Zen Buddhism, and several occultist doctrines (Swedenborgianism, Jewish mysticism, etc.).[7] As I noted of the

Colossus of Maroussi, Miller's return baggage from his European sojourn included several more or less traditional unitive visions. Some of this crops up throughout *Capricorn*: "Once this fact [of universal sentiency] is grasped there can be no more despair. At the very bottom of the ladder, chez the spermatozoa, there is the same condition of bliss as at the top, chez God. God is the summation of all the spermatozoa come to full consciousness" (204). Perhaps, then, an increase in sexual intercourse will provide an increase in divine consciousness—a charming idea. But rather than pursue further implications of Miller's methods of fantasy, now incremented by the usual occultist acrobatics around "the self and the not-self" (207), the emptiness that is unity, the change of heart in which degradation becomes angelic, etc., or Miller's insightful asides ("all department stores are symbols of sickness"), let us return to the lesser tropics of America. For it is quite likely that the occult myths so popular with twentieth-century literary visionaries are but fragments shoring the ruins of more human and social passions.

Miller's demand on America for "a life more abundant" (300), by which he means a life more individually comprehensible and humanly joyous, is transformed into a monstrous purgative edifice. Its backyard-baroque shape derives partly from the over-assertion of one who discovered himself a nullity—"just a Brooklyn boy . . . which is to say one of the last and least of men" (48)—and his change of heart becomes partly that of the underground man, resentful and perverse, and partly that of the homegrown sage, didactic and prolix. The mechanical glitter and the alienated thingness of America reflect his self-alienation, and of course deny the mystery of grace as well as of creation. His simple story, occasionally obscured by his rhetorical gestures, is merely sad: his lost first adolescent love, the pathetic affair with a maternal older woman; the disappearance of childhood heroes; the rapid breakdown of the ineffective father; the fading of the innocent vision of the primal neighborhood; disillusionment with the boy's dream of American opportunity; and the descent into the compulsions of work, sex, domesticity, and Broadway excitement. By going, in his mind anyway, to the extremity of resentment and rejection, of anger at maturity, he dismisses America and the all-too-ordinary, inverts reality to memory and fantasy, and becomes "*an angel*" free to create his own country and cosmos.

Although Miller is all too willing to dramatize himself as criminal and saint, both gratuitous acts and grace, despite hyperbolic prose, tend to buffoonery. One source arises from apparently unintentional literary parody: "I was really a brother to Dostoyevsky, . . . perhaps I was the only man in all America who knew what he meant in writing those books" (211). His peccadillos, however, are rather more those of the timid opportunist and the polymorphously perverse child—in *Capricorn,* the quick sex in the back room, the swiped pennies, the fanciful lies, the sly obscenity at a funeral, the mixed affection toward and exploitation of buddies, the puckish cheating on job, wife, friend, and principle—than of any Dostoyevskian anguish.

"I should have been a clown," he properly notes early in his laments of how the world misunderstands him; and so, as both mock underground man and synthetic angel, he is. While Miller would have achieved more art if he had stuck to direct clowning in his writing, his wrath against the American he was does sometimes provide a curious testimony of a fragmentation and a longing that belong to much of America as well as to Miller. The incomplete rebel, he suffers from the very compulsions, stridency, righteousness, ambitions, and inchoate yearnings he denounces. He does sometimes effectively present, almost in spite of himself, the mixture of glittering surfaces and soft centers that make the American experience almost incomprehensible. His cry of the heart is for the means to put the cosmic and demonic pieces of America and Miller back together. Certainly, despite some wonderful responsive flourishes, that curious documentary mélange, *Tropic of Capricorn,* does not succeed in doing it. This Brooklyn Columbus must remain perpetually at sea in the tropic of his self-pitying rages about the America of his dreams.

The Air-Conditioned Nightmare

Miller's frequently brilliant gestures—his metaphors, titles, and roles—went in search of a context. As he traveled, in memory and in fact, back and forth between Europe and America, he did not so much describe his experiences as turn out rhetorical markers indicating partly submerged fears, longings, and fancies. Of one of his trips back to the United States in the 1930s he wrote a hortatory dirge, "Glittering Pie," in which he labeled America a "nightmare" of uniformity-conformity.[8] The endless American re-doing of the cityscape, the proliferation of bland "skyscraper souls," of automated aloneness and gregariousness, of glittering and vicarious lives, end in nothingness. Only the artist, apparently, can escape, for he joyously *"plays the role of undertaker"* (345). Typically, this apocalyptic essay neither describes anything as such, nor argues any problem or point of view, but simply strings out labels, vestigial anecdotes, names, and tropes; it ends with an all-encompassing condemnation of America, except for the artist-condemner. Much of it is simply "a binge of words"[9].

The apt title of *The Air-Conditioned Nightmare* covers two volumes of miscellaneous pieces (*Remember to Remember* is vol. 2). The major subject is art and artist, and most of these sketches are marked by the point of view of the professional literary prodigal. Miller's encomia of his artistic friends and his editorials on the state of American art show him at his weakest as a writer, thinker, and person. Among the other pieces are several of Miller's best burlesques.

The Air-Conditioned Nightmare is ostensibly organized around Miller's year-long tourist travels in America, via automobile, a year after his return from Europe in 1940. Actually, except for the summary remarks in the preface and a few sketches loosely connected by the sequence of the highway, the linkage is vague and arbitrary. Another, and unintentionally amusing, frame may be seen in the epigraph and appendix to *Nightmare*. Miller starts with a long passage from Swami Vivekananda about the Sattvika (unknown and silent hero). Not only with his usual aggrandizement and noise but also in the appendix and in a number of sarcasms along the way (115, 247), Miller shows what an anti-Sattvika he himself is by displaying his anger at not being given a Guggenheim fellowship in 1941 for his trip around America, although he had a sizable advance from a commercial publisher.[10] The persistence of the author's righteous sarcasm may puzzle readers: shouldn't Miller, a longtime mocker of genteel institutional frauds, have expected the refusal, and taken it as a compliment? The ideal audience for whom he writes, however, consists neither of Sattvikas nor of sophisticates; like Miller, they apparently delight in bumptious naivete and in playing the sly child among the earnestly fraudulent adults.

Righteous stridency runs thickly through the preface of *Nightmare*. Miller's reactions to America on his return from Greece, he tells us, were full of dread, disgust, and anger; but a passing comment of typical candor, about his "wretched, sordid memories" (11), suggests that his miseries were really more internal than public. The inhospitality of America to the artist, its materialism and gewgaws, and other stock charges are sprinkled through the miscellaneous personal details of arranging the trip. Then follows a list of the best experiences of the trip, in which the primary one, for this eternal literary man, is reading a book. That year's Miller awards for best man, best woman, best soul, and so forth, show the usual overstated quaintness—a Hindu swami, the wife of a black poet, a Jewish philosopher, a theosophist, among others. The concluding half-dozen pages consist of an editorial against American mediocrity and for heroic revitalization.

"Good News! God is Love!" is an angry sermon in which Miller impatiently dismisses the largest part of his American nightmare, and the largest part of America: all that represented by Pittsburgh, Cleveland, Detroit, Chicago, and points between; all that personified by "futilitarian salesmen," Walt Disney's coy monsters, and fatuous, clean, anxious American faces; all

that found in the cruel slums, the sterile hotel rooms, and the frightening in-
dustrial landscapes. With too much thrown in—and thus not adequately
realized—the occasionally apt rhetoric generally turns blatant in dealing with
the discrepancies between the rich and the poor (corporations create these
with their "tentacles"), the frenzied productivity and the feeble culture, the
moneypower and the individual blandness, and the more evident forms of
dullness, ugliness, stupidity, and soullessness. While Miller is not altogether
wrong, neither is he quite right; and a good many of his slapdash caricatures
miss the actual America, as in linking the U.S. "status quo" with "Czarist
Russia" (24), or in using the Southern poor as the praiseworthy antithesis of
the machined souls of Detroit—as if they weren't literal brothers!—or in
holding up the synthetic religiosity of the suburban Bahai Temple as the answer to what is wrong with the South Side in Chicago (51). For the "Good
News! God is Love!" that Miller saw chalked in horrible irony on a Chicago
slum building is, for him, stock doctrine as well as bitter mockery.

Occasional bits, though never an extended piece, of invective are well
turned, such as that directed against the business-busy American: "the fat,
puffy, wattle-faced man of forty-five who has turned asexual is the greatest
monument to futility" (41). Or the condemnation of mass culture, which
doesn't even have the virtue of narcotics: "Real dope gives you the freedom to
dream your own dreams; the American kind forces you to swallow the perverted dreams" of those with only the cheapest of longings (31). Agreed, too,
"Souls don't grow in factories," or in the slick, bright ruthless ambience of
technological idolatry (37); but they may also not grow in the Indian reserva-
tions and European slums with which Miller sentimentally counters. The
sense of American actuality will run out rapidly with such large spouts as
Pittsburgh, "symbol of brutal power and wealth," versus Ramakrishna, "incarnation of love and wisdom" (24). Miller, of course, pours less of his feelings through Oriental love-and-wisdom than through the literary hysterias
of Céline, Patchen, and other *prophètes maudits* whom he imitates.[11]

"The Soul of Anaesthesia" consists largely of didactic ruminations trig-
gered by his visit to a prison in the South (Atlanta?) which he connects with
an ex-convict. Neither place nor man gets presented in any significant detail,
though Miller reacts violently to the prison and sentimentally to the ex-
convict. But the frightened Miller has two all-encompassing answers: First,
"There is only one word to remember, as you pass in and out of life, and that
word, as every great soul has said, is LOVE" (81); and second, some pages of
ornate apocalyptic prose whose verbal delirium anesthetizes Miller's fright at
nightmarishly inexplicable suffering.

At this point I might comment on Miller's long sketch, "The Alcoholic

Veteran with the Washboard Cranium." Though published in *The Wisdom of the Heart* anthology, this seems to belong somewhere in the middle of the first volume of his American trip. The "veteran" is a grotesque character whom Miller and his painter companion reputedly met one night in New Orleans. By his own report, a badly scarred and disillusioned World War I hero, this loquacious drunk also claims to have been a successful lawyer, doctor, legislator, commercial writer, convict, poet, builder, adventurer, song writer, desperado, and so on. As Miller presents himself, he took an absurdly long time to figure out that the down-and-outer was a fraud. The handling of the anecdote is weird in more than its naivete. As given, much of the veteran's fluid, fragmented, and quaint monologues on war, politics, modern society, and American food belong to Henry Miller. Yet the skidrow philosopher is treated with hostile detachment by his alter ego, and the moralizing is even more contradictory than usual in its mixture of condemnation and sympathy. The narrating author admits being cruel in the way in which he dismisses the veteran; when questioned about this by his companion, Miller gives the shoddiest rationalization, insisting (in reference to the Cosmodemonic days of several decades earlier) that he had "heard so many terrible tales, met so many guys like this . . . that I've hardly got an ounce of sympathy left in me" (128).

Yet Miller launches into lengthy philosophizing about the necessity for a true revolution of the heart, as against other forms of ameliorative change; and he attempts to demonstrate the point in a confessional double-ending. With some slyness, the author seems to admit that he belongs to those who "always know how to muster a thousand reasons for withholding their aid" to the unfortunate, as he did with the "alcoholic veteran." Yet he decides to write of the veteran, he tells us, for the didactic purpose of making "people more kindly and tolerant" (137–38). Just how his presentation of the alcoholic veteran as a fraud will encourage charity must indeed remain a puzzle. Then comes the memory of when Miller walked the streets of New York, himself a garrulous moocher, and a man in a cape and opera hat threw some change for him in the mud of the gutter. Miller's anger, before he picks up and washes off the thirty-six cents, is therapeutic. He later announces to his wife that he is joyous: "I've just been humiliated, beaten, dragged in the mud and washed in the blood of the lamb." He buys her an Easter morning hamburger in a "greasy spoon on Myrtle Avenue," and makes "a vow to remain wide awake and if possible to wake up the whole world, saying in conclusion Amen! and wiping my mouth with a paper napkin" (139).

Curious, what! as Miller loved to say. He might also *say* that the Easter morning revelation proved that human sympathy comes from suffering.

However, the ostensible moral is mostly a paper napkin to finish the literary meal. The tale, as we have it, belongs to the true confessional tradition in that it undercuts its own moral. The personal anecdote of humiliation that Miller suddenly inverts into joy we can also recognize—it takes the same form in *Cancer* and *Capricorn,* and in the volumes of *The Rosy Crucifixion*—as showing his usual perverse strategy for turning misery into ecstasy. Unlike the earlier and parallel story "Max," the "Alcoholic Veteran" is about Miller, his inability to suffer, his inability to sympathize with the sufferings of others, and his casuistry by which, representative sentimentalist that he is, he has inadequate tangible sentiments. Avowedly concerned with the wisdom of the loving heart, his superb candor reveals the joy and the "wisdom" of the loveless heart. Quite a confession!

There may be some analogical connection between this motif of the sentimentalist who cauterizes most personal sentiments and the motif of the anti-artist who spends much of his time shouting about artists. Returning to the first volume of *The Air-Conditioned Nightmare,* we find a series of five pieces about art and artists (the two just before the end, numbers 17 and 18, are also on the same subject). The longest centers on the character of Weeks Hall, who is described as a compulsive talker, full of gusto, responsiveness, and eccentricity—the same type as the Greek poets of *Colossus of Maroussi*—and who is also the proprietor of an old mansion, "The Shadows," in New Iberia, Louisiana (actually Shadows on the Teche, now a shrine open to the public). Miller's stay leads to a fairly straightforward, if touristic, adulatory account of the place and its proprietor, both seen as part of a mythic Old South of rich and bizarre culture.

Miller broadly generalizes the same theme in the concluding brief section of the book, "The Southland." "This world of the South corresponds more nearly to the dream life which the poet imagines than do other sections of the country" (248). What he has in mind are *not* the Gothic nightmares, which American writers usually have found appropriate to the South, but the fancy mansions of tourism which evoke "magical names, epoch-making events" of a plantation economy that produced a "great symphonic pageant" (252). He has, of course, granted that it was based on a vicious slave culture, but so were "India, Egypt, Rome and Greece" (25). What Miller blandly fails to emphasize is that the South never produced a good minor culture, much less a great one; however, dream can substitute for deed, for "who knows what splendours might have blossomed forth" (251). But in the long piece on "The Shadows" he noted, with rather more perception, that the idiosyncratic custodian-artist of the Southern heritage "was a self-convicted prisoner inhabiting the aura of his own creation" (101).

Miller's perceptions, as well as his genial mixed bag of artists and culture-fantasies, seem fortuitous. "Dr. Souchon: Surgeon-Painter" links a few details of New Orleans with some ranting about American philistinism and the seventyish medico-businessman who became a primitive Sunday painter. Since, for Miller, an American artist is a social eccentric "who has faith in himself" (104) and in self-expression, his qualities of mind, feeling, and art become secondary. The "artists" in "Arkansas and the Great Pyramid" are two cranks, Albert Pike, nineteenth-century Masonic Potentate and occultist, and William Hope Harvey, who wanted to build a multimillion-dollar pyramid. Miller's artless praise of them consists largely of miscellaneous information and quotations. At the other end of the American artist spectrum is a surreal apologia for avant-garde auditory experimentation, "With Edgar Varese in the Gobi Desert," which mostly sloganizes: "THE WORLD AWAKE!" (146); "Be more and more like God" (147); "Nothing is deader than the status quo" (147); "if one *believes*, miracles occur" (148); "*We are all filled with murder*" (154)—and so can only be redeemed by violently magical artists. The euphoric praise of Alfred Stieglitz as a culture-broker and of John Marin (whom Miller imitates in some of his own watercolors), or the brief blurb praising an old Paris friend, "[Hilaire] Hiler and Murals" (161), produce only sentimental indulgence.[12]

So, for the most part, does the "Letter to Lafayette," a fragmented personal polemic in which Miller praises the "genius" of several of his devotees. The center of this work seems to be righteous hyperbole, perhaps including some fractured self-pity, directed against America. If an American has any talent, shouts Miller, "he's doomed to have it crushed" (136); if the sensitive citizen of these States is "dedicated to beauty," he will spend the rest of his life "in a straight-jacket" (137). His advice to the artistic American: "Shoot yourself, young man, there is no hope for you!" Alternate advice is: "Do anything, be anything that comes into your head because it's all cuckoo" (139).

The mélange of provincial swindlers and corn-doctors, twentieth-century eccentrics and off-beat artists, in Miller's sentimental and noisy rebellion against American dullness, is a kind of home-grown dadaistic salesmanship. The art of the blurb, with the usual overstated asides about nightmarishly wicked America, also dominates the tediously written pieces in the second volume, *Remember to Remember*, on painters Varda, Beauford Delaney, and Abraham Ratner (probably, in its digressions, the best of the sketches); sculptor Benjamin Bufano; and theater director Jasper Deeter. His personal friendship with them does not encourage any complex, critical, or subtle response—thus demonstrating the very provincialism he rants against. In the thirty-page preface to *Remember* he also does passing "homage" to a series of

friends, though the lack of development means that they can have little interest to a reader. Miller's avowed affection for "the salt of the earth"—
bootblacks, AWOL soldiers, and other outcasts—seems to be only
sentimental since he does not bother to portray them in any detail.

The same limitations apply to the following pages of invective against
America. Though he rages against nationalism and statism, Miller tumbles
into an amorphous mixture of the occult, Jules Verne, and millennarian pop-
ulism. Thus he predicts a "new realm of consciousness" bursting forth in the
worst of all possible worlds: Japan soon taking over Europe, the worldwide
revolution of the "little man" ushering in a utopian "new age," and fantastic
inventions that will straighten out all practical and psychic perplexities.
Miller can get pretty silly when he practices the American vice of positive
thinking.

The matching escape into memory provides the long title sketch of *Remember to Remember*. The main subject is remembered France, not the France
of *Cancer* and "Max" but of a righteously romanticized nostalgia. The main
motif comes from the didactic novel, *The Renegade,* by Miller's Paris side-
kick, Alfred Perlès, in which the libertine hero is saved by an occultist's message, "The mission of man on earth is to remember" (295). Following Perlès
in believing that the escape from the present into memory provides both
"identity" and "eternity" (292, 300), Miller uses a few instructional aids,
such as maps of Paris and France, to get himself into the proper humor for his
anecdotes and exhortations about the natural religiosity and culturosity of
France in contrast to America (similar to the earlier "Vive La France").
Miller's overstatement of the merits of French wine, whores, scenery, spiritu-
ality, food, and books results in loose Francophile prose that lacks real
discrimination.

Another way of being outside America while in it—the apparent therapeutic function of much of Miller's writing—is to see only the dream of
America. In "My Dream of Mobile" the bookish child's version of Marco
Polo starts off a series of ruminations that include a fantasy of Farragut's Mobile. A few curious details about the actual South join the exotic substitution,
though Miller prefers the dream to actuality, especially when he can finally
collapse both into the self-mystagoguery of Henry Miller someday disap-
pearing into Tibet.

A less wilful version of Miller's child-centered cosmos appears in "Day in
the Park" where he tells several anecdotes about children. The dialogues and
details show the wryness and coyness we might expect from a lonely, genial
middle-aged tourist. He develops a tearful longing for children. Also impressed with the child's indifference to moral values—"The gift of detach-

ment" (177)—Miller finds yet another way out of anxiety and guilt besides memory-fantasy.

The next three sketches in the *Nightmare* also belong to the Americana of highway culture, and they culminate appropriately in the burlesque world of Hollywood. On the way we have a pleasant comic set-piece, "Automotive Passacaglia," in which unmechanical-minded Miller burlesques his own naivete with the motor troubles of his old Buick and ends by satirically asking for good old American kindness to animals and automobiles. But the Buick seems to get him to the Grand Canyon, which provides the scene for several anecdotes, the major one about the entitling figure, "A Desert Rat." The first few anecdotes shrewdly mock the crassness and vapidity of some standard American tourist types. Quite antithetical is Olson, the talkative, "philosophical" old-timer from the desert who tells Miller of his outsmarting the professors, of his fantastic theories about diet, of the magic power of the Indians, and of how to straighten out World War II. A typical weakness appears in the sketch: only rarely does Miller succeed in separating his persona from himself to give him independent and adequate voice. With apocalyptic hatred Miller-Olson delights in the view that Indians are better than the white Americans who are a "swiftly decaying people . . . degenerate and degraded in every way" (198). This gesture of inverting the usual tourist sentiment is elaborated in a good bit of cantankerous mythology, but tourist Miller shows little interest in ordinary American life.

Better done is the loosely woven but intensely felt next stage west, "From Grand Canyon to Burbank." The tension that gives immediacy to the descriptions here depends on the sharply changing scene as one progresses into California by anxiously pushing an overheated car across the desert. The next and best piece in the first volume of *The Air-Conditioned Nightmare,* the surreal satire "Soirée in Hollywood" uses fragmentation to provide a comic vision of Los Angeles. The Millerian catalogue of oddities, leveling religion and Coca-Cola, fusing the Marquis de Sade and right-wing Americanism, linking the *faérique* and the neon, provide the reality of Sunset Boulevard, which he describes as being "like a strip-teaser doing the St. Vitus dance" (225). With wry colloquialism, surreal metaphors of incongruity, and a speeded-up comic violence indebted to slapstick cinema, Miller presents a wealthy Hollywood dinner party where everyone is "soused," righteously phony, and childishly outrageous. The iconoclasm, the spoofing, and the earthy shrewdness of the boy from Brooklyn with an avant-garde verbal dexterity here find their natural milieu. And the ever so appropriate irreverence and irrelevance give one Los Angeles with "a feeling of the future," a "bad future" (224), as the corny penultimate of the open society and the pluralistic culture.

"Astrological Fricassée," the longer parallel party sketch in *Remember to Remember*, is one of Miller's best burlesques. Given the natural grotesques of an absurd Hollywood, and a host, Gerald(-ine), who is a snobbish, malicious, exploitative, homosexual astrologer—a dead ringer for "The Red Queen"—Miller is not distracted by ambiguities, his doctrinaire view of a stock America, or the need to defend himself from ordinary reality. We get detached observation and dialogue, plus comically artful metaphor, for each of the caricatures at the party: a rich, sickly, and officious upper-class American lady, who "might have been the twin sister of Carrie Nation done by Grant Wood in a moment of Satanic illumination" (222), with a heart "ticking away like a rusty Ingersoll" and blood "running through her veins like mucilage soaking through blotting paper"; Lady Astenbrooke, mad, trivial, rigid, British author, with three cherries on her hat and deflated leathery breasts, who bows like a "broken hinge" and stands like a "tipsy Gainesborough to which Marc Chagall had put the finishing touches" (224). Other guests include a "portly, interior decorator type of homosexual" (230) with a "yoo-hoo" voice; a strikingly beautiful and self-aggrandizing dancer, Lolita, "blank and flawless as stainless steel" (237) and with a similar hard and shiny vanity; Humberto, pawing and bewildered drunk, whom Miller introduces to a name-dropper as "the assistant gynecologist at the Schizophrenic Sanitarium in New Caledonia" (262); an ornate and sweating Cuban lady, whose posterior hung over "the seat of the chair like a piece of limp liver" (234), and who has a suspiciously dapper husband with "butter-colored gloves" and the threatening asperity of a "Neapolitan barber" (235); a pack of yapping "trained poodle" females, "terribly psychic," who talk of their reincarnations toward Karma (229) while nibbling tea cookies and thrilling to Miller's occult "aura" ("Violet . . . with a touch of magenta"); and varied other "psychopomps" of the netherworld.

Miller's bemused detachment and mocking contempt, and, perhaps most important, his general lack of pretension to being an American prophet, a unique personality, or a Great Artist—the bloated ambitions that mar so much of his writing—give him a comic command of his material. The fantasticality and incongruity of surrealist epithets, verbal displacement, and violently playful yoking produce stylistic power when turned to such concrete farce. Perhaps, too, the purlieus of Hollywood provide a most suitable locus for the more disciplined pyrotechnics of surrealist style, as we see in these two party pieces of Miller's and in the more bitter-pathetic *Day of the Locust* of Nathanael West. For the disjunctions of surrealism aptly convey the appropriate violence, sexual warping, ruthless longings, and empty dreams.

The final long episode of "Astrological Fricassée" centers satirically on

Mrs. Rubiol, pretentious wife of a rich American petroleum engineer-inventor. Miller uses most of the standup comedian's amusing repertoire in mocking her: parodied name dropping, learned non sequiturs, highfalutin jabberwocky, dead-pan fantasia, and more of his translation of surreal, visual incongruities into comic rhetoric. The sequence ends with farce deflation, the petulant homosexuals making love, drunk Humberto imitating a whale under the couch, Mrs. Rubiol in an alcoholic daze ("her eyes twittered like two desynchronized song birds" [268]), and, as a Marx brothers' fillip, a complacent undertaker arrives searching for a corpse. At the genial conclusion the characters are all looking for something to eat—Miller's common-sense focus—and are prepared to turn the place upside down.

The wild word is all. The burlesque rhetoric of "The Staff of Life" broadly satirizes American bad taste in monuments as well as in bread, inadequate spice in conversation as well as in salad, sugary weak sensuality in sex as well as in beverages, and lack of tang in life-style as well as in cheese. The comic techniques include mock-logical sequences: "poor bread, bad teeth, indigestion, constipation, halitosis, sexual starvation, disease and accidents, the operating table, artificial limbs, spectacles and baldness, kidney and bladder trouble, neurosis, psychosis, schizophrenia, war and famine" (36). Then onward and downward through "the decay and dissolution of our once glorious republic"—all because of standard American bread. The outsider's gusto for food provides the vantage point for hilarity against the American fear of "the zest for life" (51).

From the burlesque vantage point Miller can mockingly play with clichés, instead of falling into them: "it's the pie that takes the cake" (46), that standardized American machine pie with its piece of fruit "surrounded by a clot of phlegm" (47). Using the traditional device of comic displacement, it is the birds of North America, fed on our crusts, who decline—"beaks have become dull, their wing-span shortened; they are pining and drooping, moulting in season and out. Above all, they no longer sing as they used to; they make sour notes, they bleet instead of tweeting, and . . . have even been heard to cackle and wheeze" (53). The actions that take on their own mechanism—what Bergson labeled the "snowball" device; the scenery-collapsing finale of vaudeville—a favored device of Miller's in such comedy. Toward the end, he has a long parody recipe, in outrageous mockery of both our bread and our earnest desire to jazz things up, where he uninhibitedly throws in ketchup and kerosene, anchovies and urine, to improve "the staff of our unsavory and monotonous life" (52). There are appropriate asides on American fruit salad and salesmen (our crassest dishes), on the uniformity of our stock restaurants (try to get a herring or a grape, nuts, good cheese, or

Jewish bread), on how America melts down the rich foreign-born diets into
the automated pot of bland stew, and on the closely related tastes for Hollywood funerals, Christian marriage, war production, and conspicuous garbage. In describing much of our grossness of two generations ago, Miller
again displays his Thoreauvian touch, even some parallel verbal conceits.
"Earning a living," the major excuse for our hurried, prefabricated diet—the
forerunner of "fast" or "junk" food—"has nothing to do with living. It's the
beltline to the grave, without transfer or stopover" (40).

In the hyperlogic of burlesque, Miller's sweeping condemnations of everything American become meaningful in a way that his petulant rages cannot
possibly become when he poses them in more earnest forms. In comedy he
can properly ignore the multiple shadings and nuances of awareness that his
naivete, egotism, and alienation deny him in efforts at more serious writing.
"What do I find wrong with America? Everything." Only from the perspective of the saint or the fool can the total rejection of a given order of society
take on authentic shape and meaning. The rebellious wisdom of the wise
buffoon is in the detached simplemindedness and absolute logicality with
which he can annihilate all. Unfortunately, Miller frequently does not recognize his essentially comic perspective and limitations. But when he does, he
comically follows out the American logic (though not the mixed American
realities) that hates human communion even more than communism, sus-
pects rich responsiveness even more than regal simplicity, and, in creating the
world center of conspicuous garbage and hygienic nihilism, makes us super-
aesthetes who let our machines and organizations live for us.

Miller often relates his gestures of buffoonery to dadaism and
surrealism—no doubt they did provide liberating elements for natural
American hyperbole and fragmentation—and rather questionably links
himself to Petronius and Rabelais. But some more native roots nourished his
vulgate zest and wise-fool iconoclasm. Much can be found in Miller's beloved burlesque theaters and vaudeville; in the great American silent film comedians; in traditional American male obscenity, exaggeration, and
deflating jokes; and in similar urban folk styles.[13] Part of this richly mimetic
and mocking heritage goes back through several thousand years of the popular arts of fools, jesters, clowns, and buffoons. Miller's literary revolt was less a
negation of puritanism and philistinism and Americanism than of the re-
strained style, genteel sensibility, and understatement so essential to the main
Anglo-Saxon literary traditions. Miller adapts more folkish traditions of direct and outrageous humor, full of obscene and blasphemous energy, into
literature.

Until a generation ago, much of the hyperbolic and iconoclastic, mock-heroic and verbally fantastic comedy—except as rural folkloristic humor in writers like Faulkner—has, like sex and profundity, been covert in our literature. The rough comic heritage which Miller helped rediscover for literature, along with an increasing number of recent continental dramatists and American novelists—absurdists and black humorists—provides valuable laughing defiance at a world constructed on antihuman logic. The gravest limitation of Miller as comedian is that he doesn't stick with it but instead pursues romantic, metaphysical, and other literary ambitions that provide a ponderous and masked buffoonery—as when he casts an obtuse clown named Henry Miller as the tragically passionate lover in *The Rosy Crucifixion*. Except for some asides, only the few pieces just discussed, from the two lengthy volumes of his American trip, have intentional humor. The two weak anthologies are only partly redeemed by a handful of good epithets and three or four burlesque sketches.

The concluding fillip to the two-volume anthology is a joke gone ponderous, a two-page prose-poem epilogue, "The Most Lovely Inanimate Object in Existence." The provocative gesture of the title has only a synthetic context, a catalogue of allegorical (and capitalized) mythic American journeys ending in a "cold, dead mystery, like Mesa Verde" (427). The revelation is that "we are on top of the Mountain that was God, and it is extinct." What is really wrong, then, with America, the natural home of the "inanimate object," is that its God is dead. And so Miller, the cosmic outsider who, in *Tropic of Cancer* wanted to give "a kick in the pants to God" (11), is left rather spiritless on the Enchanted Mesa of America.

Horatio Alger at Big Sur

After some American touring and an extended spell in Los Angeles, Miller found his own enchanted mountaintop on the central California coast and settled down for the better part of two decades. The boy from the city streets who had, in his forties, discovered himself as a writer, had, in his fifties, discovered the simple life in nature in the American West. He also started rearing a family and identifying with a community, as well as industriously working in various roles as a professional avant-garde littérateur. Despite Miller's repeated confessions of cowardice and confusion, there is some admirable quotidian bravery in this determined pursuit of an identity and a place. That, at the end of this saga, his first book (*Tropic of Cancer*) should become a million-copy best-seller, providing him with money and other appurtenances of celebritydom, properly rounds off this American success story. Henry Miller, indignant mocker (in *Tropic of Capricorn*) at the Horatio Alger "sick dream of America" where the indomitable youth rises from rags to riches, becomes a kind of paragon of the self-made American literary man. It was, of course, a success story full of aslant comedy: our smiling young hero is a somewhat odd old man whose public success depends on notoriety as an ostensible pornographer—Horatio Alger *en marge*.[14]

In literary fact, Miller's later writings contain not only little obscenity but often little of the earlier verve, though some elements of idiosyncratic charm remain.[15] The main miscellany of the past–World Word II period is entitled *Big Sur and the Oranges of Hieronymous Bosch* (1957).[16] This volume, divided into twenty-two pieces (jottings, sketches, prose-poems, autobiographical fragments, and sermons) cannot readily be given systematic discussion. The one sustained piece, of over a hundred pages, is "Paradise Lost," a perverse memorial to Conrad Moricand (1887–1954), French astrologer-occultist and derelict-dandy, friend and intellectual mentor of the author. Miller knew Moricand in Paris in the 1930s and had him as his guest at Big Sur for three months in 1948. That visit, for which Miller brought the nearly destitute Moricand from Europe, is less a study in the tribulations of friendship than a portrait of decadence and another documentation of Miller's bumptious naivete.

With a frequently effective turn of detail, Miller sketches Moricand as an elegant conversationalist, fastidious parasite, meticulous pornographer, sickly old snob, and utterly impossible person. Images of his running psychosomatic sores, of his sexual and moral perversions, of his collaborationist wanderings through wartime Europe with two suitcases of occultist manuscripts, and of his absurdly threatening and whining demands, enlarge into a pervasive sense of the sickness unto death. Miller's motives in bringing this small-time urban decadent to his rural American retreat seem compounded of nostalgic sentimentality for his Parisian days, uninsightful sympathy, and, apparently, some obscure guilts about his own relation to suffering. Wryness—to invite Moricand was "like inviting Melancholia to come and perch on your shoulder" (296)—mixes with fascination.

In his usual chaotic way, Miller drops in scattered autobiographical musings, descriptions of memories, fragmented sensations, food, books, and sketches of several fantastical friends (a grossly energetic and lavish Hollywood cameraman, a neurotically earnest Christian Science healer, an enigmatic—undeveloped—learned recluse),[17] and several sermons on living simply and wisely. As with Miller's earlier portraits, running from "Max" through the "Alcoholic Veteran," there appears in "Paradise Lost" the usual odd mixture of Miller's sympathy and righteousness, including again the compulsive anecdotes from his own days of beggary. Yet the genteel, neuraesthenic, rigid, depressive Conrad Moricand—friendless but unable to be alone, paranoically suspicious but totally dependent—remains trapped in a misery quite alien to the healthy, garrulous, sentimental, shrewd, self-delighting, and self-appeasing Henry Miller. While the mean and miserable have no monopoly on suffering, Moricand, as Miller makes fulsomely clear, starts miserable and has only one direction to go. An implicit theme here, and through most of the self-congratulatory later writings, is that "whosoever hath, to him shall be given."

Rather than discuss again the weird synapses of sensibility characterizing Miller's sketches, we might consider some larger dimensions of Miller's portraits of grotesque outcasts. Sometimes mistakenly viewed as naturalistic documents, they are essentially studies of bad-luck figures, black fools, sacrificial blemish scapegoats. The author's rhetorical distance, underlying both the too-general moralizings and the nasty, precise detail, may, in literary terms, be related back to a pre-Christian, classical stance, as in Apuleius' Socrates episode in the *Golden Ass*. Charity in such stories is poisonous; sympathy simply increases the parasite's demands and produces outrageous results because it violates the magical order of the universe and of the magician-author that such tales presume.

Miller's portrait of Moricand also belongs to a type whose finest twentieth-century example may be D. H. Lawrence's portrait of Maurice Magnus, which Miller had admiringly read in Paris.[18] The similarity between Magnus and Moricand is striking: quasi-aristocratic background, incongruous Foreign Legion service, left-handed intellectuality, compulsive fastidiousness, genteel mooching, "unnatural" vice, resentful authoritarianism, pretentious literary ambitions, dandyism, verbal charisma, total disloyalty, miserable lonely death, and so on. Lawrence and Miller even use some of the same comparisons—the lost figure of melancholy against the beautiful landscape, the desperation of the trapped rat. But whether Miller, a devoted student of Lawrence, derives some of his treatment from the Magnus portrait is of less import than the awareness that Moricand-Magnus belongs to a fundamental type. The grotesque dandy of literary cultivation and spiritual degradation becomes a major exemplar of decadence, repulsively fascinating to Miller and Lawrence who seem to sense a kind of diabolical parody of their exacerbated and outcast sensibilities.

Miller, especially, having less character—which means less style—must defend himself at length against the diabolist who would destroy his paradisaical vision. In a long lecture in which he accepts the "poetry" and basic principle of astrological occultism ("as above, so below"), he rejects some of its arid abstractness and dehumanization. In the process, he emphasizes his

being "very much of an American. That is to say, naive, optimistic, gullible
. . . a product of this land of plenty, a believer in superabundance, a believer
in miracles" (319); he is equally a believer in "experience," in a self-righteous
quid pro quo ("I made all the mistakes . . . and I paid the penalty"), and in
the divinity of the ego and the actual world. While Miller's rather boozy exhortation in itself need not concern us, it does provide a vulgate and anti-
tragic American rejection of unrebellious European pessimism, sickness and
despair, as appropriately represented by Moricand. The Devil is a decadent
European, and Paradise is still the traditional American dream.

Most of the other pieces of the *Big Sur* volume lack art at any level—
Miller, now secure in his identity as an artist, no longer produces either art or
anti-art but simply casual jottings—and his praise of Big Sur becomes jumbled ruminations on artists, misfits, children, faith-healers, and the author's
friends and followers. While some of this could be interesting material,
Miller usually just names things rather than presents them. Though the book
is filled with shadowy figures of aspiring autobiographical writers, or their
letters in which Miller can smell "genius a mile off" (169), almost all these
people seem exceptionally pathetic, confused, self-centered, and pointless.
While part of this emphasis may be the covert side of Miller's egotism, it may
also characterize the rather passive bohemian modes of the 1950s.

In ostensibly defending Bohemia-by-the-Pacific as, rather weakly, a millennial interpretation of the pious medieval painter Bosch, Miller aims to
defend individuality, a contemporary Thoreauvianism of wise and simple
living. He does a poor job in carrying out this admirable purpose. Several examples from the final sermonic piece of what he rightly calls his "potpourri"
may characterize the whole. Aware of the nonideological stance of most of his
fellow outsiders—bohemian privateerism—he wryly observes that if they
were running things "there would be no need for revolution, they would run
the country into the ground in no time" (256)—and the country would be
better off for it. But most of his gestures lack humor and finesse, as with his
gross praise of two other groups who do not conform: gangsters and call girls
(270). This casual, and irrelevant, attempt to update his earlier sentimentality about rogues and whores overlooks the fact that gangsters and call girls
are, for the most part, notable examples of overconformance to the very
things Miller rages against.[19]

After a burlesque catalog of things patently wrong with America (250–
51), Miller gives a curious counterlist of how to truly live—curious because
he cannot decide whether to be serious or comic in recommending flight from
money, mass culture, and so forth. Among his stock adages about doing
everything in moderation are such dictums as "don't irritate your boss . . .

don't use bad language" (252). Miller's admonitions to be neighborly and loving occupy the same rhetorical margin between blandness and buffoonery. Although Miller always tripped into triteness in his writing, he now wades in clichés. Even when aware that he is trite, he is only tritely aware: "The greatest problem is . . . how to get along with one's self. Trite, you say. But true, nevertheless" (145). Similarly, his invective against America—against reading *Life* and the *Reader's Digest*, against installment buying, and against joining organizations (262)—appears as easy and empty gesturing when it is undeveloped. The pervasive deadness of writing, thinking, and awareness is rather sad, for by it Miller does a disservice to the individualism he supposedly defends—to the "lone-American" heroically willing "to live *en marge*" (255). A literary rebel gone flatulent may well be the least rebellious of all.

Miller is, with a few small exceptions, not much better than mildly quaint in his later small collection of literary and moral pronouncements, *Stand Still Like the Hummingbird* (1962). Once more the message of the artist versus America, the individual versus conformity, and God versus Americanism, lacks body and development. Why he is against the artist being "still regarded as a menace to society" (ix)—if the society is anywhere near as bad as Miller says—remains perplexing. That foundations aid mediocre and bad artists (viii), that conformists are "petted and pampered" (ix), and that America is often in the vanguard in creating a mad world may all be true enough, though Miller does nothing with those commonplace assertions. Besides miscellaneous discussions of literature, *Hummingbird* contains some sermonic essays. "Children of the Earth," starting with rather obtuse praise of France as against America, ends homiletically on the "inner peace" and "atoneness" Miller found in America but should not have according to his evaluation of America. "When I Reach for My Revolver" also finds Europe a "honey comb" and America a "desert," and ends by apocalyptically quoting Isaiah. There are many other rhetorical gestures that belong to an age several generations back in defying a stock reality of a provincial America and a Brooklyn crassness.

Even when settled into America, Miller was always in flight from ordinary reality—abroad into memory and fantasy and the occult, touring in "Art," magical gestures, and rhetorical distance. Even when ostensibly describing America, he elaborated his fantasies, France, and the atypically bizarre (Hollywood parties), or he fell into secondhand bombast. The only tangible unclichéd material in the pieces collected in *Hummingbird* is some digressive description of the old France in some ruminations around Ionesco. His major effort in several decades in the United States, the volumes of *The Rosy Crucifixion* ("Reunion in Brooklyn" is the nuclear appendix), re-creates his 1920s rages and sentiments. His later forays, with some updating of clichés, are fixated in those years, not in the realities of the 1940s, 1950s, 1960s, and 1970s. He spent nearly half a century meandering around a few of the old traumas and tropes.

Much of it is thin stuff. His stock charge against America of "materialism" misses the point. As Santayana, Lawrence, Fitzgerald, Huxley, and many others have noted, American "materialism" is often outrageously "idealistic" and romantic, in ways incomprehensible to a European shopkeeper, and therein lies its pathos and foul dust. The American "best-seller" system Miller raged against (at least half a dozen times) is patently a gross processing, so valueless that it will indifferently boost all sorts of books into irrelevant massive sales, including *Tropic of Cancer* in 1961. Miller's diatribes against American "conformity" were pathetically illustrated by his own role-playing of the bohemian-rebel Artist. His success with that role-playing provided a curious variation on the Horatio Alger pattern of how the poor American boy makes good, for his thin denunciations and sometimes suggestive rhetoric of defiance brought him nothing but fame, followers, and fortune.

For half a century Miller took an apocalyptic stance toward America. In ruminations at eighty he said that from an early age he had been convinced "that the world about me was going to pieces." "And then one day [mid-1920s?] I came across Oswald Spengler. He confirmed my convictions. (And what a good time I had reading him, reading, that is, about the decline of the West. . . . It bucked me up.)"[20] Various modernists, and especially D. H. Lawrence in the period of Miller's literary breakthrough, reconfirmed the apocalyptic role as self-sanctioning stance, and this provided the nuclear gestures of Miller's career in which he turned denunciations into affirmations. To be modern, to be "with it" in America, was to be against it rhetorically.

Ancient Ruminations

In the comfortable last two decades of his life (the 1960s and the 1970s—Miller's seventies and eighties), living in a conventional upper-suburbia house in Southern California (Pacific Palisades), raking in honors (French Legion of Honor, American National Institute of Arts and Letters, *Playboy* picture-biography, movies of his life and writings, etc.), dallying with very young aggrandizing women (his roles were rather comic-pathetic), Miller continued to write (although his whimsical watercolors seem to have been his greater passion). *Just Wild about Harry* (1963) is an awkward foray into drama.[21] Derivative from bits of Saroyan, Ionesco, and Sartre (*No Exit* seems to be the basis for the final, and most interesting, scene), Miller also draws on his own stock: the golden-hearted whore, the Brooklyn-boy thug-pimp (Harry), ancient vaudeville folderol (a dwarf, a German in long winter underwear, a double-talking doctor, etc.). In the end, sentimental love is all. There are several iconoclastic bits, such as Harry's out-of-character but commonsense polemic against the Bomb. There is much jokey stage business, not very humorous and hardly compensatory for the sloppy development, flat dialogue, and mawkish ideas.

Just Wild about Harry seems to have been Miller's most ambitious literary effort in the last two decades of his life. Most of his late writings were just slight addenda to the earlier ones. The one partial exception was the last book, the publication of which he supervised—*The World of Lawrence* (1980), a cleaned-up version of the manuscript (1932–33) from which he had published a number of essays (discussed in chapter 5). There was also a series of chapbooks, such as *On Turning Eighty* (1972), brief ruminations, with such comments as that if one is "on the way to becoming an automaton, it may do you good to say to your boss—under your breath, of course—'Fuck you, Jack!'" (7) and the concluding moral: "So, whether the world is going to pieces or not, whether you are on the side of the angels or the devil himself, take life for what it is, have fun, spread joy and confusion" (34). The rebelliousness that gave him his earlier significant role is certainly attenuated. There was an occasional spark of the defining early irreverence, as in his writing to a longtime academic correspondent (who rather expected some such) that he was considering using a Portuguese proverb for his letterhead (roughly translated, "When shit has value, the poor will be born without assholes").[22]

Insomnia, or The Devil at Large (1974) reproduces, with photographs of Miller and of a few of his watercolors (not his best), fractured ruminations on how he was taken in by, and married, a Japanese nightclub entertainer— apparently part of her purpose was to obtain American citizenship.[23] He made himself anxiously vague about it when she dumped him. Among the word and picture doodlings is an attempt to catch an old posturing with a piece called "Cadenza"—an ornate comic-surrealist bit of rhetoric (similar in manner to "The Angel Is My Watermark" of four decades earlier). Three tritely written and imperceptive little volumes were under the generic title of *Book of Friends*. The first (1976) comprised bits around the early years, the Brooklyn period, a flatter retelling of the commonplace effects on Miller (rather than the reality) of some of the kids and their mild antics in the neighborhood, with most of the point being nostalgia. A slightly later time semifocuses *My Bike and Other Friends* (1978). The third volume, *Joey: A Loving Portrait of Alfred Perlès Together with Some Bizarre Episodes Relating to the Opposite Sex* (1979) effuses vaguely about his Paris-period boon companion. The bizarreness of the added "Other Women in My Life" is the inadequately developed joke that there were some women with whom he didn't have sex. He also grants that he treated his early love meanly—"That I was a son-of-a-bitch of the first water there is no doubt" (67). But, after all, he was born to be "a very important writer" (53), an Artist, and "an artist should never marry" (67). (He had five official wives and children by two of them). Apparently his mother was partly at fault. In ruminations taking off from a dull dream about his dead mother "whom I hated all my life"—*Mother, China, and the World Beyond (1977)*—she finally in limbo learns to love him.[24] But his childhood buddies still haven't recognized that he was "even a genius" (49), not surprisingly because he patronized them while leeching off them and, he acknowledges, "I was highly indifferent to the fate of my friends" (101). There is a mostly implicit harsh confession in the unending *Book of Friends*.

He continued to be a compulsive letter writer. The posthumously published correspondence and the clichéd, flat sketches to a little magazine publisher, *From Your Capricorn Friend* (1984; written 1978–1980) affirm his belief in astrology and Nostradamus and his admiration for Marie Corelli and Sherwood Anderson (and his distaste for his rebellious Whitmanian successor, the apparently too serious and Jewish Allen Ginsberg—was it also the homosexuality?). These pieces also made a few gestures of spastic rhetoric ranting against America—"Nation of lunatics," "loony as bedbugs, destructive as lice and vermin, knowing neither peace, repose, or contentment" (98).[25] Perhaps most pertinently, he confesses that all through his childhood "I must have been a spoiled brat" (65). The posthumously published *Dear, Dear Brenda, The Love Letters of Henry Miller to Brenda Venus* (1986), a small selection from a reported 1,500 (written from 1976 until his death in 1980), show an adolescent man in his late eighties pursuing an aggrandizing young woman in poignantly silly ways. She is ambitiously and superficially accommodating—she flatters Miller by telling him that he will get the Nobel Prize in literature he has been conniving for (62)—although she directed her sexual favors only to other men (she reports briefly stripping for Miller once, as happened with the aging Groucho Marx in a somewhat parallel relationship). It is all rather pathetic and uninterestingly told. The garrulously resentful egomaniac who had not only gone on for decades too long but, as he approached ninety, still hadn't quite grown up, was not writing at all well and had very little to say. But perhaps some of the antique ruminations are of symptomatic interest about a late-nineteenth-century American writer as inverted Horatio Alger hero, or useful documentation of a spoiled Brooklyn kid who, with a curious mixture of naivete and pretension, pathos and clowning, went on and on as a kind of long-enduring lesson in what we might take as essential Americana.

Chapter Five

The Rebel-Buffoon

Dirty Books?

Miller's fame for a generation (from the publication in Paris of *Tropic of Cancer* in 1934 to its legalization and best-sellerdom in America in 1961, and beyond), was, of course, as an "obscene" author. Several brief further considerations of that role seem pertinent here. Was Miller a writer of "obscenity" or of "pornography"? The disputable distinction had prior to Miller been made by a number of writers, especially D. H. Lawrence, who had insisted on a great difference between writing graphically about sexual actions with "vulgar" language and "dirt for dirt's sake," that is, the titillating writing which equates with prostitution.[1] The obscene may be the reporting of denied truths, the pornographic (not altogether separate) the arousing for purposes of exploitation. In artistic fact, there has long been considerable difference between realistic obscenity and fantasy pornography, although often not in the minds and morals of the puritanical and authoritarian, such as the religiose petty bourgeois. Since the 1960s both forms have been widely legal and available in Westernized countries (depending on the media and other circumstances—for example, standard television programming and persons under eighteen in America are ostensibly restricted to covert pornography) so that, perhaps unfortunately, the distinctions currently are hardly clear, and certainly not socially effective in a society where nearly everything is commercialized. Still, some differences on a scale running from the seriously obscene to the exploitatively pornographic seem pertinent. (I am not arguing for any kind of censorship, which is invariably misapplied and wrong; the elimination of profit from all writing—to call on a larger moral principle—would probably eliminate much of what is usually described as the pornography problem.)

In what category do Miller's writings fall? Some of them, certainly, such as *Tropic of Cancer,* tend to the seriously (that is, considerably realistic, not just titillating) obscene. The language of "fucking", "cock-and-cunt", and so forth—primary reason for the book's restriction—no longer constitute a violation of literary decorum. Even then they were literally appropriate to the marginal male ethos presented, though not common in literature. But there was certainly something brave as well as iconoclastic about Miller following such writers as Lawrence in extensively using them. (If they helped establish his notoriety, they also long limited his commercial success, though paradoxically increasing it later.) Miller's graphic sexual descriptions have been superseded, in both exacting detail and ranging poeticization, by John Updike and Norman Mailer (among others) often with more complex awareness. However limited Miller's perspective, his obscenity may be granted appropriateness and effectiveness, literary significance, and considerable historical influence.

But Miller also wrote pornography. *Opus Pistorum* was trade-published posthumously (1983), although it was written four decades earlier (1941–42),[2] reportedly for a dollar a page, and put out in a few duplicated copies. Although it thinly uses the expatriate in Paris frame of his first book, it mostly follows the stock Sadean male porno conventions: hyperbolic sexual actions; frenziedly insatiable females; heavily repetitious fellatio, cunnilingus, and anilingus; group intercourse; taboo violations (such as father-daughter incest); a sexual black mass in a church; voyeurism with lesbians; grotesque variations (sex with a dwarf, etc.); and the gang rape of a hypocritically teasing lady.[3] There are a few bits of Miller's verbal gusto: "She's so hot, thermally as well as sexually, that I could operate the entire Metro system three hours on the energy that she's burning up" (122). Trying to stay on top of another sexually excited woman was "like trying to ride a bicycle on a catboat in a squall" (159). The accounts are traditionally misogynistic; mildly put, "all cunts are queer in the head" (159). The degradations of the female are often sadistic, though not to the extreme degree evident in Sade, Bataille, Reage, and others. *Opus Pistorum* also has a few touches of Miller's apocalyptic rhetoric and comic self-depersonalization (as discussed earlier), and a pyrrhonistic conclusion not usual to the conventions: the supersexual expatriate has had enough, wants to escape "the crazy bitches," and is "going back to America and I am going to buy or make or have made a good mechanical cunt, a fucking machine, which runs by electricity and which can be pulled out of the wall when the fuses begin to blow and the trouble starts" (286).

Whether aiming at pornography or obscenity, Miller never altogether lost his Brooklyn boy street humor—or male sexual bravado, which was partly the reactive sexual aggression against the Puritan heritage. Miller artistically exploited macho sexuality in *Tropic of Cancer*. *Tropic of Capricorn* seems to aim at going "one better"; some of its scenes of aggrandizing sex are handled as unadmitted fantasy, traditional male pornography, in the exaggerated sexual bouts with frenzied sex-hungry females. The first volume of *Sexus* at-

tempted at times to outdo *Capricorn*. Such grossness provoked the critical ire
of even such good friends as Lawrence Durrell.[4] Not accidentally, it would
seem, the following *Plexus* and *Nexus* show little obscenity, even little sexuality. And that remained characteristic for the rest of his works (partial exception: the apparent rewriting of an earlier manuscript, *Quiet Days in Clichy*,
with some casual fantasy-type sexual descriptions). Miller hardly seems clear
on what he was doing with his sexual writing.[5]

Miller's literary obscenity—in contrast to that of Lawrence in *Lady
Chatterley's Lover*, Joyce in the final section of *Ulysses*, and other serious
twentieth-century fictionists—presents almost purely, and conventionally
lower class, masculine responses.[6] Amusingly, one of Miller's very few excursions into feminine empathy is reported on in *Tropic of Cancer*; he is bored listening to Debussy in a concert hall and his mind wanders: "I find myself
wondering what it feels like, during intercourse, to be a woman—whether
the pleasure is keener, etc. Try to imagine something penetrating my groin,
but have only a vague sensation of pain" (69). His sense of women as persons
is usually painfully vague. But he knows the proper macho treatment for
them, after five wives and multitudinous whores. He concludes toward the
end of his life, "There is no denying that a woman who is screwed often and
expertly is a happy creature."[7]

Miller's obvious gross sexism was given simple, though not well-
informed, discussion by an influential feminist, Kate Millet, in her *Sexual
Politics* (1970). She rightly noted of the *Capricorn-Sexus* writings that
"much of this 'fucking' is sheer fantasy" (293), and that the dominant sexuality represented is American-style "brutalized adolescence"—"Miller's hunt
is a primitive find, fuck, and forget" (296).[8] (The obsessional marriages are
not considered, nor the historical lower-middle-class ambience and revenge
against the mother.) Millet correctly, if thinly, belabored the callous impersonality toward and degradation of women, although she ignorantly (of the
Sadean tradition) claimed that Millerean "cruelty and contempt" toward
women were greater than in most pornography (300). Of the Brooklyn and
Parisian buddies, she sensibly concluded that Miller's "strenuous heterosexu-
ality depends, to a considerable degree, on a homosexual sharing" (303).
And more generally she concluded, in awe of Miller's candor as well as his
verbal pyrotechnics, that he was a major writer who "does have something
important to tell us; his virulent sexism is beyond question an honest contribution to social and psychological understanding," however pathetically "vicious" (313).

In a harsh and considerably disingenuous counterpolemic in *The Prisoner
of Sex* (1971), Norman Mailer, who had also been attacked by Millet for his

obsessive sexism, defended Miller by pointing out some dubious Millet readings (the use of twisted quotes and, especially, her unawareness of the self-mockery in Miller's treatment of sex). But Mailer hardly met the issues of sexual denigration by twice approvingly quoting Miller's "Perhaps a cunt, smelly though it may be, is one of the prime symbols for the connection between things" (82). So, for Miller, were two turds in a bidet (*Cancer*). Mailer's further argument is that Miller uniquely, in his time and place, and exaltingly reported on male lust. In doing so "he captured something in the sexuality of men as it had never been seen before, precisely that it was man's sense of awe before woman . . . which made man detest women, revile them, humiliate them, defecate symbolically upon them, do everything to reduce them so one might dare to enter them and take pleasure of them" (86). This mystically perverse argument, like a black mass, justifies the early Miller (the latter Miller tends to self-parody) as making a "barbaric yawp of utter adoration for the power and the glory and the grandeur of the female in the universe, and it is his genius to show us that this power can survive any context and any abuse" (87).

One trouble with these arguments, both smugly male-denigrating and perversely male-exalting, is that they tend to override much of what is distinctive about Miller's treatment of sex, which, in its candid energy, self-alienation, and violation of sexual decorum, especially catches hilarious incongruities. Miller is not decent or wise about sexual relations, but he is often funny. Again, it is the power of the buffoon. Like much common lower-class male humor, the comedy certainly depends on hostility toward women, self-defeating iconoclasm about hypocrisy, unholistic amorality, and an aggrandizing egotism that result in an acrobatic, willful, grotesque, voracious, and verbally exuberant treatment of sex. Unclear about what his purposes were, Miller sometimes slid from obscenity into pornography, and out of both, unfortunately, into pretentious blandness. But, I suggest, the obscene, in several senses, is where he really was.

The Literary Life

In seeking an identity and defying an unacceptable past (as personal and social failure, as vulgar and irresponsible boy from Brooklyn, as petit bourgeois American) by taking on the role of the doer of literary "dirty books," Miller became a buffoonish self-identified "artist." He substituted writing for life. Once established in the role, he confesses in *Tropic of Capricorn*, "I realized that I had never had the least interest in living, but only in this which I am now doing" (13)—writing. The yearning to find a self to express became what he had to express. With a kind of comically heroic stubbornness, his rhetorical gestures became most of what self he had.

Because Miller viewed self-expression as heroic achievement, it also became the saving prescription—a kind of religious therapy for the injured, the sensitive, and the rebellious. Case always in point: Henry Miller, with devotees, from the young Lawrence Durrell to the old Norman Mailer, with in between a legion of common man Americans pursuing the sage of Big Sur. In the post–World War II decades, he served as somewhat of a cynosure for the bohemian and the marginal, an old hero for such writers as the later bohemian Beats.[10] Miller also seemed to believe that his way of selfhood by uninhibited self-expression of a nonself provided enlightenment for materialistic, repressed, hypocritical, and meretricious America. In this literary religiosity, reading provided the forms of devotion, art and artist provided the ark and priest, and writing or painting became the sacramental acts. While artistic bohemia should provide the community of true believers, and sometimes did, as in his Big Sur ruminations and effusions on artist-friends, true communion was with saintly victim-artists of past and present.

Miller's commitment to self-expression is sometimes mistakenly seen as making his work the verbal residue of an unusual life. But his autobiography was of more rhetorical than factual interest, even to Miller. His life, with the partial exception of his staying on in Paris after the depression drove most expatriates back to the United States, had largely been the fairly ordinary one of a not especially brave or profound American-style literary bohemian of the times. True, he liked to inflate it, even pronouncing in his last years: "I have lived like an outlaw most of my life."[11] The arch little comedian meant that he had conned, mooched, and groped his way through a few difficult years. More candidly, it was not just petty opportunism or literary talent that got him by: "I was lucky, that's all. I have a wonderful Jupiter."[12] He had been fortunate, and persistent. Actually, Miller's ordinariness provided much of his appeal; he combined common American pathos and muddle with grandiose yearnings.

His highfalutin literary role was an unusually direct adaption of his early compensatory fantasies. It was also the simple adoption of earlier romantic-subjectivist notions of the artist role. An apparently avid and responsive reader in childhood, Miller sought for bookish experiences of transcendence. Because, as he often confesses, he was not very heroic in actions on any level, literary images became the substitute personal glorification. Most literature he treated as literal personal propaganda. From adventure stories and romanticized history and biography, he quite indiscriminately moved on to the exotic-mythic sort of history (Crete, China, Atlantis); to popular romance

(Haggard, Sienkiewicz, Bellamy); to rebellious Americans (Walt Whitman, Sherwood Anderson, Emma Goldman); to, finally, the more extreme and alienated European modernists (Dostoyevski, Nietzsche, Strindberg). Inspirational writings and apocalyptic writings—Nietzsche and Spengler's *Decline of the West* were especially self-justifying for Miller in the early 1930s— mixed with avant-garde expressionism, dadaism, surrealism (and Joyce, Cendrars, Céline, et al.).[13] Bits and gestures of all these rhetorics and manners appear mixed in his "autobiographies." He often strikes the knowledgeable reader as being a reflection of the perverse geniuses, viewed in the distorting mirrors of an American carnival funhouse.

Miller wrote voluminously around his reading. His responses—and a considerable amount of his ruminations on literature—may be represented for convenience by three writers taken in the approximate chronological order of his enthusiasms: D. H. Lawrence, Honoré de Balzac, and Arthur Rimbaud. The last book whose publication Miller supervised and which appeared a few weeks after his death in 1980, was *The World of Lawrence,* "A Passionate Appreciation."[14] It was also, as a manuscript, one of his earliest books (the subtitle was probably a late, and rather defensive, addition). Half a century before, Miller had been an enthusiast not only of some of Lawrence's writings but of what he took to be the Lawrencean weltanschauung. He had planned to do a small book on a favorite serious-reputable writer, which would be published before, and pave the way to possible literary acceptance of, *Tropic of Cancer.* Encouraged by his publisher (and by his lover Anaïs Nin, who had just completed a book on Lawrence), Miller worked obsessively on his Lawrence project through most of 1933 (800 pages of manuscript, he later reported[15]), but did not have a publishable book before *Cancer* appeared in 1934. He did publish as four essays revised parts of the manuscript over the years; some years later he still viewed the incomplete project as a major personal statement.[16]

Lawrence's writings did specifically influence Miller: the justification for obscenity (*Lady Chatterley's Lover*), the rather parodistic adaption of Lawrence's Italian travel writings in his book on Greece, the long portrait of nasty Moricand in "Devil in Paradise" (paralleling Lawrence's introduction to Magnus's *Memoirs of the Foreign Legion*). There are perhaps other influences from Lawrence, particularly the sweeping apocalyptic essay form Miller was intermittently to practice (as used in Lawrence's "The Crown," *Studies in Classic American Literature,* and *Apocalypse*), but, typically, it was the sense of Lawrence as victim-of-the-age artist (*Black Spring,* 40) and rebellious culture hero that especially appealed to Miller.

Yet although he later claimed to be "truly possessed" in a nearly divine state by Lawrence, Miller also told a late interviewer that "I made the sad discovery that my idol [Lawrence] was not the writer I had imagined him to be."[17] In his apparently final addenda to the Lawrence book he noted, "The world of Lawrence now seems to me like a strange island on which for a number of years I was stranded" (259). He acknowledged having "changed" away from Lawrence; in Miller's view by this time, Lawrence had "made foolish errors, he conducted himself unwisely, he contradicted himself, he diminished himself, he was a bad friend now and then, and a bad husband and lover too. He wrote some bad books, atrocious nonsense too" (263). This could be self-description.

But something else was also at issue, both personal and metaphysical. After immersing himself in Lawrence (and some biographies), Miller found his literary hero burdened with too much "femininity": "a potent figure of a man he was not" (255)—as simple as that. He still acknowledged Lawrence as "an artist, a minor artist with a minor soul," though he "was one of the few artists of our time who possessed a soul at all" (227), but "a great life-adventurer he was not." Apparently Miller wanted to confirm a heroically "visionary" Lawrence, "an aristocrat of the spirit, like Plato, like Jesus, like Buddha." But what he had to admit was Lawrence as "a modern Don Quixote tilting against the windmills of white idealism," and an inadequate man full of "hatred" who was often "pathetic—*ridiculous*" (37, 39). Granted, some of the hatred, for Miller, was justified, for Lawrence was the kind of "mystic genius who woman always rallies round, vulgarizes, sullies and degrades," for women "don't give a real fuck for the man's philosophy, only as it effects their tickling or would be tickling cunts. They are the real vultures of the age" (42). To Miller, Lawrence was a psychological failure who in compensation became a religious "Savior." "His hope is to save the world." From early blighting, "forced into isolation, he makes himself god." "Unable to save himself he tries to save the world. The savior type is the essentially religious man who has an unusual portion of femininity in his character which comes to represent his spiritual nature" (120, 127). His faltering demands for intensification of experience, "transfigured life," led him to destructiveness and hatred in spending "himself in an effort to restore a feeling, a [religious] view of the world, which in this age seems impossible to summon" (246). Such a "neurotic-savior" is both heroic ("that last man of genius, that last individual rebel") and a human failure ("*a traitor to the human race*") (174).

In this sweeping taking up and putting down of Lawrence, the novels, stories, and poetry of Lawrence have but small (and uninsightful) part, as does the social utopianism (for which Miller had no sympathy). The ultimate metapsychological stance dominated Miller's concern—role is the only reality. Indeed, he could not abide Lawrence's actual "art," the "lesserworks"; only the "visionary" caught in "creative death" will remain of significance as "the logical culmination, the apotheosis of 2,000 years of Christian idealism, now gone over to its opposite" emphasis on the flesh and intense immediate experience in the effort to "make the world religious [yet] godless" (199).

Lawrence's literary works were hardly congenial to the Miller who had identified his writing and personal liberation with dadaistic iconoclasm, surrealistic fragmentation, and rhetorical pyrotechnics from the underside of life. The slightly earlier Lawrence (six years older) was a cosmic rebel but not an artistic vanguardist, of interest mostly as the revolting and visionary "artist," overreaching and misunderstood in uncongenial times—and therefore possible justification for Miller. Some heroic Lawrence remains—aptly enough, he whose "whole life was a struggle and his philosophy of life was based on a sense of struggle. This is the Dionysian view of truth apprehended not through the intellect, but through passionate experience" (211). But Miller concludes his *World of Lawrence* with some easy subjectivist religiosity (quite probably a much later addition), which quite lacks the intense oppositional struggle that had originally attracted him to Lawrence.

Miller's Lawrence significantly searched for a unity that he could never achieve. So, for Miller, did Balzac in a later phase of Miller's quest for an artist-visionary hero. Again we find what would by most valuations be considered an eccentric emphasis upon minor works. He dismisses Balzac's fine art of "realism" and the novels of the *Human Comedy* to focus on two minor occult tales, *Seraphita* and *Louis Lambert,* which he takes as tragic documents.[18] In "Balzac and His Double" Miller suggestively views the French novelist as victim of a cold mother and harsh schooling, of conventional ambitions and success, of a maladapted genius close to schizophrenia, of spiritual yearnings in an unsympathetic world, and (taking up a major Lawrencean notion) of the disease of "Will":

The study of society and the psychology of the individual, which form the material of the novel in European literature, served to create the illusory world of facts and things which dominate the neurotic life that began with the 19th century and is now reaching its end in the drama of schizophrenia. At the back of it is the Will, reducing through the powers of analysis all life to ashes. Balzac was himself aware of the disease which is killing us. It is the mind which is poisoning us, he says. . . . Dostoyevski gave expression to the conflict even more forcibly. Indeed, it is with him that the novel comes to an end, for after him there are no longer any individuals to write about, nor is there any society which may be said to possess a body. Proust and Joyce epitomize the dissolution of our world in their great epics. With Lawrence the novel becomes a vehicle for the Apocalyptic visions which will occupy us for the next few hundred years, as our world fades in blood and tears. (216)[19]

Not so incidentally, this tirade provides sweeping justification for his anti-novels and apocalyptic rhetoric.

Miller views the portrayal of Lambert, a hypersensitive and self-destructive occultist, as Balzac's cry of the heart against his own illusory intellectual and social will. Seraphita, an hermaphroditic Swedenborgian "Angel" who ascends to heaven in pure spiritual love, is viewed by Miller as Balzac's answer and the cure that he was incapable of fully accepting. Miller's essay "Seraphita" is mostly summary, quotation, and loose paraphrase; like most of Miller's voluminous literary ruminations, it suffers little from the "ashy powers" of analysis that he condemns. "Balzac and His Double" is more thoughtful. Neither, as usual, pays much attention to literary characteristics, though it would seem that these tract-fictions must suffer from their artistic defects (gross melodrama with stock characters) as well as from mechanical presentation of Swedenborgianism, however important that was historically (as also in its use by Blake and Baudelaire) as a defiant heterodoxy ("symbolism") against prevalent vicious rationalisms.

Post-*Cancer* (and post-Lawrencean) Miller had become an occultist fellow-traveler. In writing on Balzac, there are a number of implicit parallels with his new image of himself; in writing on Rimbaud a few years later, a major concern was in expounding the parallels between Rimbaud and Miller. Recurrently he makes much of the repressive mother in the lives of Lawrence, Balzac, Rimbaud, and Henry Miller, all of whom were poorly adapted to society, religious in egotistical yearnings, and destined for "visionary" glory. The parallels seem vague, except for the intriguing implicit suggestion that repressive mothers produce sons who long for the cosmic occult womb.

Miller's book on Rimbaud, *The Time of the Assassins,* insists on many parallels between genial old Henry Miller, who did most of his writing in middle age or later, and the violent adolescent Arthur Rimbaud, who quit writing before he even grew up.[20] The identification may strike some as comic, for Miller, unlike Rimbaud, had little of the violent thug about him; the symbiosis with a homosexual involved in assault, or running guns in the misery of East Africa, or contemptuously renouncing literature for grimly accumulating money, or miserably dying young from gangrene, seems mere fancy. While both did dabble with the occult, Miller's garrulous and rambling burlesque confessions contrast as much with Rimbaud's hard and often obscure lyrics as do the biographies of the two men, or their physical appearance, or their sense of themselves. The comic identification seems absurd when Miller insists that his sufferings "far outweighed" Rimbaud's, or when he implies that Miller is the better writer. But the real bother to Miller may be that the young *voyant* had turned antiwriter. Taking poetry as both a weapon of total revolt and total salvation, Rimbaud discovered its inadequacies for either and, I believe, accordingly renounced mere literature. When Miller pontificates that "I call that man poet who is capable of profoundly altering the world" (39) he may uncomprehendingly explain Rimbaud's renunciation of adolescent literary egotism at the age of nineteen. But Miller can't believe it; therefore, Rimbaud's "failure" must have been his mother's fault—"she who denied him, betrayed him, persecuted him" (139). Or Rimbaud's flight must have been modern society's fault, for it denies the "vision" of the artist, thus silencing him (131). Or Rimbaud's postliterary life must have been an "angel's" overdone demonic reversal into "*total* conformity" (147). Or, more generally, the misery of Rimbaud is Western history's fault, the whole ideological assassination of the artist-saint in the modern age. Why else would a great poet-hero-visionary go under like a small bourgeois adventurer? But, after all, and in spite of the rather prolix ruminations on the Rimbaud legend, the youth was rather lucid in giving up the pretentious ambitions of the literary visionary to become, in the age of imperial capitalism, the most logical of "poetic" entrepreneurs, trading in guns and slaves in Africa, to end with a gangrenous body and pious Christian soul.

For Miller, Lawrence seems to have failed in that his oppositional sensibility overrode his pieties. Miller's Balzac failed in that he could never really renounce his literary and social ambitions to become an occult angel. Rimbaud failed in that he, unlike Henry Miller, renounced literature and came to a miserable end. Both the continuity and, I would say, the decline in Miller's literary concern seem evident from this pattern, which runs from the early 1930s to the mid-1940s. Miller generally misses the point that it is the perplexity rather than the piety of his literary heroes that gives them their value. In his more serious efforts, he cultishly wanted literary saints, crudely expressing a widespread cultural religiosity of the time.

But most of Miller's writing on "artists" (including novelists, painters, belletrists, autobiographers, and literary mystics) lacks much dimension and becomes mere literary hagiography—and indiscriminately so, not only in the personal encomia of friends (as in the Greek and American travel volumes previously discussed) but in books on astrology, Dostoyevski's novels, children's potboilers, scholarly studies of oriental religion, Van Gogh's letters, Nostradamus's "prophecies," Dante, pop histories, Nijinsky's *Diary* during his madness, a minor Jewish mystic, Marie Corelli's soppy fictions, the *Tao*

Teh Ch'ing, new surrealist fads, or anything else that struck him as inspirational. Although he once in a while turns a phrase or whimsical response in a
curious way, most of the stream is mere verbiage, unbuttoned pedantry, hundreds of thousands of words around the undifferentiated enthusiasms and
endless recall of the many bookish years of a garrulous litterateur who took
literary culture as personal experience, though rarely seriously. [21]

Certainly a few of the pieces have charm, usually of a genial, reminiscent
sort—for examples, "Ionesco," "Anderson the Storyteller," and some passages
in the earlier pieces in *The Books in My Life*. But many of the reminiscent essays are very badly done—witness the long, bodiless, and nearly meaningless
catalog of theaters, plays, and actors' names recalled in "The Theater." Also,
many of Miller's would-be earnest discussions, such as the repeated ones of
Cabeza de Vaca—a Spanish explorer in the American Southwest who earnestly played witch-doctor to save his life—lack elementary awareness, with
Miller exaggerating the faith-healing while ignoring the other sides of this
ambitious courtier-soldier-adventurer.[22] What Miller seeks, especially after
his early work, is the easy enthusiasm for the simplistic messages of redeeming spiritual powers. Probably only his extreme narcissistic egotism kept
Miller from the popular American vice of joining a cult movement.

Beyond his quaintly irrelevant discussions of literary heroes, like
Whitman, it is Miller's somewhat rebellious and buffoonish asides that seem
rather more interesting. For example, the young should not be taught literature since it above all must be self-taught (*Books*, 43); besides, if much
taught officially, it will have reverse effect since "every genuine boy is a rebel
and an anarch" (82). The genuine engagement with literature is a matter of
"possession" and "obsession" (70), which can only be falsified by the genteel
authoritarianism of most of official schooling (178ff.). As for the buffoonery,
the later Miller is poorest at it when most elaborate. In "Reading in the Toilet" (*Books in My Life*, 264–86) he gives a burlesque of middle-class American compulsive reading that is rather snidely cute; the hidden joke is that the
later Miller is righteously contemptuous of reading on the john while the
more lively Miller of *Black Spring* recommended it (57). Buffoons blow, if
not with the wind, then with their own flatulence.

A less intentional but elaborate buffoonery may be seen in Miller's pro-
pensity to ponderous catalogs. One of the many in *Books* is an appendix of
"The Hundred Books Which Influenced Me Most," which includes literary
and religious classics, good-bad books (as Orwell called them) from early
years, those of various friends, and incantatory titles, but does not include the
writings of D. H. Lawrence, Sherwood Anderson, Otto Rank, L.-F. Céline,
Anaïs Nin, Michael Fraenkel, and many others who patently influenced him

in ways more important than many of those listed. (Still, it is hardly more fatuous than some academic claims.[23]) Miller, rather lacking in subject, snowballs a quaint egotistical notion such as his reading-recall into absurdity.

In much of his literary discussion Miller regularly makes pious affirmations of life over literature while pedantically covering his life with his reading. The frequent crux of this literary solipsism may be explained as a series of imbedded puns in the magical naming. In brief, "art" means writing and knowledge; therefore his writing (and reading) is knowledge-wisdom. "To imagine" means to realize and to pretend; therefore, his pretenses are great realizations. "Creator" means both god and artist; therefore, the artist is God. And so on. Thus his alternating exaggerated claims for art, artists, and imagination and his violent rhetoric disavowing literature for "direct experience of life" (*Books*, 11) simply repress the more mundane, intellectual side of the rhetorical terms in order to exalt their cultural religiosity.

Thus, too, Miller has little to say about artistry and writing as such. His pronounced aesthetic usually takes the shape of exalted therapeutics. In "Reflections on Writing" (a representative piece of dozens of such ruminations) he says that the "telling itself" (20)—the process of being the artist, not the art—is the important thing.[24] By "telling" Miller does not mean the craft, the ordering, the perception, the understanding; he means the unconscious, the fortuitous, and the purely personal associations and effects on himself while doing the writing. He catalogs the things he could say about the conditions in which he wrote but says nothing about the subject or significance of what he wrote or its relation to any fuller reality or truth. Miller is an extreme, and rather onanistic, case of art as subjectivity.

However, unlike some lucid practitioners of anti-art, Miller is no more coherent here than in other matters. He went on not only self-therapeutically writing, but also publishing and worrying about his fame and fortune. He may have more accurately described his purpose in writing when he said that the artist was "between the hero and saint," longing for "power—vicarious power." Thus he could make of his "shattered and dispersed ego" (28) a new egotism and importance. What is achieved is not art or truth but a state of personal being like a religious seizure or megalomania in which the artist becomes "a god in fact and in deed" (24). Such exalted transformation of the ordinary, whether in reading, writing, or contemplating one's self as artist, becomes the essential meaning of life. At his best, Miller enthusiastically affirmed the role of the writer as rebel and of literature as strong personal experience. But as Artist Miller was rarely at his best because he renounced mere literature to move up the blessed hierarchy, although what a god does in this world is less clear than ever. I am, of course, applying to Miller his own early standard, arrived at with one of the few authors he struggled with—D. H. Lawrence, of whose religious impetus Miller concluded: "when we eliminate God by becoming God there is no longer any struggle" into art or thought (*World of Lawrence*, 234).[25]

The Literary Saint

In his first significant publication, "Mademoiselle Claude," Henry Miller was already busy, amidst his pimping, with a comic renunciation of the desire to be a "saint." But when not putting aside his sainthood for lesser or higher being, Miller had a goodly number of pronouncements to make on the religious life. Ideas of the saint and seer provide some of his most buffoonish self-dramatizations. For he soon reversed his *Cancer* scorn for such things as that "flapdoodle which blows out of the East like the breath from a plague" (172).[26]

Miller's better religious speculations insist on the "antinomian quality of life." In the "Enormous Womb" (the basic metaphor derived from Otto Rank) he declares life to be a horrendous conflict between illusion and fear (96), with the actual, tangible world being that which must be intensely and absolutely accepted.[27] He claims to ecstatically affirm "the idea which has obsessed all the religious maniacs, the very sensible one that only in living a thing out to the full can there be an end. It is a wholly unmoral idea, a thoroughly artistic one. The greatest artists have been the immoralists, that is, the ones who have been fully in favor of living it out" (98). In a declaration probably derived from Nietzsche, he avows that *"the best world is that which is now this very moment"* (99). The comic-rebel side of this nihilistic yea-saying comes out in a short related piece, "Uterine Hunger." [28] Born wrong, he says, he naturally became "a rebel, an outlaw, a desperado. I blame my parents, I blame society, I blame God. I go through life with finger lifted accusingly. I have the prophetic itch. I curse and blaspheme. I tell the truth" (188). And in yet another apocalyptic essay of the 1930s, he takes the title from the favorite pronouncement of Father Divine (a spectacularly self-indulgent leader of a fanciful black-American religious cult in the 1930s): "Peace! It's Wonderful!"[29] Drawing yet again on the womb trope, he insists that in his early Paris experiences he "touched bottom" (2) and was reborn into the acceptance of his outcast role. No longer suffering the illusions of "hope" (a "sort of spiritual clap"), he had reached cosmic self-sufficiency and self-acceptance: "Since I have become God I go the whole hog always." This half-comic overreaching, in which the Brooklyn underground man becomes the cosmopolitan and cosmic *übermensch*, adds a footnote to Nietzsche's discovery that "God is dead." It in effect reads: Hence I am God. By such blasphemy, Miller aimed to go beyond, including beyond art ("kill off the 'artist'" in himself) and "simply *be*." Unfortunately, I think, Miller did not stay with this rebellious role. "The rebel," he later wrote, "is nearer God than the saint."[30] But he chose literary sainthood, not going beyond art but spreading himself as the gospel of it.

The occasional interesting notions and metaphors in Miller's many pronouncements are islets in murky lakes of prolixity. In one of his long, confused rambles in the 1930s, "An Open Letter to Surrealists Everywhere," he starts off with his underground verve: "Below the belt all men are brothers" (151).[31] He then intermittently attacks living by, for, and as intellectual abstractions. Defending an extreme religious individualism, he draws its consequent refusal of moral and social commitments in this age of "spiritual famine" (154). (The sociopolitical "consciousness" of the depression era is part of what is at issue.) Carried to the decisive limits, this means we should commit individual crimes rather than join in such collective ideal hatreds as fascism, communism, and Americanism. The true individual, artist, and saint (he makes them synonymous) owes allegiance only to what is "active, immediate and personal" (160). This is the position of the rebel, not the revolutionary; of the dadaist, not the surrealist; of the antinomian individualist, not the religious prophet-leader. But the stance is rather drowned in the verbiage of shouts about art, favorite prejudices (Anglophobia and astrology), and sideswipes at his contemporaries. Such tiresome idiosyncrasy may be the too-literal application of individualism, which undermines his case. In spite of the sometimes highfalutin literary locus, much of Miller's moral gesturing clearly comes out of native American dissent, as when he wrote (in the late 1930s), "I was always an out and out pacifist, and still am," for "I believe it justifiable to kill a man in anger, but not in cold blood or on principle, as the laws and governments of the world advocate."[32] But this admirable anarchism is not well developed, even when, a few years later, he elaborates it for nearly a hundred pages in "Murder the Murderer."[33] Even the ostensible war against fascism does not change the denial of allegiance to "any group or nation or cause or ideology" (129). The only authority is the "individual conscience" (179). But with more piety in the 1940s, he emphasizes less individual disallegiance to nation-state hypocrisies than self-purification: one should "murder one's own murderous self" (178). The same argument is repeated and elaborated in a monograph that followed shortly, ostensibly about Jacob Wassermann's novel, *Maurizius Forever.*[34]

It was the wisdom of dissident individualism—the source of the occasional insight in the rambling, bombast, and clowning—that gave what substance there was to Miller's saintly role. No better writing was evident in his later collection of sermonic pieces, *Stand Still Like the Hummingbird* (1962), which was published at the height of his fame. "The Hour of Man" quoted and paraphrased several arguments that men needed to meditate on the religious nature of life to paradisiacally transform it. "Lime Twigs and Treachery" stockly ranted against the popular evils of conformity. The title essay took a few loose swings at America as seen from a jet plane (what was Thoreau-Miller doing in one?), then advocated replacing mechanical technology with psychic technology (telepathy and celestial transmigration), although it concluded with invective against a somewhat more likely future, in which the world would be "one vast interlocking machine of a machine" (194). The antihomiletic homily "The Immorality of Morality" somewhat pompously argued that Jesus, the oriental wise men, and a roguish friend all make the point that one should follow spiritual impulses and not moral laws. While Miller was drastically inconsistent on whether life should be aimed at the intense present (his early view) or the unitive spiritual future (his later occult stock in trade), he did insist that saintliness was self-accepting and self-delighting, probably against his, and America's, puritanical guilt-heritage. His insistence that unitive religiousness denies both suffering and rebellion seems stock and accorded with his late, bland occult technologism.

Much of Miller's literary religious role was characterized by dabbling with various styles of occultism. From bits of popular romantic mystification Miller apparently moved into doctrinal gestures derived from writers he admired, such as Knut Hamsun (*Mysteries*) and D. H. Lawrence (*Apocalypse*). In his post-*Cancer* days he went in for religiosity wholesale: Swedenborgianism (via Balzac), Zen Buddhism (via Alan Watts), magic and madness (via the surrealists), alchemy (via Blake?), mysticisms (Jewish, Hindu, Egyptian, Tibetan, etc., via all sorts of books). Indeed, he nibbled at so many doctrines that it might be easier to note the few for which there seems to be no evidence: any standard form of Protestantism (his family heritage was German Lutheran); Jungianism (he was a devotee of the competing Otto Rank, even playing Rankian therapist for awhile in the mid-1930s); traditional Catholicism (violent Protestant antipathy, as in *Cancer*); the "orgone" sexual mysticism of Wilhelm Reich (he mentioned it several times, but to Miller there was really nothing mystical about sex); and those specialized occultisms which employ elaborate methodologies and secret codes (numerology, cabalism, cryptograms, although he does praise the *Tibetan Book of the Dead*, which has some of these, and he had a liking for Christian Science). But perhaps his most persistent doctrine for restyling actuality and gaining a literary sense of magic was astrology.

Astrology had a considerable place in Miller's writings: it provided titles (Cancer and Capricorn), grotesque characters (astrologer Moricand in "Paradise Lost"), subject matter for satiric sketches ("Astrological Fricassée"), and rhetoric for numerous burlesque passages (such as the observatory-scene mockery of science in *Colossus of Maroussi*). Miller also repeatedly thought of himself and his good luck in terms of heavenly conjunctions. To the skeptical observer, astrology provided a series of easy services for Miller: a fancifully ornate jargon; therapeutic incantations for his personal fate; arcane costuming for his role-playing of the prophet; an occasional parody device; and a means of pious hope that the universe was not the nihilistic comedy presented in *Tropic of Cancer* and similar writings.[35]

I do not mean to deny that Miller put some faith in astrology as a pseudo-science of prediction, but there is considerable pose and even jeu d'esprit in his use of it. In America, the vulgarity of astrology (it lacks the sanctions of honorific history and class, even when used by a president such as Reagan) usually causes the superior literati to avoid it (although they may similarly deploy a fashionable smattering of Zen or Jung or Reich or the Upanishads or New Age holism). It is, of course, as difficult to separate astrology from its social context—fortune-telling for those usually of narrow petit bourgeois culture—as it is to separate Christianity from the similar vulgarity of evangelical fundamentalists.

In his reported discussions with astrologer Moricand at Big Sur, Miller accepted astrological principles but, with traditional American optimism, denied their fateful applications. Elsewhere he placed his interest in astrology with occultism more generally in having the poetic utility of expanding one's "vision."[36] The later Miller also blandly asserted that "every man who is honest and sincere with himself will admit that all is not chance, not accident" (119). Astrology conveniently provided one of the imposed microcosm-macrocosm patterns of order to escape harsh chance and necessity. Although Miller granted that the cosmic "mystery" is not fully open to human interpretation, the poetic use of astrology provided him with "inexhaustible symbols"—"wheels within wheels"—for the contemplation of one's destiny. Astrology also provided him comfort in showing the mixture of "the divine in everything" and in promising "miraculous" power that could be used to "transform the world overnight" (127, 123). One's horoscope (rightly interpreted, of course) allows one to "so live each day that with fullness of being and total awareness we may enjoy the privilege of giving expression to the glorious uniqueness" of each self (124). Astrology, then, is mainly easy-sleazy inspirational rhetoric.

Why one should follow astrology rather than some other inspirational rhetoric is not a matter that Miller considers. His implied answer would seem to be that divisive intellectual discriminations are distasteful, and that all occultisms are equally valid since "common sense would decree that any role, if entered into wholeheartedly, is the right one" (126). No sense of real conflict, tragic disparity, or indifferent universe are allowed. After all, Henry Miller, self-defined as an aging Brooklyn "nonentity," chose to be an artist and literary saint—"wholeheartedly," no doubt—and was right, at least in the sense of publicly successful, in his choice of role.

The hook is that the egotistical role justification becomes spiritually catching, for "artist" really means "saint": the "artist is always surrogate for all men everywhere" (127). Since, however, the artist has no other obligations than self-discovery and self-expression, it was hard for Saint Henry—who alternately recommended quietism and rebellion, artistic production and pure spiritual being beyond art, encompassing love and total detachment—to decide what to do as holy surrogate for all mankind. In the meantime, he had an intellectually and morally easy faith in the stars.[37]

Miller's treatment of astrology (which may fairly represent all his religious interests, only it was more enduring) was fanciful and inspirational, a thin jumble and an egotistical self-glorification. Perhaps with more effect, his religiosity upgraded the artist at the expense of the art. His occult portentousness damaged his comic verve. Case in point: Miller wrote, as one of his few excursions into nonautobiographical and nonpersonal essayistic form, a clown fable, *The Smile at the Foot of the Ladder*.[38] In it, a circus clown discusses, rhetorically, some tribulations of self-discovery and ends, after a few vague adventures, destroyed, though in "seraphic" bliss, by a cruelly uncomprehending world. Ignoring the aggrandizing self-pity of the fable's autobiographical dimensions, the religious portentousness makes the art bad. The language is absurdly heavy for a fey tale ("ineffable," "simulation," "ascension," "infinitesimal," "inexplicable," "reminiscence," "pursuance," "formulate"); the phrasing is ponderous ("bring his plan to fruition," "become more manifest," "revolved his dilemma backward and forward"); the imagery is tritely melodramatic (dusk is violet, blood bubbles, truth is a fire, reality is a veil); and the allegory is absurdly heavy (the clown is the tragic artist, the simple saint, the illuminated mystic, and Jesus Christ). In an essay-epilogue Miller indicates that the story has literary-religious sources and purposes, as is too evident, and he insists that clowns are really angels and artists are really saints. His moral dictums, such as "We have only to open our eyes and hearts, to become one with that which is" (111), do not really fit the tale in which the totally anxious and unhumorous clown receives his illuminations only through punishments. Miller sadly confesses, "Perhaps I have not limned his [the angelic clown's] portrait too clearly" (114). Indeed not. Part of the failure may be put thus: Miller and his clown have not stuck to his own clown's revelation—"If he were really a clown, then he should be one through and through" (99). Much of Miller's writing suffered from not playing it straight but attempting to make a natural American clown into a literary saint.

The Legacy of Henry Miller

Miller started his writing career with an apocalyptic "kick in the pants" at the dubious and dying heroic verities. To fill the void left by the flattened idealisms, he turned out a vast and miscellaneous flood of boozy egotistical verbiage that included a small stream of provocative iconoclastic and comic rhetoric. When his marginal man's vulgate energies and verbal pyrotechnics came together he produced, I believe, some intriguing buffoonish gestures. But when he played the self-aggrandizing fundamentalist of the imagination, the result was mostly the *blagueur* man of letters and the cornball literary prophet. While this had considerable historic effects as therapeutics for American cultural gentility, and as inspirational chats for semiliterate bohemians, the overstuffed motley does not wear well, especially when camouflaging the clown as Tragic American Artist and Saint Henry.

One way of sketching out a perspective of evaluation is to suggest an anthology. Although it has obvious unevenness and prolixity, a good part of *Tropic of Cancer* might be included (but certainly no other book-length work of this essentially fragmented writer). From the sketches in the 1930s a sensitive compiler would include "Mademoiselle Claude," "Max," and perhaps "Via Dieppe-Newhaven." "The Tailor Shop" and some excerpts from the earlier sketches and the conclusion would certainly be sufficient selection from *Black Spring*. While Miller is rarely an insightful or interesting literary essayist, a couple of speculative sections from *The World of Lawrence* and "Balzac and His Double" could be included to represent that side of his work (the other half-dozen volumes of literary ruminations are best ignored, as are the many pieces around painting). From the early volumes on America, the comic pieces—"Astrological Fricassée," "Soirée in Hollywood," "The Staff of Life"—and "Reunion in Brooklyn" are the better writings. It if were to be a fat anthology, one might include from *Tropic of Capricorn* representative bits of the "ovarian fantasia" and "The Land of Fuck" and some burlesque descriptive passages (such as those of his father and Broadway and working). From the other volumes of "autobiographical romance" might come an obscene fantasy episode or two (this is one of Miller's significant contributions to American letters), such as Mona's rape narrative or a scene with the first

wife in *Sexus*. One might also include the Elfenbein portrait in *Nexus* (perhaps filled out a bit by a few anti-Semetic and philo-Semetic passages), a description or two of his Brooklyn friends, and some brief bravura bits such as
the good-bye to America. A burlesque passage—but none of the more earnest bits—from *The Colossus of Maroussi* might be added. Of the later writings in America, only the portrait of two grotesques, "Paradise Lost," might
merit inclusion, in spite of its prolixity (the rest of *Big Sur and the Oranges of
Hieronymous Bosch* is best ignored). The arty efforts, such as "Scenario," *The
Smile at the Foot of the Ladder,* and *Just Wild about Harry,* are well forgotten.
For descriptive bits, one might consider that of Lourdes from the last of the
Hamlet letters and perhaps a bawdy episode from *Quiet Days in Clichy.* The
long essays should be avoided, although if one wished to document Miller's
home-brewed philosophy, the anthologist might include an early piece such
as "Peace! It's Wonderful!" and a late rumination such as "The Immorality of
Morality." The ambitious anthologist might also include a number of titles,
asides, wild comparisons, and odd dictums to make a section of buffoonish
pensées. At best, that's it.

Another perspective can be suggested by briefly considering Miller's role
and influence in American literature. *Tropic of Cancer* and its appendages, I
have noted, belong with the idiosyncratic and rebellious poetic-prose testa-
ments of Thoreau, Cummings, Agee, and others. They can also be viewed as
a native extension of European traditions of Varronian satire and picaresque
potpourri. Many of Miller's writings of the 1930s are also an anthology of
avant-garde gestures out of dadaism, surrealism, and various apocalyptic
writings, while his later inspirational jumble was symptomatic of a swelling
cultism that became part of the American "counterculture" and then "New
Age" syncretistic ideology. Miller's major theme of artistic-spiritual self-
discovery—"*l'homme que j'etais, je ne suis*" (*Black Spring,* 39)—and the endless autobiographical project through dozens of volumes was a fancied-up
burlesque splaying of the American-as-romantic-artist-confessor. This tradition of self-sentimental and wordy naive exaltation in Sherwood Anderson,
Henry Miller, Thomas Wolfe, William Saroyan, Jack Kerouac, and others,
has been both poignant and self-parodying, literarily awkward and widely
appealing. I suppose it can be historically viewed as the exuberant—and
murky—American edge of the broader Western bildungsroman and the
quasi literature of confession and case history. The confessional strain long
crossed—in the nineteenth-century American utopians, in the Reformation-
antinomian Protestants, in some of the contemporary TV evangelists—with
fanciful metaphysics and millennial exhortation. Granted, Miller, patently
the indulgently personal and artistic sybarite, lacked heretical rigor. But his

garrulous ruminations and prophetic postures certainly contained and continued such dissident traditions.

In nearer perspective, Norman Mailer announced (in the mid-1970s) that "Henry Miller has influenced the style of half the good American poets and writers alive today" and is the largest American stylistic influence (obscenity?) other than Hemingway.[39] While Mailer was partly using Miller in apologia for his own sexual and stylistic obsessions—and thus no doubt exaggerating—his view was not imperceptive or uncritical. He granted that Miller's "polemical essays read like sludge," his "literary criticism can be pompous and embarrassingly empty," his Greek book "too nice" and thus vague, his 1,600-page romance a narcissistic failure, *Black Spring* and *Tropic of Capricorn* vainly overwritten into "all vices of avant-garde" manners, much of his work "repetitive," "loud," "corny," and dominated by "an enormous ego, false, weak, posturing," and finally lacking the courage of its personality." But against all this criticism Mailer asserted that *Tropic of Cancer* is one "of the ten or twenty great novels of our century." Mailer modestly cites writers strongly influenced by Miller: Burroughs, Bellow, Roth, Jong—and Norman Mailer. This is fair enough, though a more disinterested list might include a good many rather less stylish writers in the narcissistic-confessional manner. An obvious one would be that Miller is a probable source of (as well as admirer of) the embracing "bop" prose of the confessional literary "saint" Jack Kerouac (and other Beat and following writers).[40] In another direction, such bawdy but poetically mannered comedy of the rebellious American abroad as J. P. Donleavy's *The Ginger Man* seems clearly indebted in its nihilistic humor to *Tropic of Cancer*. And so on, to a probably widespread effect in the mid-twentieth-century literary generation.

But I suggest summarizing a significant part of Miller's role and influence in another way. Early Miller, not least because of his large public role as the daringly forbidden author, provided *ground* not only for the "obscene" in language and subject but for the fusion of the high and the low, the colloquial and the ornate—if you will, the dirty mandarin. Otherwise put, Miller offered the poeticization of the naturalistic. Only in some such broad sense can one recognize Miller's significant effects on such diverse figures as Isaac Bashevis Singer (a fervent admirer), Nelson Algren (in his later poetic-naturalist fictions), Lawrence Ferlinghetti (whose parody-pastiche volume, *A Coney Island of the Mind,* took its title from Miller[41]), Lawrence Durrell (his *Black Book* is a rococo use of *Cancer* in bohemian confession and rhetoric before he became the devout friend), Kenneth Rexroth (dissident naturalistic egotist who also anthologized Miller), Norman Mailer (*Advertisements for Myself* does Millerean things long before the apologetics of *The Prisoner of*

Sex and *Genius and Lust*), Karl Shapiro (who came with late hyperbole to trumpet "the greatest living author" as he reacted against his role as "the bourgeois poet"), and even satiric women novelists (Erica Jong, Eleanor Rackow). (Miller has also had considerable readership, admiration, and probably influence, abroad.) Although Miller was not the only impetus to the poetic-obscene and the comedy of exuberant self-alienated incongruity, he was undoubtedly a pervading spirit.

One of Miller's bemusements was to preen himself before the mirror of an imagined future and see that great artist and saint Henry Miller being admired by posterity. His reputation and influence, however, probably reached their apogee in the 1960s (boosted by the censorship furor and the rebellious ambience) and seem unlikely to achieve such proportions again, given that they must bear the burden of an immense amount of bad writing. Although Miller still has imperceptive devotees, it should be evident to the knowledgeable reader that even at his best he was limited in scope, insight, human types, imaginative order, range of feeling and intelligence—in short, a minor writer.[42] I do not intend this as simple put-down but rather as a summing-up that it would be specious to discuss his work as if it presented a major style and attitude in itself, a primary form and force of sensibility. After all, to the degree that Miller found himself, hype-forged an identity, it was by a commitment to the marginal and grotesque. His oddity must properly remain his definition. To predict what the future will do with him and his legacy, as a means of evaluation, would be dubious. Literary history is probably no more honest and wise than much of the rest of history. The critic need not, then, attempt seriously to locate Miller's place in some American bureaucratic-style literary pantheon, even though it houses many anomalous and weird writers with whom Miller would be at home.

Miller's main contribution, I suggest, is the rhetoric of grotesquerie. He did open it up. In several senses, there is little behind his rhetoric—not much of a dramatic world of autonomous characters and patterns, not much major moral or social engagement, and not a unique way of knowing or living. Part of his distinctive quality may be the Americanization of the literature of extreme rebellion in which he modified defiance by bumptiousness, eloquence by crass confession, nihilism by geniality, iconoclasm by easy optimistic faiths. Miller's American ordinariness does separate him from the radical explorers of sensibility and the world. He was a buffoonish version of that great tradition, upon which he so patently drew. The mind-loose and fancy-wild American talker, he transcended the fatally ordinary American lower-middle-class ambience—out of which he came but always remained part of—by his eloquent and grandiloquent gestures. Miller's buffoonish rhetoric became his identity (however pathetically failing him in the end) and his legacy.

Miller's words exaggerated much, probably including his own foolishness as well as lust and faith, thus fulfilling the role of buffoonery. Such a role had its poignancy, not least in displaying (as do every one of his portraits and self-portraits) the loss of all authentic heroism. His figures lack most tragic, moral, and unified consciousness. Miller, of course, was a bit of a con man about his comic nihilism, declaiming all sorts of artistic and religious values. But his poses as great artist and saint, rather than producing a pornography of the spirit, hardly need to be taken seriously. In a way more willy-nilly than a great artist or person, Miller testified effectively to the loss of values and to a drastically incomplete humanity. Such grotesqueness has its profound truth in a world in which individuality is increasingly marginal and heroism is gratuitous. Adventure into a closed world and rebellion against amorphous doom are obviously foolish. But the Miller grotesque made the rhetorical gestures of adventure, and it rebelled by refusing heroic poses as well as victimization. Thus to insist on one's grotesqueness is to insist on one's being—a residual, inverted, yet finally crucial heroism.

The buffoon is often a desperate and sly rebel: the more earnest-appearing his poses, the more absurd he seems. Is this why, knowingly or not, Miller played at gigantic roles of great artist and prophet and saint and divinely unique human being? While such buffoonery is of ancient lineage, it is hard to recall anyone else quite so exhaustively playing the role as self-important writer. Miller put into books hundreds of thousands of bombastic, ruminative, casual, pretentious, foolish, obscene words that have not usually been put into books at all. While the result is occasionally striking amidst the tediousness, such literary buffoonery also has its salutary effect. For when we turn from Miller to many pretentious confessions and pronouncements and arts, they justly appear weak. Miller pronounced in his old age: "Ninety percent of what is called the works of the old masters could be thrown on the junk heap. The same for books"[43] (and the same or more for his own writings?). The wisdom of the buffoon may be to swell himself up until we see him, and much else, in truer proportion. Good old American hyperbole.

Miller's best writing, those fractured bits, and most distinctive gestures may produce a grotesque catharsis. The rebel-buffoon's real heroism is his own defiant absurdity, amidst the rest of what he sees as the "fucking absurdity," as he dances in his torn rhetoric. It provides a legacy of motley for other rebel-buffoons, and perhaps for more sardonically acute comedians. The topsy-turvy gesture is all, but it may be taken as a suggestive and amusing affirmation of the lively human.

Notes and References

Chapter One

1. *Tropic of Cancer* (New York: Grove, 1961), Black Cat paper edition, the most widely distributed. References in text.

2. The biographical information, of course, is drawn from Miller's many accounts, with skeptical qualifications, from published letters, and from a number of memoirs, such as Alfred Perlès, *My Friend, Henry Miller* (New York: John Day, 1956). The fullest biography is Jay Martin, *Always Merry and Bright: The Life of Henry Miller* (1978; New York: Penguin, 1980), which fully draws upon documentary collections but is partly in florid novelistic manner and is often intellectually inaccurate and foolish (sometimes comically so, as with saying that Max Stirner's *The Ego and His* [sic] *Own* provided Miller with "summaries of the leading ideas of other major anarchists such as Kropotkin, Baukunin, Tolstoy, and Johann Most" [38], which would be quite a feat for a writer who wrote before all of them, and drastically differed from them).

3. See, for example, Edmund Wilson, "Twilight of the Expatriates [1938]," *Shores of Light* (Garden City, N.Y.: Doubleday, 1952), 705–10. A detailed, pedestrian discussion of the theme is Annette Kar Baxter's *Henry Miller, Expatriate* (Pittsburgh: University of Pittsburgh Press, 1961), the first academic book on Miller.

4. George Orwell, in an essay highly influential in the growth of Miller's serious reputation, emphasizes the sociology of Parisian and lower class life: "Inside the Whale [1940]," *A Collection of Essays* (Garden City, N.Y.: Doubleday, 1954), 215–56. Amidst his praise of Miller, Orwell also suspected "charlatanism." George Wickes, in "Henry Miller Down and Out in Paris," *Americans in Paris* (Garden City, N.Y.: Doubleday, 1969), provided a pleasantly polite summary of the Paris period.

5. Thoreau is not, unlike Emerson and Whitman, quoted in the book, although Miller later wrote a praising piece on him, "Henry David Thoreau," *Stand Still Like the Hummingbird* (New York: New Directions, 1962). A number of critics (such as Brown and Gordon) have followed my suggestion in viewing Miller partly as an American transcendentalist autobiographer.

6. According to Martin (*Always Merry,* 260), the real-life Miller only kept less than a third of the money, sending the rest to the abandoned Frenchwoman. The amoralist exaggeration, which also applies to a number of other episodes, may be part of the roguish role Miller was creating.

7. But when "his command of the colloquial style faltered, he produced some of the most awkward prose of the age. His surrealistic effusions could become utterly confusing; his dadaistic pastiches puerile and self-indulgent" (J. D. Brown, *Henry Miller* [New York: Unger, 1986], 107). Miller's switch from "naturalistic" to

"surrealistic" styles generally comes as a subjective escape. After describing a repulsive scene and then going to a movie, he connects the two in a verbal splay of association (such as the one of the eye [*Cancer,* 57] probably drawing on his favorite Dali-Buñuel film, *Le Chien Andalou*).

8. *The World of Lawrence* (Santa Barbara, Calif.: Capra, 1980), 94. Joyce's "Revolution of the Word" is "the logical outcome of this sterile dance of death" and expresses "a profound hatred of humanity" (103, 106). He extends this charge to other modernists he ambivalently admired and felt competitive with, such as Proust, Eliot, and Pound.

9. George P. Elliot, in a ponderously obtuse memoir-essay parody of Miller, emphasized the delight in "muck" ("A Brown Fountain Pen," *Kenyon Review* 24 [Winter 1962]:). Various memoirs emphasize his contrary compulsive cleanliness. For an incisive description of the maternal compulsions Miller verbally rebelled against, see his own "Reunion in Brooklyn" (in *Sunday after the War* [New York: New Directions, 1944]).

10. E. E. Cummings's *The Enormous Room* (1922) is probably a direct source here, a point needing emphasis because literature often plays a larger role than other experiences in forming Miller's episodes. The tradition of poetic memoir-essay has more generally not been given its influential due. See my "Timeless Prose," *Twentieth Century Literature* 4 (July 1958).

11. Miller's inability to accept "humdrum" life has often been insufficiently acknowledged. One of the few to note it was philosopher Paul Weiss in his essay "Art and Henry Miller" (in *The Happy Rock,* ed. Bern Porter [Berkeley, Calif.: Porter, 1945], 133–35). In a later interesting argument, Don Kleine suggested that Miller's plain/colloquial style stultified his perceptions of the ordinary and drove him to an excessively florid counterstyle, "Innocence Forbidden: Henry Miller in the Tropics," *Prairie Schooner* 33 (Summer, 1959): 125–30.

12. Miller's later explanation of the title was that "Cancer" was used because it was the zodiacal sign of the crab, who moves in all directions (*Henry Miller Recalls and Reflects,* LP recording, ed. Ben Grauer [New York: Riverside Records, 1956]). According to Martin (*Always Merry,* 260), Walter Lowenfels, an influential writer friend of Miller's in the Paris period, suggested the title.

13. Orwell, ("Inside the Whale," *A Collection of Essays* [New York: Doubleday, 1953], 215–256), thinking in political terms, rather overemphasized the passivity, as did Frederick Hoffman (*Freudianism and the Literary Mind* [Baton Rouge: Louisiana State University Press, 1945], 299–305). The resentment motive is given another twist in Miller's later statement that "Rome has to burn in order for a guy like me to sing" (in Henry Miller and Victor Fraenkel, *Hamlet,* vol. 1 [New York: Carrefour, 1943], 109). He was not above shouting "fire" to have something to sing about.

14. Other sources indicate that this material, which provided his first publication of note (see chapter 2), was about a supportive prostitute named Claude. I have largely ignored Miller's "womb" (rather than "cunt") motif—he is pregnant with this

book, etc.—because its main use is in post-*Cancer* writings. In an essay Miller wrote, he said of this book, "The strong odor of sex which it purveys is really the aroma of birth" (*The World of Sex* [Paris: Olympia, 1940])—hardly true of the actual book, which emphasizes sexual impersonality and grotesqueness. When Miller makes more positive claims (*World of Sex,* 44), he is imposing on the material. He is not to be separated from the gross sexuality, for Miller, "too, is one of the male clowns and scoundrels in the circus arena of sex" (Donald Gutierrez, "'Hypocrite Lecteur': *Tropic of Cancer* as Sexual Comedy," *The Maze in the Mind and the World* [Troy, N.Y.: Whiston, 1985], 78). Gutierrez is no doubt right, too, in pointing out that even when Miller uses women as "symbolic" of the positive it turns into the "hostility towards women that idolization typically produces" (83).

15. Various biographers and editors (Martin, *Always Merry,* 250ff.), provide bits of information on the real-life sources of the caricatures. Michael Fraenkel ("Boris"), an erudite and speculative writer on death themes who had great influence on Miller's ideas and imagery, touches on some of this not only in the *Hamlet* dual correspondence but also in "The Genesis of the Tropic of Cancer" (*The Happy Rock,* 38–56). Samuel Putnam, translator and editor ("Marlowe"), who published unknown Miller, and otherwise helped him, returns the compliments in his comments on Miller as coward, plagiarist, and "expounder of the Philosophy of universal Filth" in his memoir *Paris Was Our Mistress* (New York: Putnam's, 1947), 113–14. Patron and friend Richard C. Osborn ("Fillmore") gives a different version of several of the episodes drawn on in *Cancer,* and highlights Miller's egotism, in "#2 Rue Auguste Barthodi" (*The Happy Rock,* 28–37). Alfred Perlès ("Carl") genially covered the period of his intimate friendship with Miller in his memoir-biography. There are other such accounts, mostly of interest to the participants and the biographer rather than the reader. The "Kreuger" episode, with Miller as the gross parasite, has an ironic reversal in Miller's tribulations as host to Moricand many years later (discussed in chapter 3).

16. For further discussion of the "American Joe," see the chapter on the archetype in my *The Literary Rebel* (Carbondale: Southern Illinois University Press, 1965). Kenneth Rexroth early noted the dominance of the lower class Brooklyn male ethos in his "Reality of Henry Miller," *Bird in the Bush, Obvious Essays* (New York: New Directions, 1959), 154–67.

17. Of the many comments on *Cancer* later tossed off by Miller, perhaps the most apt is his noting that "hatred and vengeance were the main spring," and the book was dominated by "the idea of separation. I had to break with the past" (*Hamlet,* 1:354). Since Miller was being pushed into the admissions by his knowing friend Fraenkel, the remarks are probably more candid than some later comments.

18. I am not objecting primarily to the silly brutality but to the weak narrative: Collins, for example, is never adequately developed, and although we are teasingly told that "he was never to see America again," he just disappears from the account in the confusion of personal life and narrative coherence. Similar weakness pervades the first two chapters.

19. Such points were usually lost in the imbalances of the censorship discussions. As Dr. Eleanor Widmer, main defense strategist and witness in the San Diego acquittal of *Cancer* summarized, "There are fundamental disparities between sexual and literary facts and public and legal processes." See, also, her "My Day in the Censoring Tropic," *Freedom and Culture,* ed. Eleanor Widmer (Belmont, Calif.: Wadsworth, 1970). For other details of the trials of that period, see the dual correspondence of Miller and the pretentious attorney Elmer Gertz, *Henry Miller: Years of Trial and Triumph, 1962–1964,* ed. Elmer Gertz and Felice Flanery Lewis (Carbondale: Southern Illinois University Press, 1978); also E. R. Hutchison, *"Tropic of Cancer" on Trial: A Case History of Censorship* (New York: Grove, 1968); and, more broadly, Charles Rembar, *The End of Obscenity* (New York: Random House, 1968).

20. The 1928 manuscript was printed in *Gliding into the Everglades* (Lake Oswego, Oreg.: Lost Pleiade, 1977). The title piece is stilted, sometimes florid, often trite, and weak on visualization, including the hostile priest episode (33ff.). The writing not only confirms Miller's negative view of his earlier writing, and the drastic change a couple of years later in Paris, but also shows why he had such difficulty with his down-and-out role in Paris. It concludes: "Old man, you came perilously near making a bum of yourself" (48). The petit bourgeois gentility took much overcoming, thus part of the sense of accomplishment in *Cancer.*

21. Céline's novel, *Journey to the End of Night,* was published to considerable attention and response from Miller in 1932 while Miller was revising his manuscript; the passage (in the John Marks Englishing) is the one ending that people have good hearts—"sods, with so much love inside . . . they die of love—still inside." See my discussion of Céline in chapter 5 of *Edges of Extremity: Some Problems of Literary Modernism* (Tulsa, Okla.: University of Tulsa, 1980).

22. For an example of his sardonic gusto switching to a fatuous play with exotic words, see the end of the concert episode (*Cancer,* 70–71). Elsewhere, Miller rightly noted his proclivity for "verbal jags" (*The Time of the Assassins* [New York: New Directions, 1956], 18).

23. The Thoreau analogue and the use of Whitman, Rabelais, and Céline have been pointed out earlier. The Lawrence is summarized in chapter 5. Joyce seems important primarily for several metaphors and the combination of verbal high life with urban low life. Other specific literary sources include nineteenth-century confessional literature (Strindberg and Van Gogh in his letters); surrealism (especially André Breton's *Nadja* and manifestos, Dali, and Buñuel, whose films Miller later wrote about, and the general ambience and many of the mannerisms of the group); some of the French late naturalists (Phillipe, *Bubu of Montparnasse*); Sherwood Anderson's "grotesques" (Miller's favorite contemporary American author, as cited below); Gallic travel writers and polemicists, such as Morand and Duhamel (a number are cited from manuscript sources by Martin, *Always Merry,* 250ff.); the writings as well as personal friendships of Anaïs Nin (who subsidized the book as well as Miller); Michael Fraenkel (who endlessly discussed it with him); Walter Lowenfels

(likewise); and his boon companion Alfred Perlès. As is clear in his language of denunciation, Nietzsche and Spengler were also crucial to him. The point still needs
emphasis that Miller was a highly "literary" and intellectualized writer in *Cancer,*
with books often his most crucial experiences.

24. The Muir was in *The Present Age from 1914* (London: 1939), 149ff.; the
Durrell in *The Happy Rock,* 4. All the others cited here may most conveniently be
found reprinted in two anthologies: *Henry Miller and the Critics,* ed. George Wickes
(Carbondale: Southern Illinois University Press, 1963); *Henry Miller: Three Decades
of Criticism,* ed. Edward B. Mitchell (New York: New York University Press, 1971).
These also include other commentaries, some critically and historically important in
developing Miller's substantial literary reputation, primarily for *Tropic of Cancer.*

25. Norman Mailer, *Genius and Lust: A Journey through the Major Writings of
Henry Miller* (New York: Grove, 1976). Mailer's commentary is discussed more
fully in chapter 5.

Chapter Two

1. *The Henry Miller Reader,* ed. Lawrence Durrell (New York: New Directions, 1959), 3. Oddly, Miller said of this ornately "experimental" book that it
"came nearer to being myself, I believe, than any book I have written before or since"
(*The Books in My Life* [New York: New Directions, 1952], 98).

2. *Black Spring* (Paris: Obelisk, 1958). Page references in text.

3. While praising the nostalgic descriptions of New York, George Orwell in
"Inside the Whale" (*Collection,* 218) noted Miller's tendency to slide into "mere ver-
biage." Of Miller's avant-gardist verbalism, Ihab Hasson reasonably concluded:
"Miller brings that tradition to a close less by revolution than by sheer indiscrimi-
nancy" (*The Literature of Silence: Henry Miller and Samuel Beckett* [New York:
Knopf, 1967], 67).

4. The piece has also been several times reprinted with reproductions of
Miller's watercolors; see his *Watercolors, Drawings, and His Essay, "The Angel Is My
Watermark"* (New York: Abrams, 1962). Further writing around his watercolors appears in the posthumously published *The Paintings of Henry Miller,* ed. Noel Young
(San Francisco: Chronicle, 1982). This includes "The Painting Lesson" (ca. 1935),
"The Waters Reglitterized" (1939), "To Paint Is to Love Again" (1960) (although
apparently the love is narcissistic since he acknowledges that all his heads turn into
self-portraits, [Young, *Paintings,* 66]), and "Paint as You Like and Die Happy"
(1965). The volume includes reproductions (apparently selected by Miller) of examples of his painting from the 1930s to the 1970s. From a limited survey (from an immense number) of his visual works, I find some of the early ones (under the influence
of Paul Klee, perhaps by way of Miller's teacher-friend Hans Reichel), rather better
than most of the late, knocked-off, meanderings into quaintness and cuteness. Overall, there is a mishmash of styles (out of Chagall, Marin, surrealists, et al.) though
much is simply *faux-naif.*

5. Friend Wallace Fowlie discusses the last part of this painting description as

an example of surrealism (*Age of Surrealism* [New York: Duell, Sloan, 1950], 184–87), but essentially Miller lacked the surrealist's revolutionary intentions.

6. Miller indicated that he was a devoted reader of *transition* (avante-garde journal), to which his mixed mannerisms are indebted (*Books in My Life,* 204).

7. Considerable skepticism should be applied to the autobiographical side of this material (the substitution of a half-wit brother for his retarded sister is an obvious example). The title and other things seem to derive from Anaïs Nin.

8. Many of the details and motifs reappear in somewhat varying form in other writings. Cleo, for example, provides a motif in *Sexus* (Paris: Obelisk, 1960), 588ff.

9. Miller's sense of modernism, reasonably enough, was that one had to be socially critical; here, in the conclusion, it is the Nietzschean "individual as against the collectivity." This statement, and other pseudo-organized jottings, may be seen in material published as "Work Schedule," one of many indications that Miller wrote not so much spontaneously as out of a fragmentation marked by desperate efforts at organization (*Henry Miller Miscellanea,* ed. Bern Porter [Berkeley, Calif.: Bern Porter, 1945]).

10. There is an "Epilogue to Black Spring," apparently never published with the book, with a spray of surrealist images—"celluloid sky," "green carpet made of the foam and snot of the epileptic," etc. (*Miscellanea,* 31–33). A similar piece, "The Brooklyn Bridge," appears to have been written shortly after the book, on which it draws (Tante Melia, again), including yet another stillborn rebirth announcement—"The thug in me is dead, and the fanatic and lunatic also" (*The Cosmological Eye* [Norfolk, Conn.: New Directions, 1939], 345–56).

11. Many were soon reprinted, with other material, in his first American anthology, *The Cosmological Eye.*

12. "Mademoiselle Claude," *The Wisdom of the Heart* (New York: New Directions, 1941), 140–50, originally appeared in a friend's *New Review* [Paris] in the fall of 1931. In the later *Tropic of Cancer,* in a switch, Claude is unfavorably contrasted with Germaine because Claude was a too "*delicate* whore" (43). Miller much later said (to Bradley Smith, who told me that he consciously elicited such opinions) that "Mlle. Claude was a charming prostitute . . . with whom I fell in love for a time" (*My Life and Times* [Chicago: Playboy, 1971], 148). Another prostitute portrait, apparently not written until much later, appears in the "Mara Marigan" series of minor sexual anecdotes in *Quiet Days in Clichy* (Paris: Obelisk, 1958). A revised version appears as "Berthe" (*Henry Miller Reader,* 190–99). In a prefatory note, Miller links it with the Claude piece, although it is far more sentimental.

13. "Max," *Cosmological Eye,* 8–46. On this, as on most of Miller's best shorter pieces, there is little significant comment.

14. In a later prefatory note on "Max," Miller says that it was from such suffering ones that he "learned about life, about God, and about the futility of 'doing good.'" He adds that he does not know about what happened to the original Max, al-

though he assumes that he must have been killed by the Nazis (*Henry Miller Reader*, 134).

15. *Wisdom of the Heart*, 13–18. Perhaps a bit better, because more concrete, is the paean to the *naif*, Miller's painter friend Hans Reichel, in the entitling essay of *Cosmological Eye* 357–64.

16. *Cosmological Eye*, 75–106. Nin's rather lush prose poem attempted to project a serious sense of narcissistic and incestuous longings. Miller seems to burlesque it unintentionally by mechanical loading with dream symbolism and fantasy imagery from, I would guess, "B" movies, H. Rider Haggard, astrology, and so forth, for a redundant nightmare.

17. Miller published three essays on cinema (and various digressive comments elsewhere) in his early anthologies: "The Golden Age" (*Cosmological Eye*, 47–62), properly high praise of Luis Buñuel and a defense of cinema as art; "Reflections on Extasy" (*Cosmological Eye*, 63–74), a brief explication of Machaty's film; and "Raimu" (*Wisdom of the Heart*, 47–62), comparisons of America and France via actors. Discursive (with some usual bombast), they take the then "highbrow" position on movies. In a later interview Miller said he soon gave up seeing films, but allusions in letters, show this to be untrue ("Henry Miller," with George Wickes, *Paris Review* [Summer–Fall, 1962]: 129–59). In the late and embarrassingly bad "On Seeing Jack Nicholson for the First Time" he ruminated about *Five Easy Pieces* (*Gliding into the Everglades*, 71–76), and during the 1930s he took some enthusiastic but thin interest in American jazz.

18. The 1938 pamphlet has been reprinted (as in *Stand Still*, 119–56). Miller attributed the notion to a question from economics-mad Ezra Pound; Perlès says that the impetus was a wager with Fraenkel that he could convincingly sound scholarly without making sense (Perlès, *My Friend, Henry Miller*, 92). Somewhere Miller says that it was the only piece of his that was read—and taken seriously—by his father.

19. Miller did some similar minor parodies for *Booster* (a periodical he co-edited with Perlès in Paris for a few issues in the late 1930s). "Fall and Winter Fashions," portentous-sounding nonsense in the manner of male fashion commentary of an earlier period (he had worked in his father's gentlemen's tailor shop), was reprinted in *Miscellanea*, 37–41.

20. *What Are You Going to Do about Alf?* (I am using the reprint: Berkeley, Calif.: Porter, 1944). Perlès says that Miller must have appropriated any contributions that came in, which is just what Miller justifies in his usual amoralist claims of the prerogatives of "the artist" (Perlès *My Friend, Henry Miller*, 173).

21. In a 1939 letter he gave, as a conservative estimate of his letters, the number 25,000 (*Henry Miller Literary Society Newsletter* [November 1960]). There were many thousands more later.

22. The first volume of *Hamlet*, omitted a number of letters included in the second edition (New York: Carrefour, 1943); Volume 2 of *Hamlet* (New York: Carrefour, 1941) was complete. Among many other published collections were *Aller*

Retour New York (Paris: Olympia, 1935), a bombastic ninety-page quasi-essay directed to Perlès, and the more genial recollections of the parallel *Reunion in Barcelona* (Northwood, England: Scorpion, 1959). A selection of Miller's dry-run letters for *Cancer,* to Emil Schnellock, was published as *Semblance of a Devoted Past* (Berkeley, Calif.: Bern Porter, 1944). George Wickes edited a selection, *Lawrence Durrell— Henry Miller: A Private Correspondence* (New York: Dutton, 1963), which has since been replaced by the less bowdlerized *The Durrell-Miller Letters, 1935–80,* ed. Ian S. MacNiven (New York: New Directions, 1988). Gunther Stuhlmann edited Miller's *Letters to Anaïs Nin* (New York: Putnam's, 1965). Later, and lesser, collections will be cited below. Most were done under Miller's control.

23. When discussing himself, as he often did, as a "genius," he noted: "When I write something I like extra well I smack my lips and look over my shoulder. I am already with the man of A.D. 2500 . . . enjoying this great guy Henry Miller who lived in the 20th century" (*Hamlet,* 1:313).

24. *Cosmological Eye,* 197–288.

25. *Colossus of Marousi* (Norfolk, Conn.: New Directions, 1941). Page references in text. Miller later published a notebook from the trip (*First Impressions of Greece* [Santa Barbara, Calif.: Capra, 1973]), which includes hyperbolic praise of Greece and friends, ponderous prejudiced asides, and not much ordered description.

26. A later Greek writer appropriately objected to Miller's romanticizing the harsh poverty, almost completely ignoring the nasty Metaxas dictatorship and displaying much ignorance (Minica Cranaki, *Greece,* trans. N. C. Clegg [London, 1959], 77–90).

27. *Colossus* seems to have been the most widely, though cursorily, praised of Miller's books. One of the earliest studies of Miller, however, did not find it among his "best" and thought it uninformative on Greece (Nicholas Moore, *Henry Miller* [Wigginton, England: privately printed, 1943], 20). In one of the more obtuse American studies, William Gordon judged the book to be "perfect" (*The Mind and Art of Henry Miller* [Baton Rouge: Louisiana State University Press, 1967], 180). Norman Mailer viewed it as too vague and "too nice," perhaps in Miller's an attempt to be popular, for which there seems to be historical evidence (Mailer, *Genius and Lust* [New York: Grove, 1976], 395). An incisive summary of the book is that of Jeffrey Meyers, who called it poorly and ignorantly written around a "literary persona . . . *faux-naif,* intellectually pretentious and banal" (Meyers, *The Legacy of D. H. Lawrence,* [London: Macmillan, 1987], 98–100).

28. *Sunday after the War* (Norfolk, Conn.: New Directions, 1944), 107–15.

29. *Wisdom of the Heart,* 61.

Chapter Three

1. *The Henry Miller Reader,* 384. Elsewhere Miller wrote that that day he was working at an easy clerical job in the Park Department office (*Nexus* [Paris: Olympia, 1960], 159) or digging a ditch (*Colossus,* 150) or something else (*Books in*

My Life, 98). Miller repeatedly called his life story "autobiographical romance," apparently to indicate that it is not literal autobiography.

2. Miller had said, in interviews over the years, that there would be further volumes of *Nexus*. He had also announced yet another book dealing with the obsessional self-dramatization of the 1920s, to be called "Draco and the Ecliptic," which would give the occult significance of the multivolumed work. None was apparently done.

3. In yet another summary of his life, Miller explained that "rosy crucifixion" meant the "transmutation" of suffering into understanding ("My Life as an Echo," *Stand Still*, 81). He also noted that he no longer knew what was true and what was not in his "autobiographical romances": "If I lie a bit now and then it is mainly in the interest of truth" (83). When it comes to many of the sexual descriptions (and other episodes as well), I characterize them as fantasies simply because that seems the most appropriate literary term for the way they are handled.

4. *Quiet Days*, 110. Much of it seems to have been written some years earlier. It is a series of minor good-humored anecdotes of his Paris days after *Cancer:* a trip to Luxembourg, Clichy prostitutes, miscellaneous bohemian adventures. It lacks the apocalyptic tone and the intense writing of *Cancer,* although it has touches of comic iconoclasm; of stolid Luxembourg, he concludes, "Now I know what makes the world civilized: it's vice, disease, thievery, mendacity, lechery" (89).

5. In *Cosmological Eye*, 197–202, she is just called his "wife." The specifics (most of the concern, of course, is Miller's responses) seem more sordid-pathetic than mythic, but the portrayal is hardly consistent. Jay Martin's documentary-source biography shows considerable variance from Miller's account (*Always Merry*).

6. *Books in My Life*, 96–97. Perhaps some of the mystification in Miller's treatment is indebted to H. Rider Haggard's fictions, such as *She*, to Breton's *Nadja,* and to the heroines of Claude Houghton, among others whom he assiduously admired.

7. *Sunday after the War*, 291–94. Miller's other pieces on Nin are burbling encomiums, including a letter in the same volume (276–84) and "Un Etre Etoilique" (*Cosmological Eye*, 269–91).

8. Miller calls it the "Amarillo Dance Hall"; here and elsewhere the source is probably the Roseland Ballroom, Times Square. In an author's copy of Nin's *The Winter of Artifice* (Paris, 1939) in the "Special Collections" of the UCLA library there is a list, apparently in Nin's handwriting, called "Identification of Characters." Hans is given as Miller, Djuna as Nin, Johanna as June Mansfield Miller, Andre as Perlès, and Lilith as sometimes Nin, sometimes Mrs. Miller. In this shapeless and overfervent account of the personal history, the main emphasis seems to be on polymorphous sexuality and feelings, and on Miller's overwhelming self-love. A composite figure with Mona/Mara characteristics appears in other Nin works, as does a Miller-like figure called Jay. For another account by her, censored from her diaries while Miller was alive, see *Henry and June: From the Unexpurgated Diaries of Anaïs Nin* (San Diego: Harcourt Brace Jovanovich, 1986).

9. See Miller's comments about Balzac, who wrote his occultist *Louis Lambert* in his thirty-third year, no doubt imitating an earlier self-important story-teller (*Wisdom of the Heart*, 211–12).

10. For a sexual fillip, Miller casually sketches in an orgy with two other women friends (*Sexus*, 523). While I have not counted, a scholarly student informs me that the protagonist of Miller's "autobiographical romances" has a distinguished sexual record that includes five women in one day, nine orgasms in one night, and other sterling performances. The sexual performance principle may be judged as undercutting the romance emphasis.

11. I know of no detailed literary commentary on the role of the destructive-desirable Jewish Dark Lady in literature, although the iconography runs at least from the Renaissance through Iris Murdoch's witty novel *A Severed Head* (1961). Near the end of his life, Miller reportedly told a lady friend that his second wife endlessly had sex with other men and lied about it. Miller also did a playlet showing her as a compulsive whore (*Dear, Dear Brenda, The Love Letters of Henry Miller to Brenda Venus*, with text by Brenda Venus [New York: Morrow, 1986], 114–22). In an earlier letter attempting to justify his literary treatment of "Mona," Miller decided that "the confusion or conflict in me was in confounding the Muse and the *femme fatale.*" But then he went on to deny the obvious—that he had showed her as monstrous—and claimed as proof that he knew readers who found her charming and "truly feminine" (see William A. Gordon, "A Correspondence with Henry Miller," *Writer and Critic* [Baton Rouge: Louisiana State University Press, 1968], 66). Surprisingly, women critics on Miller have not picked up on the slander. Jane A. Nelson held that Mona/Mara should be recognized (contrary to such skeptical critics as K. Widmer) as "the anima figure described by Jung" (*Form and Image in the Fiction of Henry Miller* [Detroit: Wayne State University Press, 1970], 87).

12. Wallace Fowlie notes, in an otherwise weak essay, that Miller's fear of domineering women encouraged him to reduce them to prostitutes ("Shadow of Doom," *Of-by-and-about Henry Miller* [Younkers, N.Y.: Gotham, 1947], 23).

13. I do not recall any sexual scene in the first 400 pages of *Plexus* (Paris: Olympia, 1959), and even the friendly "orgy" started then is soon replaced by a discussion of the aesthetics of Gottfried Benn (historically displaced?). The absence of sex may have been partly in response to the criticisms of Durrell.

14. See also the hopelessly narcissistic aesthetic of *Colossus:* "I have always felt that the art of telling a story consists in so stimulating the listener's imagination that he drowns himself in his own reveries long before the end. The best stories I have heard were pointless" (71).

15. The lesbianism is first brought out as a minor motif in several of the dream fantasies in *Plexus*, 272–95. In spite of Miller's later reasonable statements (such as *Nexus*, 19), the presentation usually suggests a fearful masculinity in which the woman's female choice points to male inadequacy.

16. The lesbian friend, Anastasia, appears to be the same as Thelma (origi-

nally Jane), a Rimbaudean who died in an insane asylum, described in *The Time of the Assassins* (New York: New Directions, 1956), 3.

17. Miller seems to have had a special fondness for such set pieces of artifice, reprinting this in *Sunday after the War,* 161–88.

18. Voicing the common view of Miller devotees that the work cannot be criticized because of its unique fusion of good and bad, Claude Mauriac held that the autobiographical romances were major because of the size of the effort (*The New Literature,* trans. S. F. Stone [New York: Braziller, 1959], 59). Durrell seemed to hold a similar view, as did (more negatively) Mailer (see chapter 5).

19. There has been much less personal recollection by those who knew Miller in the Brooklyn period than in the Paris period (many of the latter were writers). Emil Schnellock published a genial personal reminiscence, "Just a Brooklyn Boy" (*The Happy Rock,* 7–24), which, however, notes that Miller's portraits of his friends show "viciousness" and "monstrous cruelty."

20. Sexual fascination with the Jewish woman appears in other scenes, as in his lavish praise of Rebecca (wife of Arthur Raymond) as superior to all ordinary American women (*Sexus,* 431ff., 490ff.). A Jewish male is also given a speech explaining that Jewish women develop a passion for a "lost gentile" (*Sexus,* 532). There are also gross sexual fantasies concerning hyperpassionate Jewish women.

21. In a note to the reprinting of this piece, Miller said that the ghetto was his favorite part of the city, an inspiration, and the only place to meet an "interesting character" (*Miller Reader,* 72). He sentimentally fails to note negative aspects of the ghetto.

22. Another aspect of Miller as imaginary Jew comes out in his identification with the prophetic role and Old Testament rhetoric (as in *Plexus,* 31ff.). For Miller's ecstatic account of the effect of some Yiddish literature on him, see *Books in My Life,* 260ff. Is this why the more skillful Isaac Bashevis Singer has been such an admirer of Miller? See also Miller's lavish praise of two Jewish friends in *Big Sur and the Oranges of Hieronymous Bosch* (New York: New Directions, 1957), 196, 203–4. For some rather odd praise of Jewish religiosity, see Miller's comments in *Hamlet,* 1:263. Fraenkel, in turn, acutely points out the hostility also in Miller's notions of the Jewish heritage. That Miller's family and his own earlier feelings were anti-Semitic becomes cumulatively emphatic in the scattered episodes about his early days and in a number of scenes in *Tropic of Cancer.* It seems that a long anti-Semitic concern, made more knowledgeable by his Paris associations, became an increasingly mythic identification *after* his return to the United States, and culminates in the re-creation of his past as an imaginary Jew. I published some of this discussion as "The Imaginary Jew: Henry Miller" (*International Henry Miller Letter* 3, 1963) and was attacked in print by several devotees, but in such general and inaccurate terms that a reply does not seem profitable.

23. Few of the readers of the later works found them much good, much less better than the earlier. However, William A. Gordon typically claims that *Plexus* "is on the whole one of the best things Miller has written" (*The Mind and Art of Henry*

Miller [Baton Rouge: Louisiana State University Press, 1967], 138). Leon Lewis (apparently loosely borrowing again from Widmer) judged *Plexus* as "complete . . . failure" (*Henry Miller: The Major Writings* [New York: Schocken, 1986], 164).

24. Longtime friend and admirer Lawrence Durrell, however, wrote (5 September 1949) vehemently attacking *Sexus* as "moral vulgarity" and a "childish explosion of obscenity." Perhaps more important, he saw it as a "puerile narrative" with "little real feeling." Miller's defense (28 September 1949) weakly discussed the great time he had devoted to it and his sincerity (Wickes, *Lawrence Durrell—Henry Miller,* 264–66).

24. In another letter to Durrell (3 October 1959), Miller wrote that he so desperately wanted to be a writer that he "sinned" against everything, even denying reality and religious beliefs. He makes a somewhat more restricted admission in *Art and Outrage,* "A Correspondence about Henry Miller between Alfred Perlès and Lawrence Durrell (With an Intermission by Henry Miller)" (London: Putnam, 1959), 56ff.

25. In his two letters in *Art and Outrage* (28, 60–61) Miller in effect grants most of the criticisms of his defective art but justifies himself in terms of his spiritual "break-through" into new being. As purely individual therapy, there is not much room for argument. But Miller seems on foolish ground when he goes on to justify publishing what he did because his readers have been "unanimous in writing of the therapeutic value of my work" (29). Not a proper sample, and therapy is a two-way street, which, by its own logic, can damage as much as delight. Still, Miller's role as vicarious figure for a bumptious and not very demanding "liberation" into vulgarity and "art" may account for considerable of the devotion to him for more than a generation.

Chapter Four

1. *Sunday after the War,* 63–106. A few commentators have properly noted this work's importance. Herbert Read called it a "masterpiece" (*The Tenth Muse* [London: Faber, 1957], 250–55). J. D. Brown (apparently drawing on Widmer) named it "the finest personal essay he [Miller] would write" (*Henry Miller,* 63). Unfortunately, some of the critical imbalance about Miller comes from so many (Mailer, Gordon, Lewis, et al.) inappropriately concentrating on the book-length works.

2. This episode, repeated in *Sexus,* would seem to be crucial to Miller's overstated hostility between America and the artist. Annette Kar Baxter summarized some of his other points on the artist in America (*Henry Miller, Expatriate* [Pittsburgh: University of Pittsburgh Press, 1961], chapter 4).

3. In a suggestive, though a bit cranky, essay on Miller, Kenneth Rexroth overpraised the Cosmodemonic section because he agreed with its view of our "insane and evil society" with "its orgy of human self-alienation." Perhaps tricked by memory, Rexroth also claimed Valeska as a "Beatrice" and "one of the most real women in fiction," although she is hardly developed by Miller (Kenneth Rexroth, Introduction

to *Henry Miller, Nights of Love and Laughter* [New York: New American Library, 1955], 10).

4. In adapting surrealist dogma, Miller had repeatedly stressed the involuntary nature of parts of his writing, especially the "Interlude" section of *Capricorn*. He wryly, and perhaps disingenuously, describes the "Voice" of unconscious dictation working against his will in this section of *Capricorn* (*Big Sur*, 126–30).

5. See, for a handful of Miller's many references to it, *The Henry Miller Reader*, 384; *Books in My Life*, 306; *My Life and Times*, 190; and "It was a world-shaking event for me to hear Emma Goldman" (Henry Miller, *Joey: A Loving Portrait of Alfred Perlè's Together With Some Bizarre Episodes Relating to the Opposite Sex* [Santa Barbara, Calif.: Capra, 1979], 64). It is repeated twice, including the insistence that he went to a "series" of her lectures, which led to his becoming a writer, in *Book of Friends* (Santa Barbara, Calif.: Capra, 1976), 72, 135. Richard Drinnon (and the sources he cites) in his biography of Goldman, *Rebel in Paradise* (Chicago: University of Chicago Press, 1961), 136, confirms my view of this, as does the detailed account of Goldman's and Reitman's visits to San Diego, based on archives, by Roger A. Bruns, *The Damndest Radical* (Urbana: University of Illinois Press, 1987), chapter 12, 300–1. Goldman did briefly lecture in San Diego in 1915 (Reitman was not with her), but Miller, according to all accounts, was back in New York from 1914 on. Jay Martin (apparently aware of my 1963 note on this) typically tried to slide around the matter by saying "Henry managed to exchange a few words with her" (Martin, *Always Merry*, 38). But that is not listening to a series of lectures, buying books from Reitman, etc., besides being highly improbable in the known circumstances. Possibly Miller heard her somewhere else; most likely he got the lectures considerably later in Goldman's book, *The Social Significance of Modern Drama* (1914). The issue is not only a matter of accuracy but of recognizing Miller's typical self-aggrandizement. The gesture of claiming Miller's personal-intellectual descent from Goldman (with whom he had little in common) has been, with arrogant ignorance, repeated by most of the commentators in the past quarter century.

6. Miller several times refers to the impact made on him by Otto Rank's *Art and Artist*, as, for example, in *Stand Still*, 84. While he does not cite other writings, such as those around Rank's most famous notion, the "birth trauma," the effect seems likely, given that Miller in the mid-1930s briefly conned his way as a Rankean therapist. (He was brought to Rank by Nin during the period he was her lover.) Rank's exalted German-romantic notions of the artist had substantial and lasting effect on Miller. Incidentally, Miller's use of psychoanalytic notions and tropes is usually fantastic rather than analytic, as in his laudatory essay on an inspirational analyst, E. Graham Howe, in the entitling piece of *Wisdom of the Heart*, 31–46, and his dithyrambic use of womb imagery elsewhere.

7. Just when and to what degree the occult influences became substantial is debatable. In "Autobiographical Note" in *Cosmological Eye*, he emphasized that his early reading was mostly religious and "philosophical." *Books in My Life* does not confirm this. He did dabble, pre–World War I, in theosophy for a while. The *Ham-*

let letters show him quite involved in Eastern religious notions in 1936. Generally, the importance of occult religiosity seemed to increase with each book in the 1930s. Further summary of some of this appears in Chapter 5.

8. *Cosmological Eye*, 337–45. Other comments by Miller on America appear in his account of part of a mid-1930s visit, *Aller Retour New York*, a letter-essay addressed to Perlès which has a Céline-like violence and disgust. In another exercise, *Semblance of a Devoted Past*, "America must be destroyed" (21). In his high praise of Georges Duhamel's *America the Menace* (one of the most extreme of the 1920s attacks on America as the epitome of modern dehumanization), we may have a major rhetorical source. Miller cultivated the role of the American as anti-American, partly as proof of his "modernism," partly as self-pitying resentment.

9. Philip Rahv, *Image and Idea* (New York: New Directions, 1957), 160.

10. In a note to reprinting one of the burlesques from *Nightmare*, Miller complained about an advance of "several hundred dollars." (It was more likely a thousand dollars, a very substantial sum in the early 1940s when, as I can testify, a machine operator in a factory might earn less than three dollars a day.) Improvident Miller's frequent complaints about money should not be taken literally; given the kind of writer he was, he was both widely published and considerably paid, although, of course, he went through several periods of economic hardship.

11. Or displacement, as in "Vive la France!" where he associates around Alain Fournier's *Le Grand Meaulness* as a profound child-vision of the world; his earlier published comment called it "feeble" and an illustration of the "inherent weakness of the French character"—soft fantasy (*Wisdom of the Heart*, 48). A similar switch occurs in his early and late remarks on the French and their culture. There seems to have been a reverse relationship in his role-playing the artist and his effective astringency.

12. A better portrait of Hilaire Hiler appears in the letters in *Semblance of a Devoted Past* (25–34).

13. See also my "Twisting American Comedy: Henry Miller and Nathaneal West, among Others" *Arizona Quarterly* 43 (Autumn 1987): 218–229.

14. Karl Shapiro called *Tropic of Cancer* the "Horatio Alger story with a vengeance" (*In Defense of Ignorance* [New York: Random House, 1960], 317). It seems more ironically applicable to the later Miller. There are numerous chatty descriptions of Miller at Big Sur by his friends. Jay Martin also provides a range of information in *Always Merry*, 402ff.

15. As to the high proportion of bad writing, it may have been due not only to Miller's role as uncritically praised artist-sage of Big Sur but to a decline in sexual impetus, the lack of much confrontation with harsh reality, the ease with which he could get almost anything published, and his occultist preoccupations. His own defense of bad writing was that the "slag" was justified as part of life processes (Durrell, Perlès, and Miller, *Art and Outrage*, 40ff.). But why it also should be published was not clear.

16. The loosely controlling motif comes from Wilhelm Franger's *The Millennium of Hieronymous Bosch* (Chicago: University of Chicago Press, 1951), which

most scholars consider an eccentric interpretation, but the fancifully millennial and antinomian often appealed as quaint to Miller.

17. In a note elsewhere, Miller expressed regret at not having developed his portrait of Jaiame de Angulo (apparently a cultivatedly wild misanthrope) (*The Henry Miller Reader,* 77); but the lack of adequate development is pervasive.

18. M[aurice] M[agnus], *Memoirs of the Foreign Legion,* with an introduction by D. H. Lawrence (1925; *Phoenix II,* ed. Warren Roberts and Harry T. Moore [New York: Viking, 1970] 303–64). Miller praisingly refers to this work in *The World of Lawrence,* ed. Evelyn J. Hinz and John J. Teunissen (Santa Barbara, Calif.: Capra, 1980), discussed in chapter 5.

19. Miller's discussion of call girls is neither very pertinent nor witty. For general information on the subject at that time, see Harold Greenwald, *The Call Girl* (New York: Avon, 1958). For a confession of a prostitute, which shows up the traditional male sentimentality that blinds Miller, see the poignantly insightful anonymous *Streetwalker* (New York: Bantam, 1961).

20. Henry Miller, *On Turning Eighty* (Santa Barbara, Calif.: Capra, 1972), 31–32.

21. Henry Miller, *Just Wild about Harry: A Melo-Melo in Seven Scenes* (New York: New Directions, 1963). Since this play came at a period of his high fame, it has a history of some performances.

22. *Letters of Henry Miller and Wallace Fowlie (1943–1972)* (New York: Grove, 1975), 155.

23. Miller's new interest in things Japanese led to a number of inconsequential essays, including *Reflections on the Death of Mishima* (Santa Barbara, Calif.: Capra, 1972).

24. Henry Miller, *Mother, China, and the World Beyond* (Santa Barbara, Calif.: Capra, 1977). The "China" here is ruminations on the metaphor he had used now and again (from *Black Spring* on) for the "marvelous." "To say China was to stand things upside down." And he notes (in reference to his slightly "Oriental" face) that he always thought he had some "Oriental blood" (*Mother, China,* 27).

25. *From Your Capricorn Friend: Henry Miller and the "Stroker", 1978–1980,* ed. Irving Stettner (New York: New Directions, 1987). Besides letters, this volume includes a story and several pieces of rambling ruminations originally published in the little magazine *Stroker.*

Chapter Five

1. See D. H. Lawrence, "Pornography and Obscenity" and "A Propos of *Lady Chatterley's Lover*" (*Sex, Literature and Censorship,* ed. Harry T. Moore [New York: Twayne, 1953]). For a recent discussion, see Donald Gutierrez, "D. H. Lawrence's 'Pornography and Obscenity': Sex, Society, and the Self," *The Dark and Light Gods* (Troy, N. Y.: Whitston, 1987). My discussion is necessarily abbreviated here.

2. *Opus Pistorum* (New York: Grove, 1983), with brief information on its genesis in an appended affidavit by the original contractor. References in text.

3. For further examples and discussion of the Sadean tradition, see my "Pornotopianizing" (*Counterings: Utopian Dialectics in Contemporary Contexts* [Ann Arbor, Mich.: UMI Research Press, 1988], 132ff.). One of the more elaborately obscene serious contemporary novelists, John Updike, has his theologian Roger find "comfort and inspiration in pornography," specifically "the late Henry's *Opus Pistorum,* so vile it was posthumous . . . for me had redeeming qualities . . . exalting . . . the damp underside" (John Updike, *Roger's Version* [New York: Fawcett, 1987], 42).

4. Durrell, Perlès, and Miller, *Art and Outrage.*

5. Miller wrote about sex in his writings, as in *The World of Sex,* a mixture of reflections and absurd anecdotes. The erotic-spiritual remarks, apparently indebted to D. H. Lawrence, not only run contrary to the sexual descriptions in his other books but to the personal details and stories he gives in this book. Similar incoherence applies also to Miller's defenses of obscenity-censorship, as in "Obscenity and the Law of Reflection" (*Remember to Remember* [New York: New Directions, 1947], 274–91); "Letter to the Norwegian Supreme Court" (*The Henry Miller Reader,* 372–79); and the trite invective of "I Defy You" (*Playboy,* January 1962).

6. The claim has been made that Miller was searching for the "absolute" by way of sex, as by Pierre Fanchey, "*Un Epopee du Sexe,*" (*Of-by-and-about Henry Miller,* 41), but, while it might apply to Lawrence, Mailer, et al., there seems little evidence for it in Miller. Georges Villa more appropriately noted Miller's simple, traditional masculine bias, (*Miller et L'Amour* [Paris, 1947], 115). Murray S. Davis appropriately included Miller among his representatives of "naturist" pornography (as against the Manichean-spiritualist) (*Smut: Erotic Reality/Obscene Ideology* [Chicago: University of Chicago Press, 1983]).

7. *Book of Friends* (Santa Barbara, Calif.: Capra, 1976), 97.

8. Kate Millet, *Sexual Politics* (Garden City, N.Y.: Doubleday, 1970). Page references in text.

9. Norman Mailer, *The Prisoner of Sex* (New York: New American Library, 1971), 71–115. Some of the material is repeated and expanded upon in Mailer's anthology of Miller, *Genius and Lust.*

10. Warren French appropriately noted that Miller had become a "patron saint" of the Beat Movement ("The Age of Salinger," *The Fifties,* ed. Warren French [Deland, Fla.: Everett/Edwards, 1970], 17).

11. Stettner, *From Your Capricorn Friend,* 60.

12. *Book of Friends,* 87.

13. I am summarizing from most of Miller's writings, not just from the sometimes arbitrary account in *Books in My Life.* On the basis of his early manuscripts, Jay Martin summarizes the early influence of Dreiser and Sherwood Anderson (*Always Merry* 74ff., 91ff.). Miller's reiteration over many decades that Anderson was always his "favorite" American writer might suggest such influence as "The Book of the

Grotesque" (Sherwood Anderson, *Winesburg, Ohio*), but, given Miller's obsessive emphasis, what he probably had in mind was Anderson's *role* (as in *A Story Teller's Story*), the myth of breakout from restrictive America and self-discovery and self-sanctioning as an expressive writer.

14. I am drawing some information from the editors, Evelyn J. Heinz and John Teunissen; inconveniently for critical scholarly purposes, they do not indicate cuts and Miller's final additions (the work apparently was done under his supervision). For a fuller discussion of Miller's use, see my "Lawrence's Rebellious American Progeny: Henry Miller and Norman Mailer," *D. H. Lawrence's Literary Inheritors*," ed. Keith Cushman and Dennis Jackson, forthcoming.

15. *My Life and Times*, 156.

16. "Creative Death" was published in a periodical and then as the lead piece in *Wisdom of the Heart* (1941), and it seems also heavily indebted to various works of Michael Fraenkel, such as *Death Is Not Enough* (1939); *Wisdom* also included another essay around Lawrence (as essentially Jesus Christ), "Into the Future"; "Shadowy Monomania" appeared in *Sunday after the War* (1944); the first American publication of "The Universe of Death" was in *The Cosmological Eye* (1939)—influential critic Philip Rahv called it "a truly inspired piece of criticism" (*Image and Idea*, 166). Later, Miller spoke several times of finishing the Lawrence book as the summation of his writing life and its meaning (mentioned, for example, in a letter to Anaïs Nin [1941] cited in the introduction to *World of Lawrence*, 22). Jay Martin gives an extended account of the stages of Miller's Lawrence work (though without much attention to content) in *Always Merry*, 285ff. There has also been the printing of Miller's thin little jottings on a Lawrence novel, *Notes on "Aaron's Rod"*, ed. Seamus Cooney (Santa Barbara, Calif.: Capra, 1980). (There are numerous other trivial publications of Miller, often in the form of notebooks and letters—markers of his cult status as well as egotism—which I have examined but do not cite.)

17. Letter in William A. Gordon, *Writer and Critic* (Baton Rouge: Louisiana State University Press, 1968), 68; *My Life and Times*, 150.

18. Miller later wrote that "Seraphita remains the high peak of my experience in the world of books" (*World of Sex*, 7). Admittedly, the enthusiast has made similar claims about other books.

19. *Wisdom of the Heart*. "Balzac and His Double" is in the same volume.

20. The two essays combined in *The Time of the Assassins* were originally written and published in the 1940s. In my comments I am drawing, as does Miller, not just on Rimbaud's writings but also on Enid Starkie's biography, *Rimbaud*. Miller's insistent illumination by French literature for an essentially quite different literary ambience seems to me a recurrent (and underrated) crux in American writers. Karl Shapiro was one of the few to praise the Rimbaud book (*In Defense of Ignorance* [New York: Random House, 1960], 334). Bertrand Mathieu treated it as part of a mystical gospel (*Orpheus in Brooklyn: Orphism, Rimbaud, and Henry Miller* [The Hague, Netherlands: Mouton, 1976]).

21. For example, Miller discusses Erich Gutkind, *The Absolute Collective*, in

an essay of that title in *Wisdom of the Heart* (78–93), in "The Hour of Man" (*Stand Still*, 61ff.), and in *Books in My Life* (231ff.). This minor theological rhapsody had similarities to the ideas of Martin Buber in its emphasis on religious communion with immediate physical life and in an antinomianism that often appealed to Miller.

22. See Miller's preface to Haniel Long, *The Power within Us* (1944), a selective summary of Cabeza de Vaca's *Relacion*. See also Miller's comments elsewhere, such as *Books in My Life* (171ff.). For a sense of the figure, I am also drawing on a later translation of de Vaca's work—*Adventures in the Unknown Interior of America*, trans. Cyclone Covey (New York: Collier, 1961).

23. The ponderously obtuse William A. Gordon elaborated the inappropriate analogue of Wordsworth (*The Mind and Art of Henry Miller*, 240ff.).

24. *Wisdom of the Heart*, 19–30.

25. "I would one day give up writing altogether, give it up voluntarily—in the moment when I would feel myself in possession of the greatest power and mastery" (*Colossus*, 205). There are many similar claims that Miller is on the way to spiritual power, which had the unfortunate effect of excusing him from being on the way to achieved art. Miller also often points more slyly to his deification, as, for example, in praising Claude Houghton (Oldfield), who wrote bland occultist allegories in which the artist figure turns out to have protean salvational powers. See Houghton's *I Am Jonathan Scrivener* (1935). Miller says that Houghton's *Hudson Joins the Herd* (1947) reveals the secret story of Miller's own life (*Books in My Life*, 46). The artist there has a sensitivity too great for this world; also appealing to Miller might have been a schizophrenic and nymphomaniacal heroine who commits crimes for the artist, though he is the world's savior.

26. "I don't care particularly anymore whether I am a saint or not" (*Wisdom of the Heart*, 147). Apparently such encouraged the gross cultism, as in Robert Fink's calling Miller not only a "saint" but "a nearly perfect man" (*The International Henry Miller Letter* 1 [June 1961]: 3).

27. *Wisdom of the Heart*, 94–103.

28. Ibid., 187–91.

29. *Cosmological Eye*, 1–7.

30. *Books in My Life*, 95.

31. *Cosmological Eye*, 151–96. Some of Miller's early work could be related to surrealist dicta, such as "automatic writing" (which Miller several times avows) and the conclusion to André Breton's *Nadja* (1928), "*Le beauté sera convulsive ou ne sera pas*" (215). One catch with the exaltation of the artist is that anyone who claims the role is to be comfortably state-supported for life—a dubious position for an avowed anarchist ("Artist and Public," *Remember to Remember*, 407–24). A similar nonfunctional demand is made amidst the ranting of *The Plight of the Artist in the United States of America* (Berkeley, Calif.: Porter, 1944).

32. *Cosmological Eye*, 367. He evaded the draft in World War I and was overage in World War II.

33. *Remember to Remember*, 126–216.

34. *Maurizius Forever* (San Francisco: Colt, 1946) is a rambling, didactic monograph on Jacob Wasserman's *Maurizius Case*, which is taken not as a novel but as "propaganda" for "a new vision of things" in which love apocalyptically supercedes justice, evil, and the murderer in every man. As with many novels that had a magical appeal to Miller, there is a destructive witch-woman (Anna Jahn) and violent rhetoric against America.

35. In his published notes from the Clichy period, Miller advised himself to exploit both psychoanalysis and astrology for satire, of which he did a bit (Porter, *Miscellanea*, 24).

36. Miller's fullest comment on astrology originally appeared as "A Great Writer Talks about Astrology," *1958 Guidebook to Astrology*, ed. Sidney Omarr (Los Angeles), 116–27, from which my quotations are taken. It was later reprinted as the foreword to Omarr's *Henry Miller: His World of Urania* (London: Villiers, 1960), which is paraphrase, quote, and praise. There would seem to be no other commentary on the indecorous subject.

37. Even good buddy Perlès dismissed Miller's religious interests (*My Friend, Henry Miller,* 228ff.). Miller's later remarks on religion were usually conventional and vague; he said in a Paris interview in 1969, "I am fundamentally a religious man without a religion. I believe in the existence of a supreme intelligence" (Quoted by Wallace Fowlie, "Introduction," *Letters of Henry Miller and Wallace Fowlie,* 13). But the astrological flapdoodle continued to the end.

38. *The Smile at the Foot of the Ladder* (New York: Duell, Sloan, Pearce, 1948), with an appreciative introduction (mostly praise of *Cancer*) by Edwin Corle, and an epilogue comment by Miller. Miller's ham-handed attempts at traditional forms in this period include heavy burlesques of fairy tales (*Plexus,* 454–63; *Big Sur,* 81ff.).

39. Mailer, *Genius and Lust,* 5. The following quotes are from later pages of Mailer's commentary.

40. See Miller's preface to Jack Kerouac, *The Subterraneans* (New York: Avon, 1959), 5–7. Kerouac, of course, was indebted to Miller not only for the late version of surrealist automatic-writing in an American context but for his fractured life-style, including an attempted withdrawal to *Big Sur* (the cynosure and Kerouac's 1962 "novel" of that name), and the fatal postbohemian descent into middle-class conventional living, on which Miller, but not Kerouac, thrived.

41. Such rhetorical gestures may be seen to have their own tradition. I recall that in some piece written in the 1920s, Maxwell Bodenheim, the archetypal Greenwich Villager and self-destructive bohemian (whom Miller apparently knew then), used the phrase "the Coney Island of the soul." So, perhaps, is there also the traditional function of inspirational defense for C[+] minds.

42. A less discriminating and more negative evaluation (however indebted to mine) is that of Ihab Hassan (*Literature of Silence,* 204), who concluded that Miller's writings were "maudlin, egotistical, blind," "combine callousness with sentimentality," and were mostly "tedious, slapdash, repetitious . . . narrow." Since it is

autobiographical material, we should conclude of the man that "his intelligence is not of the first order. And we also sense that his courage in the face of life's pain is moderate".

43. *My Life and Times*, 127. As usual with his later statements, Miller was flattening out earlier rhetorical gestures: "Ninety-nine percent of what is written—and this goes for all our art products—should be destroyed" (*Cosmological Eye*, 371). Although as usual lacking development and discrimination (which ten, or one, percent is genuine?), the response may be taken as not only authentic but important and a considerable truth, which it may be one of the functions of buffoons to announce.

Selected Bibliography

Most of the book publications of Henry Miller are listed in alphabetical order since usual typologies are not appropriate to his mixtures of memoirs, letters, sermons, parodies, etc. Some indication of the type of material is briefly indicated. The current, hardcover, U. S. edition is given, following the parenthetical early (usually foreign in English) edition (unless there was no later American edition). No translations are given. The secondary material is highly selective, for representative works, excludes commentaries in other languages, and does not repeat many of the items given in the notes.

PRIMARY WORKS

The Air-Conditioned Nightmare. New York: New Directions, 1945. Miscellany of memoirs, essays, etc., relating to trip in United States.

Aller Retour New York. Paris, Obelisk, 1935. Letter-essay about United States.

Art and Outrage: A Correspondence about Henry Miller (with Lawrence Durrell and Alfred Perlès). London: 1959; New York: Dutton, 1961. Includes replies by Miller.

Big Sur and the Oranges of Hieronymous Bosch. New York: New Directions, 1957. Miscellany of memoirs and essays.

Black Spring. Paris: 1936; New York: Grove, 1963. Memoirs and rhetorical experiments.

Book of Friends: A Tribute to Friends of Long Ago. Santa Barbara, Calif.: Capra, 1976. Childhood memoirs.

The Books in My Life. Norfolk, Conn.: New Directions, 1952. Book lists, bits of memoirs, and ruminations.

Collector's Quest: The Correspondence of Henry Miller and J. Rives Childs, 1947–65 (with J. Rives Childs). Edited by Richard Clement Wood. Charlottesville: University Press of Virginia, 1968.

The Colossus of Maroussi. Norfolk, Conn.: New Directions, 1941. Travel memoirs of Greece.

The Cosmological Eye. Norfolk, Conn.: New Directions, 1939. Miscellany of reviews, personal essays, and reprints from other books.

Dear, Dear Brenda, The Love Letters of Henry Miller to Brenda Venus (with Brenda Venus). New York: Morrow, 1986. A selection with some text by Venus.

A Devil in Paradise. New York: New American Library, 1956. Profile; also in *Big Sur and the Oranges of Hieronymous Bosch.*

The Durrell-Miller Letters, 1935–80 (with Lawrence Durrell), ed. Ian S. Mac-Niven. New York: New Directions, 1988.

First Impressions of Greece. Santa Barbara, Calif.: Capra, 1973. Notebook jottings preliminary to *Colossus of Marousi.*

From Your Capricorn Friend: Henry Miller and the Stroker, 1978–1980. Edited by Irving Stettner. New York: New Directions, 1987. Small miscellany: stories, essays, and letters.

Gliding into the Everglades. Lake Oswego, Oreg.: Lost Pleiade, 1977. Brief memoir of early Florida trip.

Hamlet (with Michael Fraenkel). 2 vols. 1939; New York: Carrefour, 1941. Personal essays in the guise of letters on a variety of topics, not including Shakespeare.

Henry Miller on Writing. Edited by Thomas H. Moore. New York: New Directions, 1964. Anthology of pontifical bits.

Henry Miller: Years of Trial and Triumph, the Correspondence of Henry Miller and Elmer Gertz (with Elmer Gertz). Carbondale: Southern Illinois University Press, 1978. With pretentious annotations by Gertz.

Insomnia, or, The Devil at Large. Euclid, Ohio: Loujon, 1971. Illustrated notebook of responses to desertion by fifth wife.

Joey: A Loving Portrait of Alfred Perlès Together with Some Bizarre Episodes Relating to the Opposite Sex. Vol. 3 of *Book of Friends.* Santa Barbara, Calif.: Capra, 1979. Memoir of Paris days, plus early nonsexual relations with women.

Just Wild about Harry: A Melo-Melo in Seven Scenes. New York: New Directions, 1963. Playlet.

Letters to Anaïs Nin. Edited by Gunther Stuhlmann. New York: Putnam's, 1965.

My Life and Times. Chicago: Playboy, 1972. Picturebook with text by Bradley Smith.

Letters of Henry Miller and Wallace Fowlie, 1943–1972 (with Wallace Fowlie). New York: Grove, 1975.

Maurizius Forever. San Francisco: Colt, 1946. Personal essay around literary work.

Max and the White Phagocytes. Paris: Obelisk, 1938. Earlier version of *Cosmological Eye* miscellany.

Money and How It Gets That Way. Paris: 1938; Berkeley, Calif.: Bern Porter, 1945. Parody essay.

Mother, China, and the World Beyond. Santa Barbara, Calif.: Capra, 1977. Brief reminiscences on mother problem and associations.

My Bike and Other Friends. Vol. 2 of *Book of Friends.* Santa Barbara, Calif.: Capra, 1978. Brief memoir of youth.

Nexus. Book 3 of *The Rosy Crucifixion.* Paris: 1960; New York: Grove, 1965. Memoir-novel.

Opus Pistorum. Privately printed, 1943; New York: Grove, 1983. Sexual fantasies.

The Paintings of Henry Miller. Edited by Noel Young. San Francisco: Chronicle, 1982. Reprint of various Miller texts focusing on painting, with selection of reproductions.

To Paint Is to Love Again. Alhambra, Calif.: Cambria, 1960. Personal essay with reproductions.

Plexus. Book 2 of *The Rosy Crucifixion.* Paris: 1953; New York: Grove, 1965. Memoir-novel.

Quiet Days in Clichy. Paris: 1956; New York: Grove, 1965. Rewritten Paris-period memoir.

Reflections on the Death of Mishima. Santa Barbara, Calif.: Capra, 1972. Brief personal essay on Japanese novelist.

Remember to Remember. New York: New Directions, 1947. Follow-up miscellany to *Air-Conditioned Nightmare.*

Reunion in Barcelona. Northwood, England: Scorpion, 1959. Memoir-letter.

Scenario (A Film with Sound). Paris: Obelisk, 1937. Nonscenario surrealist pastiche, reprinted in *Cosmological Eye.*

Semblance of a Devoted Past (with Emil Schnellock). Berkeley, Calif.: 1944. Letter essays.

Sexus. Book 1 of *The Rosy Crucifixion.* Paris: 1949; New York: Grove, 1965. Memoir-novel.

The Smile at the Foot of the Ladder. New York: Duell, Sloan and Pearce, 1948. Earnest parody-fairy tale.

Stand Still Like the Hummingbird. New York: New Directions, 1962. Miscellany of essays, reviews, and reprints from books.

Sunday after the War. Norfolk, Conn.: New Directions, 1944. Miscellany of essays, reviews, and reprints.

The Time of the Assassins: A Study of Rimbaud. Norfolk, Conn.: New Directions, 1956.

Tropic of Cancer. Paris: 1934; New York: Grove, 1961. Paris memoir.

Tropic of Capricorn. Paris: 1939; New York: Grove, 1962. New York memoir.

On Turning Eighty. Santa Barbara, Calif.: Capra, 1972. Personal essay.

What Are You Going to Do About Alf? Paris: 1935; Berkeley, Calif.: Bern Porter, 1944. Parodistic essay.

Wisdom of the Heart. Norfolk, Conn.: New Directions, 1941. Miscellany of essays and sketches.

The World of Lawrence. Edited by Evelyn J. Hinz and John J. Teunissen. Santa Barbara, CA: Capra, 1980. Rewrite of early literary study.

The World of Sex. 1940; rev. ed., Paris: Olympia, 1957; New York: Grove, 1965. Fiction-memoir of Paris period.

Writer and Critic: A Correspondence with Henry Miller (with William A. Gordon). Baton Rouge: Louisiana State University Press, 1968.

SECONDARY WORKS

Bibliographies

Moore, Thomas H. *Bibliography of Henry Miller.* Minneapolis: Henry Miller Literary Society, 1961.

Renken, Maxine. *Bibliography of Henry Miller, 1945–1961.* Denver: Swallow, 1962.

Riley, Esta Lou. *Henry Miller, an Informal Bibliography 1924–1960.* Hays, Kans.: Fort Hays Kansas State College, 1961.

Schifreen, Lawrence J. *Henry Miller: A Bibliography of Secondary Sources.* Metuchen, N.J.: Scarecrow, 1979.

Biographies

Martin, Jay. *Always Merry and Bright: The Life of Henry Miller.* Santa Barbara, CA: Capra, 1978.

   The only full-scale biography, it is heavily researched in Miller archives, with his cooperation, rather floridly written, and often intellectually inadequate.

Perlès, Alfred. *My Friend, Henry Miller.* New York: John Day, 1956.

   By his closest Paris-period companion, this is mostly genial memoir.

Anthologies of Criticism

Porter, Bern, ed. *The Happy Rock: A Book about Henry Miller.* Berkeley, Calif.: Bern Porter, 1945.

   This is mostly reminiscences by friends and brief comments by devotees.

Wickes, George, ed. *Henry Miller and the Critics.* Carbondale: Southern Illinois University Press, 1963.

   Includes historically influential essays by George Orwell, Herbert J. Muller, Philip Rahv, Kenneth Rexroth, and others.

Mitchell, Edward B., ed. *Henry Miller: Three Decades of Criticism.* New York: New York University, 1971.

   In addition to some of the above, includes interesting essays by Frederick J. Hoffman, Aldous Huxley, Karl Shapiro, David Littlejohn, and others.

Selected Other Studies

Baxter, Annette Kar. *Henry Miller, Expatriate.* Pittsburgh: University of Pittsburgh, 1961.

   First American academic study, this is a compendium on the expatriate theme.

Brown, J. D. *Henry Miller.* New York: Ungar, 1986.
   One of the better short introductions, this is reasonably well-informed and unpretentious.
Gordon, William A. *The Mind and Art of Henry Miller.* Baton Rouge: Louisiana State University Press, 1967.
   A pretentious—and historically and critically silly—treatment of Miller as great romantic artist, to be linked with Wordsworth, etc.
Gutierrez, Donald. "'Hypocrite Lecteur': *Tropic of Cancer* as Sexual Comedy." *The Maze in the Mind and the World.* Troy, N.Y.: Whitson, 1985.
   This suggestively argues that early Miller provides constructive satire of the typical American male brutal attitude towards women.
Hassan, Ihab Habib. *The Literature of Silence: Henry Miller and Samuel Beckett.* New York: Knopf, 1967.
   Linking Miller with Beckett, and with silence, is extremely arbitrary, but some of the criticism is sophisticated and apt.
Kleine, Don. "Innocence Forbidden: Henry Miller in the Tropics." *Prairie Schooner* 33 (Summer 1959): 125–30.
   An argument that early Miller has a split attitude towards his material which resulted in antithetical styles.
Lewis, Leon. *Henry Miller: The Major Writings.* New York: Schocken, 1986.
   This earnestly ponderous restatement (and requoting) of some earlier criticism discusses only the longer Miller works; it is uninsightful.
Mailer, Norman. *Genius and Lust: A Journey through the Major Writings of Henry Miller.* New York: Grove, 1976.
   This anthology of selections, unfortunately confined to the long works, also has ten prefatory essays combining sweeping enthusiasms, special pleading for traditional male sexual views, and some acute criticisms.
Millet, Kate. *Sexual Politics.* Garden City, N.Y.: Doubleday, 1970.
   This is the most influential, though thin, feminist polemic using Miller to document male sexual chauvinism.
Mathieu, Bertrand. *Orpheus in Brooklyn: Orphism, Rimbaud, and Henry Miller.* The Hague, Netherlands: Mouton, 1976.
   A crass overreading of some loose Orphic analogies applied to Miller's writings on Greece, this book is earnestly cultish.
Meyers, Jeffrey. "D. H. Lawrence and Travel Writing." In *The Legacy of D. H. Lawrence,* edited by Jeffrey Meyers. London: Macmillan, 1987.
   Sophisticated dismissal of Greek book.
Nelson, Jane A. *Form and Image in the Fiction of Henry Miller.* Detroit, Mich.: Wayne State University, 1970.
   Obsessive Jungian allegorizing, especially of Miller's female figures, this book attempts to present him as archetypally profound.

Omarr, Sidney. *Henry Miller: His World of Urania.* London: Villiers, 1960.
   A cultish compilation of Miller on astrology by one of the more commercially successful practitioners.
Widmer, Eleanor Rackow. "My Day in the Censoring Tropics." In *Freedom and Culture,* Edited by Eleanor Widmer. Belmont, Calif.: Wadsworth, 1970.
   This is an amusing account of a *Tropic of Cancer* censorship trial.
Winslow, Kathryn. *Henry Miller: Full of Life.* Los Angeles: Jeremy P. Tarcher, 1986.
   A devotee-dealer's collection of trivia by and around Miller.

Index